Chinese literature has been extensively preserved in an unbroken cultural tradition for nearly 2,500 years. Its extent easily surpasses that of all other ancient literatures put together. This definitive anthology contains tales expressing numerous aspects of Chinese culture. There are supernatural and fantastic tales, parables and fables, tales of morality and justice, love and marriage, and Taoism. They capture those elements which are of the essence of Chinese literature: intensity of imagination, wit, and human concern.

A Chinese Anthology

A collection of Chinese folktales and fables

edited and with an introduction by
RAYMOND VAN OVER

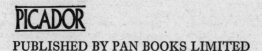

PUBLISHED BY PAN BOOKS LIMITED

First British edition published 1973 in Picador by
Pan Books Ltd, Cavaye Place, London SW10 9PG
2nd Printing 1974
© Fawcett Publications Inc 1972
Printed in Great Britain by
Richard Clay (The Chaucer Press), Ltd, Bungay, Suffolk

ISBN 0 330 23736 5

CONTENTS

ACKNOWLEDGEMENT

There are always many people involved in the creation of any book, but special thanks are due to Jim Trupin of Premier Books for his insight and consideration, and to C. C. Chambers for research and editorial assistance. And of course, S.D.G., without whose help nothing could have been accomplished.

'Outsides', from *A History of Chinese Literature* translated by Herbert A. Giles, reprinted by permission of William Heinemann Ltd.

DYNASTIES AND PERIODS OF CHINESE LITERATURE

Name of Period or Dynasty	Dates	Principal Characteristics
Chou	1122?–221 BC	Confucian classics, philosophical prose
Ch'in	221–207 BC	
Han	206 BC–AD 220	Historical prose, *Shih* poetry (five-word verse)
Minor dynasties	AD 221–618	Supernatural tales, *Shih* poetry
T'ang	AD 618–906	*Shih* poetry (five- and seven-word verses), neoclassicism, literary tales, Buddhist tales
Five dynasties	AD 907–960	
Sung	AD 960–1279	Neoclassical prose, vernacular tales, drama and variety plays
Mongol dynasties	AD 1279–1368	Drama, poetry
Ming	AD 1368–1644	Fiction, drama
Ch'ing	AD 1644–1911	Fiction, drama (Peking theatre)

Let's talk nonsense and listen as we please!
Outside, beans and melons 'gainst a trellis, and rain like silk strands.
Speaking of human affairs surely is irksome,
But fain would we hear, in the hush of a tomb, spirits singing their
  songs.

– WANG SHIH-CHEN (AD 1634–1711)

Introduction

Chinese literature has been extensively preserved for nearly twenty-five hundred years in an unbroken cultural tradition. Its volume surpasses all other ancient literatures combined, yet Western attempts to study and anthologize Chinese literature were begun only within the past century. Archaeological evidence indicates that China had an advanced writing system and a well-developed technology of bronze casting as early as 1400 BC. But much of the Chinese culture, built upon a feudal system not unlike that of early Europe, developed during the incomparably long eight-hundred-year Chou dynasty (1122?–221 BC). By the third century BC, Chinese civilization had developed to the degree that the Chou era is now considered the classical period in both philosophy and poetry. Chinese culture during this epoch flourished primarily around the Yellow River and Yangtze regions. The two thousand years of Chinese history that followed this Golden Age were torn by civil strife, changing dynasties, political upheavals, and conquest by the barbarians from the North beyond the Great Wall; yet the culture that was established during those early years remained unimpaired. It is a peculiarity of Chinese culture that from the Han period (206 BC–AD 220) through the T'ang (AD 618–906) and Sung (AD 960–1278) eras to the end of the Ch'ing dynasty in 1911 the essence of Chinese life remained intact. Numerous invaders conquered China (the Toba and Tungus during the fourth and sixteenth centuries, the Kitans and Jurchens during the tenth to thirteenth centuries, the Mongols in the thirteenth and fourteenth centuries, and the Manchu from the seventeenth to the twentieth century), only to find that their own culture was assimilated and utilized by the Chinese. Foreign cultures certainly had an impact upon China, but not in the sense of conquering, for the conquerors merely added new dimensions that enhanced rather than impoverished or destroyed Chinese life. Buddhism, for example, which was brought to China from India, stimulated the Chinese creative drives in painting, sculpture, and literature as well as influencing Chinese philosophy and way of life. Thus, the Chinese absorbed new ideas and techniques that sustained and revitalized them throughout their long history. All these fluctuating influences can be found in Chinese literature. There you will find traditional Confucianism, Buddhist ideas, and esoteric Taoism fused in a way of life that is at once reflective and functional; absorbed with the rhythms and fluctuations of natural phenomena, of which man himself is but a part. While the flexible, eclectic techniques of Chinese culture can most easily be seen in this fusion of divergent teachings of Confucianism, Taoism, and Buddhism, which existed for centuries side by side in Chinese everyday life, it is Confucianism that most strongly influenced the morality and customs of China; and it is Confucianism, in a broad sense, that dominates much of Chinese literature. Most writers conformed to Confucian principles, and found their inspiration in the Confucian concepts of morality and proper social behaviour. To the practical Chinese, literature was a vehicle by which Confucianism was communicated to the people. There is often, consequently, a moral lesson to be found in Chinese fiction. Confucius' strong influence can be seen in the fact that, in a Chinese library, one of the four major divisions was the Confucian classics, alongside history, philosophy, and *belles lettres*. But even with this strong Confucian element, Chinese fiction incorporated Taoist beliefs, Buddhist canon, and a great variety of demons, demigods, spirits, animals with supernatural powers, and ghosts who not only intermingle with humans in this earthly existence, but do so with charm and elegance.

The range of these tales is broad and incorporates most aspects of Chinese life, which is proper, since Chinese fiction pervaded everyday existence. Unlike the West, China had no aristocracy of birth in its ancient world. At the peak of the social system there stood the emperor, and beside him stood the scholar, who, through annual state-conducted examinations, could reach the highest offices in the land. Merchants, on the other hand, no matter how wealthy, were not considered the social equal of a talented scholar of advanced degree. The system of competitive literary examinations dominated Chinese social life for more than two thousand years and was not abolished until 1903.

The state examinations were open to all and were used by officials to find able and talented men to serve the state. After passing tests as to his character, a candidate then had to pass through three levels of examination: the first, or bachelor's degree, the second, or master's degree, and the third, or doctorate degree. The third degree led in turn to the highest literary honour, the Hanlin degree, which resulted in the scholar's being taken before the emperor and suitably rewarded.

From this curious system, that rewarded literary excellence with high government responsibility, came two distinct types of traditional Chinese tales. The first, or *ch'uan-ch'i*, is written in classical Chinese, established in the Chou period, by and for the well-educated. Another type, the *p'ing-hua*, had its origins in the storyteller's art and was eventually written down in the vernacular. As in ancient Greece, storytellers would ply their trade on busy street corners in large cities or wander the hamlets and villages of China telling their stories verbatim, rarely missing a phrase, to all who would pay them a small fee. The storyteller as carrier of a literature in the process of refinement was popular as early as the T'ang dynasty, but it was not until the twelfth and thirteenth centuries that he came into his own. The storytellers of the next, or Sung period, developed oral narration to a fine art that rivalled Homer. This type of colloquial tale led to independent literary creations, for its influence was found primarily in the village marketplace or teahouse, where the storyteller had to hold his audience or starve.

Narrative prose, however, was not considered by the literati as a branch of serious literature, and unlike the writings of the *ch'uan-ch'i*, or the formal essay and philosophical tract, *p'ing-hua* writing could not lead the scholar to social prestige or government position. This was an important distinction in a society where the educated person, the winner of literary distinction and state examination, was at the same time a civil servant. The free-lance writer, represented most clearly by P'u Sung-ling in this anthology, was the exception rather than the rule, for he could win an audience, could achieve popular fame, but was generally barred from high public office.

Supernatural tales dominated the attention and tastes of the early Chinese people. Most of the late Ming dynasty (1368-1644) writers fell in with the seventeenth century mania for tales of the weird, miraculous, and supernatural. The most famous collection of such tales is the *Liao Chai Chih I*, which is still accepted in China as the 'best and most perfect model' of this type of literature. For more than two centuries these tales have been known throughout China, and are as familiar to the Chinese as are the adventures of Alice in Wonderland to English-speaking school children.

The *Liao Chai Chih I*, or *Strange Stories from a Chinese Studio*, as

Herbert Giles translates it, is the source of many of the stories in this anthology, for two basic reasons. First, because of their literary excellence and clear representation of everyday Chinese life, and, second, because they have been largely ignored by contemporary anthologists. The writer of the *Liao Chai*, as these tales are informally known, was a seventeenth-century poet of the fantastic, P'u Sung-ling (1640–1715), or 'Liu-hsien, the last of the Immortals' as his friends called him. P'u Sung-ling failed the all-important master's examinations and suffered in poverty his whole life, dying in obscurity. The *Liao Chai* was circulated in manuscript for many years, because the author was too poor to have it printed. Not until 1740, after P'u Sung-ling's death, did his grandson print and publish his collection of now-classic tales. P'u Sung-ling wrote the 431 short stories that constitute the *Liao Chai* by gathering traditional tales in much the manner of other fiction writers. But P'u Sung-ling retold them with a subtlety and accuracy of imagery and expression that brought the Chinese popular tale to a height never before achieved.

Commenting on P'u Sung-ling's tales, the respected Sinologists, Winberg and Ch'u Chai remark: 'After nearly eight hundred years of development, this genre of writing [the *p'ing-hua*] reached perfection with the appearance of *Liao Chai Chih I*, which surpasses any previous collection of ghost and fairy tales in scope, literary merit, and profundity of ideas, serving as a landmark in the history of Chinese fiction.'

Herbert Giles, a turn-of-the-century Sinologist, was one of the first to recognize the merit of these tales, and wrote that the *Liao Chai* must raise P'u Sung-ling 'to a foremost rank in the Chinese world of letters'. The Jewish philosopher, Martin Buber, admired the strange tales of P'u Sung-ling so much that he wrote an introduction to a translation of the *Liao Chai* and described the work as 'a classic'. Why then, one must ask, has P'u Sung-ling been so clearly ignored in most modern anthologies? Herbert Giles, Lin Yutang, the Chais, and Rose Quong are among the few who give this Chinese writer due attention and appreciation. The answer to such a question remains elusive, but, as one learns more about him, one tends to take the fatalistic, almost mystical view of P'u Sung-ling himself. He wrote at one point in gentle despair: 'Our house was cold and bare as a monastery, and there, toiling with my pen, I was as poor as a monk with his alms-bowl . . . I was driven hither and thither, at the wind's pleasure, like a flower beaten down into the mud. But truly the six paths of man's pilgrimage are inscrutable and I have no right to complain. Be that as it may, the midnight hour finds me beside my flickering lamp, while the storm wind whistles its tragic tune; and seated at my joyless table I piece together my stories.' In another place he seems to foretell his fate, initially in China while he was alive, and later in the West, 'Alas, I am only a bird trembling before the winter frost and finding no refuge in the bare branches. I am only a cricket chirping to the moon and pressing close to the door to gather itself a little warmth. For where are they that know my name?'

P'u Sung-ling's tales were originally the creation of the Chinese people, and he had sought out traditional, orally transmitted tales wherever he could find them. 'Each time I hear one, I jot it down,' he wrote, 'and later write the material up into tales. For a long time, too, friends from different parts of the country have been sending me stories, so my collection is growing all the time.'

The retelling of traditional tales was common in China, and often numerous versions, each retold according to the distinct style of the writer, would develop around a single theme that moved the Chinese spirit. In this anthology one of the most popular themes can be found in 'The Wolf Dream', where a popular literary device is used again to great effect by P'u Sung-ling. (See the second footnote on page 56 for other dream themes in Chinese fiction.) According to Winberg and Ch'u Chai, P'u Sung-ling's distinction lies in his command of the classical language, 'which he uses for detailed descriptions, as well as in his rich imagination, which dramatizes the development of the story'. And while the terseness of the *ch'uan-ch'i* type of writing was the most respected and the common literary form in China, the *p'ing-hua* or popular tale was incorporated and pushed to its limits with P'u Sung-ling. According to Giles, P'u Sung-ling frequently develops new and original combinations in his writing, that invest words and ideas 'with a force [they] could never have possessed except under the hands of a perfect master of his art'. Those who do not read Chinese will never know the force of P'u Sung-ling's original, but it is clear even in translation that one is reading a master storyteller and a craftsman of his art. Unlike those of much other Chinese fiction, P'u Sung-ling's characters are developed, his story lines consistent, yet intensely imaginative. He does not fall prey to heavy moralizing, a natural failing in a culture dominated by Confucian moral philosophy, but views Chinese life in all its complexity. His tales embrace common folk and emperors, yet are frequently filled with devils, spirits, and people possessed by the supernatural. But most importantly, the order of nature, so frequently abused in supernatural fiction, is never broken, for P'u Sung-ling was too good a storyteller to upset his reader in such a fashion. What he did was to extend the reader's awareness into a world alien to his everyday environment, into a world at once purely Chinese and also an integral and natural part of the human imagination. The boundaries of reality are extended in P'u Sung-ling's writing, and remind one of the pantheistic world of Celtic folklore. Parallels in the Western world can be found in Poe's imaginative tales of the supernatural, and the filigree of human and superhuman interfacings of Ambrose Bierce and H. P. Lovecraft. Such a singular fact of Chinese life and history as that thirty-six thousand minor gods live in and govern the human body, emerges in P'u Sung-ling in the form of minute people taking up residence in the eyes of a scoundrel whose sight was struck from him for impudence. Although it is true that P'u Sung-ling was heir to the best traditions of folk literature, he created a unique place for himself in Chinese fiction by perfecting and enriching Chinese classical literature.

But the greatest value in all the tales collected here (not just those by P'u Sung-ling) resides in their detailed expression of Chinese culture and beliefs. Only writers of reputation and excellence have been included in this collection. The range of these tales is broad, and the division of the book into such categories as *Supernatural and Fantastic* and *Love and Marriage*, provides only a simple guide to the general framework of the stories. Too many elements overlap to indicate successfully the contents or direction of Chinese fiction, and especially of the traditional tales. The range of authors and topics is intentionally broad (even though a volume devoted exclusively to P'u Sung-ling would be justifiable), in order that the anthology should express the widest sample of the spirit of Chinese culture. This was one of the primary criteria for including particular stories in this anthology. Another consideration was the problem of translation. Some modern translators demean what even they call 'fine translations of decades ago' because their English style may be 'dated'. Fine translations are so difficult to come by, especially from Chinese, that this seemed a foolish rule to follow; for this reason, many of the translations to be found in this volume may seem to be in 'dated' English, but have been included because of their exceptional quality and reputation. This is particularly true in the case of turn-of-the-century Sinologists of great sensitivity, such as Herbert Giles. In essence, the decision was made always to include a proven, sensitive translation at the small and occasional sacrifice of modern English usage.

These tales are from a China past. Since the period of civil wars, and the ravages suffered during World War Two, China is no longer the land of superstition, whimsy, and artistic originality. Today, art is a function of the state, and for that reason much modern Chinese writing seems limited in scope and lacks the creative imagination of the earlier literature. Today's China, however, cannot sever itself from its heritage. The Chinese temperament, as expressed in these tales, can be seen in the puritanical tone of the present Communist state, and this is only one indication of continuity of character. The Chinese are a people used to subjugating the individual to the mass good. This also has not changed. Acceptance of one's role in a rigid social and political structure can be seen both in Chinese conformity to strict Confucian dogma in the past and in their rigid role acceptance in the present society. Reading these tales, one begins to understand China's roots – and thereby gains some insight into her always mysterious and multi-faceted character.

1 Supernatural and Fantastic

The Lady of Tung-t'ing Lake

The spirits of the Tung-t'ing lake* are very much in the habit of
borrowing boats. Sometimes the cable of an empty junk will cast itself
off, and away goes the vessel over the waves to the sound of music in the
air above. The boatmen crouch down in one corner and hide their faces,
not daring to look up until the trip is over and they are once more at
their old anchorage.

Now a certain Mr Lin, returning home after having failed at the
examination for a master's degree, was lying down very tipsy on the deck
of his boat, when suddenly strains of music and singing were heard. The
boatmen shook Mr Lin, but failing to rouse him, ran down and hid
themselves in the hold below.

By and by the noise of the various instruments became almost deafen-
ing, and Lin, partially waking up, smelt a delicious odour of perfumes
filling the air around him. Opening his eyes, he saw that the boat was
crowded with a number of beautiful girls; and knowing that something
strange was going on, he pretended to be fast asleep. Someone then
called for Chih-ch'êng, upon which a young waiting-maid came forward
and stood quite close to Mr Lin's head. Her stockings were the colour
of the kingfisher's wing, and her feet were encased in tiny purple shoes,
no bigger than one's finger. Much smitten with this young lady, he took
hold of her stocking with his teeth, causing her, the next time she moved,
to fall forward flat on her face. Some one, evidently in authority, asked
what was the matter and when he heard the explanation was very angry
and gave orders to take off Mr Lin's head. Soldiers appeared and bound

* Tung-t'ing lake was famous in the province of Hunan as the source for many
tales and legends which grew up around it.

Lin. On getting up, he beheld a man sitting with his face to the south, and dressed in the garments of a king.

'Sire,' cried Lin, as he was being led away, 'the king of the Tung-t'ing lake was a mortal named Lin – your servant's name is Lin also. His Majesty was a disappointed candidate – your servant is one too. His Majesty met the Dragon Lady, and was made immortal – your servant has played a trick upon this girl, and he is to die. Why this inequality of fortunes?'

When the king heard this, he bade them bring him back, and asked him, 'Are you, then, a disappointed candidate?' Lin said he was, whereupon the king handed him writing materials and ordered him to compose an ode upon a lady's head-dress.

Some time passed before Lin, who was a scholar of some repute in his own neighbourhood, had done more than sit thinking about what he should write, and at length the king upbraided him. 'Come, come, a man of your reputation should not take so long.'

'Sire,' replied Lin, laying down his pen, 'it took ten years to complete the Songs of the Three Kingdoms; whereby it may be known that the value of compositions depends more upon the labour given to them than the speed with which they are written.'

The king laughed, and waited patiently from early morning till noon, when a copy of the verses was put into his hand, with which he declared himself very pleased. He now commanded that Lin should be served with wine; and shortly after there followed a collation of all kinds of curious dishes, in the middle of which an officer came in and reported that the register of people to be drowned had been made up. 'How many in all?' asked the king. 'Two hundred and twenty-eight,' was the reply. The king inquired who had been deputed to carry it out, whereupon he was informed that the generals Mao and Nan had been appointed to do the work. Lin here rose to take leave, and the king presented him with ten ounces of pure gold and a crystal square,* telling him that it would preserve him from any danger he might encounter on the lake. At this moment the king's retinue and horses ranged themselves in proper order upon the surface of the lake and His Majesty, stepping from the boat into his sedan-chair, disappeared from view.

When everything had been quiet for a long time, the boatmen emerged from the hold, and proceeded to shape their course northwards. The wind, however, was against them, and they were unable to make any headway when all of a sudden an iron cat appeared floating on the top of the water.

'General Mao has come,' cried the boatmen in great alarm, and all the

* An instrument used by masons is meant here.

passengers on board fell down on their faces. Immediately afterwards, a great wooden beam rose up from the lake, nodding itself backwards and forwards, which the boatmen, more frightened than ever, said was General Nan. Before long a tremendous sea was raging, the sun was darkened in the heavens, and every vessel in sight was capsized. But Mr Lin sat in the middle of the boat, with the crystal square in his hand, and the mighty waves broke around without doing them any harm.

Thus were they saved, and Lin returned home. Whenever he told his wonderful story he would assert that, although unable to speak positively as to the facial beauty of the young lady he had seen, he dared say that she had the most exquisite pair of feet in the world.

Once, upon having occasion to visit the city of Wu-ch'ang, Lin heard of an old woman who wished to sell her daughter but was unwilling to accept money, stating that any one who had the exact match of a certain crystal square in her possession should be at liberty to take the girl. Lin thought this very strange, and taking his square with him sought out the old woman, who was delighted to see him, and told her daughter to come in. The young lady was about fifteen years of age and possessed of surpassing beauty. After saying a few words of greeting, however, she turned round and went within again.

Lin's reason had almost fled at the sight of this peerless girl, and he straightway informed the old woman that he had such an article as she required, but could not say whether it would match hers or not. Lin and the old woman compared their squares and found there was not a fraction of difference between them, either in length or breadth. The old woman was overjoyed, and inquiring where Lin lived, bade him go home and get a bridal chair,* leaving his square behind him as a pledge of his good faith. This he refused to do, but the old woman laughed and said, 'You are too cautious, sir; do you think I should run away for a square?' Lin was thus convinced to leave it behind him, and hurrying away for a chair, made the best of his way back. When he got there, however, the old woman was gone. In great alarm he inquired of the people who lived near as to her whereabouts; no one, however, knew and it being already late he returned disconsolately to his boat.

On the way, he met a chair coming towards him, and immediately the screen was drawn aside and a voice cried out, 'Mr Lin! why so late?' Looking closely, he saw that it was the old woman, who, after asking him if he hadn't suspected her of playing him false, told him that just after he left she had had the offer of a chair; and knowing that he, being only a stranger in the place, would have some trouble in obtaining one, she had sent her daughter to his boat. Lin then begged her to return

* A specially decorated sedan-chair used to transport a bride to her new home.

with him, to which she would not consent. Not fully trusting what she said, he hurried on himself as fast as he could, and jumping into the boat, found the young lady already there. She rose to meet him with a smile, and then he was astonished to see that her stockings were the colour of a kingfisher's wing, her shoes purple, and her appearance generally like that of the girl he had met on the Tung-t'ing lake. While he was still confused, the young lady remarked, 'You stare, sir, as if you had never seen me before!' but just then Lin noticed the tear in her stocking made by his own teeth and cried out in amazement. 'What! are you Chih-ch'êng?' The young lady laughed at this, whereupon Lin rose, and making her a profound bow, said, 'If you are that divine creature, I pray you tell me at once, and set my anxiety at rest.'

'Sir,' replied she, 'I will tell you all. That personage you met on the boat was actually the king of the Tung-t'ing lake. He was so pleased with your talent that he wished to bestow me upon you; but, because I was a great favourite with Her Majesty the Queen, he went back to consult with her. I have now come at the Queen's own command.' Lin was highly pleased, and washing his hands, burnt incense, with his face towards the lake, as if it were the Imperial Court, and then they went home together.

Subsequently, when Lin had occasion to go to Wu-ch'ang, his wife asked to be allowed to avail herself of the opportunity to visit her parents. When they reached the lake, she drew a hair-pin from her hair and threw it into the water. Immediately a boat rose from the lake, and Lin's wife, stepping into it, vanished from sight like a bird on the wing. Lin remained waiting for her on the prow of his vessel, at the spot where she had disappeared. By-and-by he beheld a houseboat approach, from the window of which there flew a beautiful bird, which was no other than Chih-ch'êng. Then some one handed out from the same window gold and silk, and precious things in great abundance, all presents to them from the Queen. After this, Chih-ch'êng went home regularly twice every year, and Lin soon became a very rich man, the things he had being such as no one had ever before seen or heard of.

P'u Sung-ling (Ch'ing Dynasty)
From *Liao Chai Chih I*

The Fighting Cricket

During the reign of Hsuan Te,* cricket fighting was so much in vogue at court that levies of crickets were exacted from the people as a tax.

Wishing to make friends with the Governor, a magistrate of Huayin presented him with a cricket that displayed remarkable fighting powers, so much so, that the Governor in a rather ungrateful way commanded the magistrate to supply him regularly with more crickets. The magistrate in turn ordered his beadles† to provide him with crickets. Before long, it became the practice of the people with time on their hands to catch and rear crickets for fighting. Thus, the price of them rose exceedingly high. In fact, when a beadle's runner came to exact even one cricket, it was enough to ruin several families.

There lived in a village a student named Ch'eng, a rather stupid fellow who had often failed his examinations for a bachelor's degree, and it was quite natural that his name be sent in for the post of beadle. He tried his best to squirm out of it, but in vain, and by the end of the year his small patrimony was gone. Regrettably, a call for crickets came just at this time. Ch'eng was at his wit's end, and determined to commit suicide.

'Why kill yourself?' said Ch'eng's wife. 'You had better go out and try to find a cricket instead!'

In the early morning, Ch'eng, armed with a bamboo tube and a silk net, went off in search of a cricket. He searched about in tumbledown

* Ming Dynasty, reigned AD 1426–1436.
† The post of beadle was a sensitive one. Chosen by officials from among the respectable and substantial, it was not a post that could be easily refused. Although the post held honour and some financial reward, the beadle was responsible for his territory and could be harshly punished if anything went wrong within his jurisdiction that displeased his superiors. If there were too many robberies, or if the beadle failed to capture a malefactor the magistrate wanted, the beadle was beaten with bamboo. For less serious failings, or simply for displeasing his superior, the beadle was often fined. His main duties were to handle all petitions presented to the authorities, all mortgages, transfers of land and goods, etc, which needed the beadle's official seal or signature.

walls, in bushes, under stones, and in holes, but caught only two or three, and those weak, unimpressive specimens.

The magistrate, upon seeing such unsatisfactory crickets, gave Ch'eng a time limit. Several days later, poor Ch'eng was bambooed one hundred blows for having failed to find the crickets within the time allotted, and this made him so sore that he lay upon his bed unable to search any more. As he lay tossing and turning upon his bed, he determined once again to take his own life.

At this time a humpbacked fortune-teller of great skill and renown came into town. Ch'eng's wife seized what pittance she could find and went off to seek his assistance. When she arrived the door was blocked with fair young girls and white-headed old ladies. Peering over the crowd, she saw the room within was darkened and a bamboo screen hung at the door; an altar was arranged outside so that the fortune-seekers could burn incense in a brazier. Each prostrated herself twice, while the soothsayer stood by her side, and prayed for an answer. Looking up into vacancy, his lips opened and shut, but no sound came forth. All stood in awe waiting for the answer. In a few moments, a piece of paper was thrown from behind the screen, and the soothsayer said that the petitioner's desire would be accomplished in the way she wished.

When her time came, Ch'eng's wife advanced, placed the money on the altar, burnt her incense, and prostrated herself. After a few moments, the screen began to move, and a piece of paper was thrown down on which no words were written, only a picture. In the middle was a temple-like building, and behind this, a small hill and a number of curious stones with the long, spiky feelers of innumerable crickets appearing from behind. Nearby was a frog posing in various attitudes. The good woman had no idea what it meant, but she did notice the crickets and ran home to show her husband.

'Ah!' said he, 'This is to show me where to hunt for crickets.' Looking more closely at the picture, he realized that the building very much resembled a temple to the east of their village.

So he forced himself to get up, and leaning on a stick, went out to seek crickets behind the temple. Rounding an old grave, he came upon a place where stones were lying scattered about as in the drawing. He set himself to watch attentively, but he might as well have been looking for a needle or a mustard seed. He soon became exhausted when suddenly an old frog jumped out. Ch'eng was startled but managed to pursue the frog into the bushes. He saw a cricket at the root of a bramble and grabbed for it. But the creature seemed to escape him permanently when it ran down a hole. Ch'eng poured some water into the hole and finally the creature came out. It was a magnificent specimen, strong and handsome, with a fine tail, green neck, and golden wings. Putting him into his basket, Ch'eng returned home in high glee to receive the congratulations of his family.

Ch'eng was overwhelmed with delight. He would not have taken anything for this cricket. He put it into a bowl, and fed it white crab's flesh as well as the yellow kernels of the sweet chestnut. He tended it with love, waiting for the day of triumph when the magistrate should call upon him for it.

One day, Ch'eng's son, aged nine, decided to open the cricket's bowl as his father was not at home. In an instant, the cricket sprang forward and was gone, and all the efforts to catch him seemed in vain. Finally, in desperation, the boy seized one of its legs which broke off, and the little creature soon died.

When Ch'eng's son told his mother amidst many tears what had happened to the cricket, she turned deadly pale. 'What will your father say?' she cried. The boy ran away crying bitterly.

When Ch'eng returned home and heard his wife's story, he felt as if he were turned to ice. He went out to find his son, and after much effort finally found him lying at the bottom of a well. The anger of the two parents was thus turned quite suddenly to grief.

As they sat facing each other over the body of their ill son, it seemed that death would almost be a pleasant relief to them. At evening, they prepared to bury their boy. On touching him, however, they discovered there was still life in him. Overjoyed, they placed him on the bed and towards the middle of the night he came around. But he seemed strange in the head, and only wished to continue sleeping.

Ch'eng's eyes then chanced to settle on the empty cricket bowl and he ceased to think about his son. He lay awake all night long, stiff and stark. As day began to break, he heard the chirping of a cricket outside the house door. Jumping up, he saw his lost cricket. He tried to catch it, but it hopped away. At last, he caught it in his hands, but when he opened them up there was nothing. So he went chasing up and down until he finally cornered it against a wall. But when he looked closer, it seemed small and of a dark red colour. Ch'eng just looked at it without even trying to catch such a worthless specimen. Suddenly, the creature hopped into his sleeve. Examining it again, he found that it was a very handsome insect after all, with a well-formed head and neck. He quickly took it indoors.

Ch'eng was anxious to try its prowess at fighting and it so happened that a young fellow of the village had a fine cricket, which used to win nearly every bout, and he called on Ch'eng that very day. He laughed heartily at Ch'eng's companion, and producing his own cricket, placed them side by side. The comparison made Ch'eng's heart fall and he no longer wished to back his cricket against such opposition. But his friend urged him on, and Ch'eng decided that there was no use in rearing a feeble insect, and that he might as well sacrifice him for a laugh. So they put them together in a bowl.

Ch'eng's little cricket lay quite still, like a piece of wood. The young fellow roared with laughter when it would not move even after being tickled with a pig bristle. After much tickling the small cricket suddenly became quite aroused and fell upon its adversary with such fury that in a moment the young fellow's cricket would have been killed outright had he not quickly interfered.

The little cricket then stood up and chirped to Ch'eng as a sign of victory. Overjoyed, Ch'eng was discussing the fight with his friend when a cock caught sight of his cricket and ran up to eat it. Alarmed, Ch'eng watched as the cock missed its aim. The cricket hopped away, the cock following. In another moment it would have been snapped up, when to his great astonishment, Ch'eng saw his cricket seated on the cock's head, holding firmly to its comb.

He then put the cricket into a cage, and soon sent it to the magistrate, who became furious when he saw the small size of the insect. Ch'eng told the story of the cock, but the magistrate refused to believe such nonsense and set it to fight with other crickets. It vanquished them all without exception. Now the magistrate was willing to try it with the cock, and when it turned out as Ch'eng had said, he gave him a present and sent it in to the Governor.

The Governor then put it into a golden cage, and forwarded it to the palace, accompanied by some remarks on its performances. It was found that of all the splendid collection of His Imperial Majesty, not one cricket was worthy to be placed alongside of this one. It could even dance in time to music, and thus became a great favourite. The Emperor in return bestowed magnificent gifts of horses and silks upon the Governor. Nor did the Governor forget the magistrate. And the magistrate also rewarded Ch'eng by excusing him from the duties of beadle, and by instructing the Literary Chancellor to pass him for the first degree. A few months afterwards Ch'eng's son recovered his intellect. He said that he had dreamed he was a cricket and had proved himself a very skilful fighter. The Governor, too, rewarded Ch'eng handsomely, and in a few years he was a rich man, with flocks and herds, houses and acres, quite one of the wealthiest of men.

P'u Sung-ling (Ch'ing Dynasty)
From *Liao Chai Chih I*

The Talking Eye Pupils

At Ch'ang-an there lived a scholar named Fang Tung, who, though by no means destitute of ability, was a very unprincipled rake, and in the habit of following and speaking to any woman he might chance to meet.

The day before the spring festival of Clear Weather,* he was strolling about outside the city when he saw a small carriage with red curtains and an embroidered awning, followed by a crowd of waiting-maids on horseback, one of whom was exceedingly pretty and riding on a small palfrey. Going closer to get a better look, Fang noticed that the carriage curtain was partly open, and inside he beheld a beautifully dressed girl of about sixteen, lovely beyond anything he had ever seen before. Dazzled by the sight, he could not take his eyes off her; and, now before, now behind, he followed the carriage for many miles. Presently he heard the young lady call out to her maid, who then came alongside. 'Let down the screen for me,' she said to her maid. 'Who is this rude fellow that keeps on staring so?' The maid accordingly let down the screen and, looking angrily at Fang, said, 'This is the bride of the Seventh Prince in the City of Immortals going home to see her parents, and no village girl that you should stare at so.' Then taking a handful of dust, she threw it at him and blinded him. Rubbing his eyes, he looked around, but the carriage and horses were gone.

This frightened him and he hurried off home, his eyes feeling very uncomfortable. He sent for a doctor to examine his eyes and on the pupils was found a small film, which increased by next morning. His eyes were watering incessantly. The film went on growing and in a few days was as thick as a cash.† On the right pupil there came a kind of

* One of the twenty-four solar teams, Ching Ming, meaning clear and bright. A special time for worshipping at family tombs, it falls during the first part of the month of April.

† 'Cash' is the common European translation for the only Chinese coin. Each coin has a square hole cut in the centre for the convenience of stringing them together. In many Chinese stories you will come across the expression a 'string of cash'.

spiral, and as no medicine was of any avail, the sufferer gave himself up to grief and wished for death. He then thought of repenting his sins, and hearing that the *Kuang-ming* sutra could relieve misery, he got a copy and hired a man to teach it to him. At first it was very tedious work, but by degrees he became more composed and spent the whole day in a posture of devotion telling his beads.

At the end of a year he had achieved a state of perfect calm. Then one day he heard a small voice, about as loud as a fly's, calling out from his left eye: 'It's horridly dark in here.' To this he heard a reply from the right eye saying, 'Let us go out for a stroll and cheer ourselves up a bit.' Then Fang felt a wriggling in his nose which made it itch, just as if something was going out of each of the nostrils; and after a while he felt it again as if returning up his nostrils. Then he heard a voice from one eye say, 'I hadn't seen the garden for a long time! The epidendrums are all withered and dead.'

Now Fang was very fond of these flowers and had planted a great number which he watered himself; but since the loss of his sight he had never mentioned them. Hearing these words, however, he at once asked his wife why she had let the epidendrums die. She asked him how he knew they were dead, and when he told her she went out to see – and found them all withered away. They were both astonished at this, and his wife decided to quietly conceal herself in the room. She then saw two tiny people,* no bigger than a bean, come down from her husband's nose and, shimmering like sparks, fly out of the door, where she lost sight of them. They soon came back and flew up to his face, like bees or beetles seeking their nests.

This went on for some days until Fang suddenly heard from the left eye: 'This roundabout road is not at all convenient. It would be better for us to make a door.' To this the right eye answered, 'My wall is too thick: it wouldn't be at all an easy job.' 'I'll try to open mine,' said the left eye, 'and then it can do for both of us.'

Fang then felt a pain in his left eye as if something was being torn, and in a moment he found he could see the tables and chairs in the room. He was delighted and told his wife, who examined his eye and discovered an opening in the film through which she could see the black pupil shining out beneath, the eyeball itself looking like a cracked peppercorn. By next morning the film had completely disappeared, and when

---

* Herbert Giles, the renowned Sinologist and translator of this story, tells us that 'the belief that the human eye contains a tiny being of human shape is universal in China'. He believes it originated, sensibly enough, from the reflection of oneself seen when looking into the pupil of someone's eye – or even, with the help of a mirror, when looking into one's own.

his eye was closely examined it was discovered to contain two pupils. But as the spiral on the right eye remained as before, they knew that the two pupils had taken up their abode in one eye. Now although Fang was still blind in one eye, the sight of the other was better than the two eyes of most people.

From this time on he was more circumspect in his behaviour, and acquired the reputation of a virtuous man in his part of the country.

P'u Sung-ling (Ch'ing Dynasty)
From *Liao Chai Chih I*

The Ghost of a Hanged Woman

While Chen Peng-nien was still unknown, he was good friends with his fellow countryman Li-Fu. One autumn evening he took advantage of the bright moonlight to call on Li for a chat. This Li, who was a poor scholar, said to Chen, 'I have asked my wife for some wine, but she has none. Just wait a moment while I go out to buy some, and then we can enjoy the moonlight together.'

So Chen took up his poems and sat reading while he waited. Presently a tousled-haired woman in blue came along and opened the door, but shrank back at the sight of Chen. Thinking she was some relative of his host who would not come in because a stranger was there, Chen turned in his seat away from her. Then the woman entered with something in her sleeve, which she hid by the threshold before hurrying in. Chen, curious to know what it was, went to the door to look. It was a rope, foul-smelling and stained with blood. He realized that this was the ghost of some woman who had hanged herself; and putting the cord inside his boot, he resumed his seat.

In a little while the woman with the tousled hair came out and felt for the rope she had hidden, but could not find it. In anger she rushed up to Chen, crying, 'Give that back!'

'Give what back?' Chen demanded.

Instead of answering, she opened her mouth as she stood erect and blew its breath at Chen. The gust of wind was icy cold. Chen's hair stood on end and his teeth chattered, while the lamp turned pale and was on the point of going out.

Chen thought, 'So even ghosts have breath! I have breath too, haven't I?' He took a deep breath and blew back, and wherever his breath touched the woman it made a hole, piercing first her belly, then her breast, and finally making away with her head. In a twinkling she had been blown away like thin smoke, never to appear again.

Soon Li, back with the wine, cried out that his wife was hanging by the bed.

'Don't worry,' said Chen with a laugh. 'I've got the ghost's cord in my boot.' He told Li what had happened. And they went in together to revive Mrs Li, pouring ginger soup down her throat till she came to.

Asked why she had tried to take her own life, she replied, 'Poor as we are, my husband is always entertaining guests. He took the only hairpin I had left to buy wine. I was very upset, but with a guest in the house I couldn't make a scene. Then a woman with tousled hair was standing beside me. She said she was a neighbour living to our left, and told me that my husband didn't take the pin because of the guest, but to go to a gambling den. That made me even more angry. I thought: he won't be back till late and this guest won't go – I can hardly send him packing. Then the woman with tousled hair made a ring with her hands and said, "You can pass through this to the realm of Buddha, where you will have joy untold." But when I tried to get through the ring, her hands would not close tightly enough and it kept breaking. At last she said, "I'll get my Buddha belt to help you achieve Buddhahood." She went out to fetch the belt, but didn't come back. I was in some sort of trance when you came to my rescue.'

Yuan Mei (Ch'ing Dynasty)
From *What Confucius Did Not Talk About*

Miss Quarta Hu

Mr Shang was a native of T'ai-shan and lived alone quietly with his books. One autumn night when the Silver River* was unusually distinct and the moon shining brightly in the sky, he was walking up and down under the shade, his thoughts wandering, when lo! a young girl leaped over the wall, and smilingly asked him, 'What are you thinking about so deeply, Sir?'

Shang looked at her, and seeing that she had a pretty face, asked her to walk in. She then told him her name was Hu and that she was called Tertia. When he wanted to know where she lived, she only laughed and would not say. So he did not inquire any further.

By degrees they struck up a friendship and Miss Tertia used to come and chat with him every evening. He was so smitten that he could hardly take his eyes off her and at last she said to him, 'What are you looking at?' 'At you,' cried he, 'my lovely rose, my beautiful peach. I could gaze at you all night long.'

'If you think so much of poor me,' she answered, 'I don't know where your wits would be if you saw my sister Quarta.'

Mr Shang said he was sorry he did not know her and begged that he might be introduced. So, the next night Miss Tertia brought her sister, who turned out to be a young damsel of about fifteen with a face delicately powdered and resembling the lily, or like an apricot-flower seen through mist. She was altogether as pretty a girl as he had ever seen. Mr Shang was charmed with her, and inviting them in, began to laugh and talk with the elder, while Miss Quarta sat playing with her girdle and keeping her eyes on the ground. By and by, Miss Tertia got up and said she was going, whereupon her sister naturally rose to leave also. Mr Shang begged her not to be in a hurry, and requested the elder to help him persuade her. 'You needn't hurry,' she said to her sister

* Giles translates this word, 'Silver River', as meaning the Chinese equivalent of the Milky Way – an unquestionably more poetical description than our own.

with a smile and accordingly Miss Quarta and Mr Shang remained chatting without reserve, until finally she told him she was a fox.*

Mr Shang, however, was so occupied with her beauty that he didn't pay much heed to this. Then she added: 'And my sister is very dangerous. She has already killed three people. Any one bewitched by her has no chance of escape. Happily, you have bestowed your affections on me, and I shall not allow you to be destroyed. You must break off your acquaintance with her at once.'

Mr Shang was very frightened, and implored her to help him. She replied, 'Although a fox, I am skilled in the arts of the Immortals † and I will write out a charm for you which must be pasted on your door, and in this way, you will protect yourself from her.' And she immediately wrote down the charm and in the morning when her sister came and saw it, she fell back crying out, 'Ungrateful minx! Throw me aside for him, will you! As you two are destined for each other, what have I done to be treated like this?' She then went away.

A few days afterwards Miss Quarta too said she would be absent for a day, so Shang went out for a walk by himself and suddenly beheld a very nice-looking young lady emerge from the shade of an old oak that was growing on the hillside. 'Why so dreadfully pensive?' she asked and then added, 'Those Hu girls can never bring you a single cent.' She then presented Shang with some money, and bade him go on ahead and buy some good wine, adding, 'I'll bring something to eat with me and we'll have some fun.'

Shang took the money and went home, doing as the young lady had told him. By and by, she herself came in and threw a roast chicken and a shoulder of salt pork on the table, and at once began to cut them up. They now set to work to enjoy themselves, and had hardly finished when

---

* The Chinese spirit world possesses the fullest pantheon of any peoples. Within this wondrous world of spirits who can actively interplay with mortals in 'this' world are 'fox spirits'. Fox spirits have numerous characteristics but their particular role is that of a beautiful young girl who seeks to win the love (and eventually marriage and even children) of a mortal man. Through this union, and the opportunity it affords for 'right conduct', the fox spirit can obtain a brighter future existence. Martin Buber, in his admiring article on P'u Sungling's storytelling art, remarks that this strange preference for the fox has been accounted for by the fact that in winter, 'when this animal crosses a frozen lake or river, he continually lowers his head to the ice and listens to the water flowing beneath it'. In this way, Buber theorizes, the Chinese saw the fox as combining the dark primeval realm under the ice, the domain of Yin, with the bright, upper world of Yang, the masculine and constructive element.

† The Taoists were considered the 'Immortals' in Chinese cosmology. See Herbert Giles, *A History of Chinese Literature* (William Heinemann, London, 1901), p 56, 'Taoism – The *Tao-Te-Ching*'.

they heard someone coming in, and the next minute in walked Miss Tertia and her sister.

The strange young lady did not know where to hide and managed to lose her shoes as well. The other two began to revile her saying, 'Out of here, you base fox! What are you doing in this place?' They chased her away with a certain amount of difficulty. Shang began to excuse himself to them until at last they forgave him and they all became friends again.

One day, however, a Shensi* man arrived riding on a donkey, and coming up to the door said, 'I have long been in search of these evil spirits and now I've got them.' Shang's father thought the man's remarks rather strange, and asked him from where he had come. 'Across much land and sea,' he replied, 'for eight or nine months out of every year I am absent from my native place. These devils killed my brother with their poison. Alas! Alas! And I have sworn to exterminate them, but until now have never been able to find them although I have travelled many, many miles. They are now in your house and if you do not cut them off, you will die even as my brother did.'

Now Shang and the young ladies had kept their acquaintanceship very dark but his father and mother had indeed guessed that something was up and, much alarmed, bade the Shensi man walk in and perform his exorcisms. Producing two bottles, the Shensi man placed them upon the ground and proceeded to mutter a number of charms and caballistic formulae, whereupon four wreaths of smoke passed two by two into each bottle.

'I have the whole family,' cried he in an ecstasy of delight and proceeded to tie down the mouths of the bottles with pigs' bladders, sealing them with the utmost care. Shang's father was equally pleased and kept his guest to dinner. Shang, however, was sadly dejected and approaching the bottles unperceived by the others, bent his ear to listen.

'Ungrateful man,' hissed Miss Quarta from within, 'to sit there and make no effort to save me.' This was more than Shang could stand and he immediately broke the seal. But he found he could not untie the knot.

'Take down the flag that now stands on the altar,' advised Miss Quarta, 'and with a pin prick in the bladder I can easily get out.'

Shang did as she bade him and in a moment a thin streak of white smoke issued forth from the hole and disappeared in the clouds. When the Shensi man came out and saw the flag lying on the ground, he started violently and cried out, 'Escaped! This must be your doing, young man.' He then shook the bottle and listened, finally exclaiming, 'Luckily, only one has got away. She was fated not to die and may therefore be pardoned.' Thereupon he took the bottles and went his way.

* A province in Northern China.

Some years afterwards Shang was one day superintending his reapers cutting the corn when he spied Miss Quarta at a distance sitting under a tree. He approached and she took his hand saying, 'Ten years have rolled away since last we met. Since then I have gained the prize of immortality, but I thought that perhaps you had not quite forgotten me, and so I came to see you once more.'

Shang, of course, wished her to return home with him, to which she replied, 'I am no longer what I was that I may mingle in the affairs of mortals. We shall meet again.' And as she said this, she disappeared.

Twenty years later, when Shang was one day alone, Miss Quarta simply walked in. Shang was overjoyed and began to address her but she answered him saying, 'My name is already enrolled in the Register of the Immortals and I have no right to return to earth. However, out of gratitude to you, I determined to announce to you the date of your dissolution so that you may put your affairs in order. Fear nothing, for I shall see you safely through to the happy land.'

She then departed and on the day named Shang actually died. A relative of a friend of mine, Mr Li Wen-yu, frequently met the above mentioned Mr Shang.*

P'u Sung-ling (Ch'ing Dynasty)
From *Liao Chai Chih I*

Wei Pang

During the Ta Li Era† in the T'ang Dynasty, there was a scholar named Wei Pang who possessed unusual strength, and who travelled at night without fear. He was a good horseman and archer, and never left home without his bow and arrows. He not only cooked all the birds and beasts he caught, but even ate snakes, scorpions, earthworms, dung beetles, mole-crickets and the like.

* Many Chinese authors end their tales with this type of personal note.
† AD 766–779.

He was out at dusk once in the capital when the sounding of the evening drum surprised him still far from his destination, and he did not know where he could find a lodging. Then he noticed a respectable-looking family in that neighbourhood moving out of their house and about to lock the gate. Wei asked if he might spend the night there.

The master of the house said, 'There is a dead man next door. As the saying goes, this house is under the influence of an evil spirit. If anyone goes in, he will be hurt. So we are moving into a relative's house nearby to keep out of harm's way till tomorrow. I cannot conceal this from you.'

'Just let me stay here for the night,' said Wei. 'You need not worry about anything. If there is an evil spirit, I shall bear the brunt of it.'

The owner of the house led him inside, opened up the hall and kitchen and showed him where a bed, food and drink were to be had. Wei told his servant to stable his horse and light a candle in the hall, then prepare a meal in the kitchen. After eating, he made his man sleep in another room while he put his couch in the hall and opened the door. Then he blew out the candle, held his bow ready, and sat there to wait for the ghost.

Towards the end of the third watch, a bright object resembling a large disc, shining like fire, flew down from the air to the door. When Wei saw this he was delighted.

Drawing his bowstring to the full in the dark, he let fly an arrow which hit the target in the centre. There was a crackling and then flames darted out. He shot three times in succession, till the light grew dim and the thing ceased to move. Bow in hand, he went to pull the arrows out. Suddenly the shining object fell to the ground.

Wei called his servant to fetch a light and found it was a lump of flesh with eyes all over it. When these eyes flickered they emitted sparkling gleams.

Wei said with a laugh, 'So, the master of the house was right when he said that this place was under the influence of an evil spirit!' And he told his man to cook the lump of flesh.

The meat smelled most appetizing and, well cooked and chopped into a mince, it proved delicious. He shared it with his servant, leaving half to show the master of the house. At dawn, when the owner came back, he was pleased to find Wei safe, and when Wei told him about the ghost and showed him the meat, he was greatly amazed.

Huangfu (T'ang Dynasty)
From *Tracing the Changes*

The Princess Lily

At Chiao-chou there lived a man named Tou Hsun, otherwise known as Hsiao-hui. One day he had just dropped off to sleep when he beheld a man in serge clothes standing by the bedside, apparently anxious to communicate something to him. Tou inquired his errand, to which the man replied that he was the bearer of an invitation from his master.

'And who is your master?' asked Tou.

'Oh, he doesn't live far off,' replied the other.

So they went away together, and after some time came to a place where there were innumerable white houses rising one above the other, shaded by dense groves of lemon-trees. They threaded their way past countless doors, not at all similar to those usually used, and saw a great many official looking men and women passing and repassing. They all called out to the man in serge, 'Has Mr Tou come?' to which he always replied in the affirmative.

Here a mandarin met them and escorted Tou into a palace, upon which the latter remarked, 'This is really very kind of you but I haven't the honour of knowing you, and I feel somewhat diffident about going in.'

'Our Prince,' answered his guide, 'has long heard of you as a man of good family and excellent principles, and is very anxious to make your acquaintance.'

'Who is your Prince?' inquired Tou.

'You'll see for yourself in a moment,' said the other. Just then two girls with banners came out and guided Tou through a great number of doors until they came to a throne, upon which sat the Prince. His Highness immediately descended to meet him, and made him take the seat of honour. Then exquisite viands of all kinds were spread out before them. Looking up, Tou noticed a scroll, on which was inscribed *The Cassia Court*. He was just beginning to feel puzzled as to what he should say next, when the Prince addressed him: 'The honour of having you for a neighbour is, as it were, a bond of affinity between us. Let us, then, give ourselves up to enjoyment and put away suspicion and fear.' Tou murmured his acquiescence, and when the wine had gone round several times, there arose from a distance the sound of pipes and singing – unaccompanied, however, by the usual drum and very much subdued in volume. Thereupon the Prince looked about him and cried out, 'We are about to set a verse for any of you gentlemen to cap! Here you are: *Genius seeks the Cassia Court.*'

While the courtiers were all engaged in thinking of some fit antithesis,* Tou added, '*Refinement loves the Lily flower*', upon which the Prince exclaimed, 'How strange! Lily is my daughter's name, and, after such a coincidence, she must come in for you to see her.'

In a few moments, the tinkling of her ornaments and a delicious fragrance of musk announced the arrival of the Princess, who was between sixteen and seventeen, and endowed with surpassing beauty. The Prince bade her make an obeisance to Tou, at the same time introducing her as his daughter Lily.

As soon as the ceremony was over the young lady moved away. Tou remained in a state of stupefaction, and when the Prince proposed that they should pledge each other in another bumper, paid not the slightest attention to what he said. Perceiving what had distracted his guest's attention, the Prince remarked that he was anxious to find a consort for his daughter, but that unfortunately there was the difficulty of *species*, and he didn't know what to do. But again Tou took no notice of what the Prince was saying, until at length one of the bystanders plucked his sleeve and asked him if he hadn't seen that the Prince wished to drink with him, and had just been addressing some remarks to him. Thereupon Tou started, and, recovering himself at once, rose from the table and apologized to the Prince for his rudeness, declaring that he had taken so much wine he didn't know what he was doing. 'Besides,' said he, 'Your Highness has doubtless business to transact. I will therefore take my leave.'

'I am extremely pleased to have seen you,' replied the Prince, 'and only regret that you are in such a hurry to be gone. However, I won't detain you now, but if you don't forget all about us, I shall be very glad to invite you here again.' He then gave orders that Tou should be escorted home. On the way one of the courtiers asked Tou why he had said nothing when the Prince had spoken of a consort for his daughter, as His Highness had evidently made the remark with an eye to securing

* This was a favourite pastime of the literati in China. Giles explains that the important point is that 'each word in the second line should be a proper antithesis of the word in the first line'.

him as his son-in-law. The latter was now sorry that he had missed his opportunity.

Meanwhile they reached his house and he himself awoke. The sun had already set and there he sat in the gloom thinking of what had happened. In the evening he put out his candle, hoping to continue his dream; but, alas! the thread was broken and all he could do was to pour forth his repentance in sighs.

One night he was sleeping at a friend's house when suddenly an officer of the Court walked in and summoned him to appear before the Prince. He jumped up and hurried off at once to the palace, where he prostrated himself before the throne. The Prince raised him and made him sit down, saying that since they had last met he had become aware that Tou would be willing to marry his daughter, and hoped that he might be allowed to offer her as a handmaid. Tou rose and thanked the Prince, who thereupon gave orders for a banquet to be prepared.

When they had finished their wine it was announced that the Princess had completed her toilet. Immediately a bevy of young ladies came in with the Princess in their midst, a red veil covering her head, gliding with tiny footsteps as they led her up to be introduced to Tou. When the ceremonies were concluded, Tou said to the Princess, 'In your presence, Madam, it would be easy to forget even death itself. But tell me, is not this all a dream?'

'And how can it be a dream,' asked the Princess, 'when you and I are here together?'

Next morning Tou amused himself by helping the Princess to paint her face, and then with a girdle he began to measure the size of her waist and with his fingers the length of her feet.* 'Are you crazy?' cried she, laughing.

Tou replied, 'I have been deceived so often by dreams that I am now making a careful record. If such it turns out to be, I shall still have something as a souvenir of you.' While they were thus chatting, a maid rushed into the room, shrieking out, 'Alas! alas! a great monster has got into the palace: the Prince has fled into a side chamber: destruction is surely come upon us.' Tou was in a great fright when he heard this and rushed off to see the Prince, who grasped his hand and, with tears in his eyes, begged him not to desert them. 'Our relationship,' cried he, 'was cemented when Heaven sent this calamity upon us, and now my kingdom will be overthrown. What shall I do?'

---

* It is a well-known fact that small feet were admired in China. But it is also true that small waists were considered highly desirable. Chinese women, however, unlike their European counterparts, avoided any stays or corsets to achieve this.

Tou begged to know what was the matter and then the Prince laid a dispatch upon the table, telling Tou to open it and make himself acquainted with its contents. This dispatch ran as follows: 'The Grand Secretary of State, Black Wings, to His Royal Highness, announcing the arrival of an extraordinary monster, and advising the immediate removal of the Court in order to preserve the vitality of the empire. A report has just been received from the officer in charge of the Yellow Gate stating that, ever since the 6th of the 5th moon, a huge monster, 10,000 feet in length, has been lying coiled up outside the entrance to the palace, and that it has already devoured 13,800 and odd of your Highness's subjects, and is spreading desolation far and wide. On receipt of this information your servant proceeded to make a reconnaissance, and there beheld a venomous reptile with a head as big as a mountain and eyes like vast sheets of water. Every time it raised its head, whole buildings disappeared down its throat; and, on stretching itself out, walls and houses were alike laid in ruins. In all antiquity there is no record of such a scourge. The fate of our temples and ancestral halls is now a mere question of hours; we therefore pray Your Royal Highness to depart at once with the Royal Family and seek somewhere else a happier abode.' *

When Tou had read this document his face turned ashy pale. Just then a messenger rushed in, shrieking out, 'Here is the monster!' at which the whole Court burst into lamentations as if their last hour was at hand. The Prince was beside himself with fear. All he could do was to beg Tou to look to his own safety without regarding the wife through whom he was involved in their misfortunes.

The Princess, however, who was standing by, bitterly lamenting the fate that had fallen upon them, begged Tou not to desert her. After a moment's hesitation, he said that he should be only too happy to place his own poor home at their immediate disposal if they would only deign to honour him.

'How can we talk of *deigning*,' cried the Princess, 'at such a moment as this? I pray you take us there as quickly as possible.'

So Tou gave her his arm, and in no time they had arrived at Tou's house, which the Princess at once pronounced to be a charming place of residence and even better than their former kingdom.

'But I must now ask you,' said she to Tou, 'to make some arrangement for my father and mother, that the old order of things may be continued here.' Tou at first offered objections to this, whereupon the

---

* In translating this 'fanciful document' Herbert Giles tells us that it is couched in language 'precisely such as would be used by an officer of the Government in announcing some national calamity; hence the the value of these tales – models as they are of the purest possible style'.

Princess said that a man who would not help another in his hour of need was not much of a man, and immediately went off into a fit of hysterics, from which Tou was trying his best to recall her when all of a sudden he awoke and found that it was all a dream. He still heard a buzzing in his ears, however, which he knew was not made by any human being, and, on looking carefully about, he discovered two or three bees which had settled on his pillow.

He was very much astonished at this and consulted with his friend, who was also greatly amazed at his strange story. Then Tou's friend pointed out a number of other bees on various parts of his dress, none of which would go away even when brushed off. His friend now advised him to get a hive for them, which he did without delay, and it was immediately filled by a whole swarm of bees, which came flying from over the wall in great numbers. On tracing whence they had come it was found that they belonged to an old gentleman who lived near and who had kept bees for more than thirty years previously. Tou thereupon went and told him the story and when the old gentleman examined his hive he found the bees all gone. On breaking it open, he discovered a large snake of about ten feet in length inside, which he immediately killed, recognizing in it the 'huge monster' of Tou's adventure. As for the bees, they remained with Tou and increased in numbers every year.

P'u Sung-ling (Ch'ing Dynasty)
From *Liao Chai Chih I*

The Ghost in the Privy

Mr Hsu Nan-chin of Nanpi has great courage. While studying in a monastery once, he was sharing a bed with a friend when two torches blazed out from the north wall at midnight. Looking closely, he saw emerging from the wall a man's face as large as a winnowing fan. The two torches were its eyes. His friend shook with fear and nearly died of fright, but Hsu threw his coat over his shoulders and got up slowly remarking, 'I was wanting to read but my candle had burned out. It was very good of you to come!' He picked up a book and sat with his back to the creature to read aloud. He had not read many pages, when little by little the light from the eyes faded. Though he knocked on the wall and called out, it did not come back.

Another night he went to the privy, followed by a servant boy carrying a candle. Without warning, the same face emerged from the ground to grin at him. The boy dropped the candle and fell flat on the ground, but Hsu picked it up and put it on the spectre's head saying, 'My candle has no stand. It was very good of you to come again.' When the spectre just looked at him without moving, Hsu said, 'Can't you take yourself somewhere else, instead of coming here? By the sea there are men who hanker after foul smells.* I suppose you are one of them. Well, I mustn't disappoint you.' He smeared a filthy paper on its mouth. The spectre belched, uttered frantic roars, and disappeared after knocking over the candle. And since that day it has never been seen again.

Chi Yun (Ch'ing Dynasty)
Originally titled 'Hsu Nan-Chin of Nanpi'
From *Notes of the Yueh-wei Hermitage*

Wang Chi-ming

Wang Chi-ming of Wuyuan once moved into the Scholar's Mansion at Shangho, formerly the home of his kinsman Wang Po, a metropolitan scholar. During the night of the first day of the fourth month of the thirty-ninth year of Chien Lung,† he had a long nightmare from which he woke to find a ghost tall as the room standing by his curtain. Since Wang was a brave man, he leaped up to grapple with the ghost. It

* The translators of this tale note that in *The Annals of Lu Pu-wei* there is the story of a man who smelled so obnoxious, owing to a disease, that none of his family could endure his company. He was forced to live alone by the seashore where he met a man who, 'fascinated by his stench, stuck closely to him'.
† AD 1774.

rushed towards the door, but hurtled by mistake against the wall and seemed stunned. Wang had just seized hold of its waist when a cold gust of wind made the lamp flicker and go out. Unable to see the ghost's face, he could only feel that its hands were icy cold, its waist as thick as a barrel. He wanted to shout for his family, but not a sound could he utter. It was some time before, mustering all his strength, he managed to raise a shout at which his whole household assembled. The ghost by then had shrunk to the size of an infant. When they held a lamp up to it, they found that Wang was holding a roll of tattered silk wadding. Then tiles and bricks rained down outside the window, and Wang's terrified family urged him to let the ghost go.

Wang laughed and said, 'This ghostly crew is trying to scare us, but what can they do? If I let it go, it will help the rest to make trouble. We'd better kill this one as a warning to all other ghosts.'

So holding the ghost with his left hand, he took a torch from one of his family with his right and burned it. There was a crackling, blood spurted out, and the stench was unbearable. The next morning his neighbours, who had been disturbed, gathered. But they all had to hold their noses because of the stench. Blood as sticky as glue lay more than an inch thick on the ground, and no one knew what manner of ghost this was. Mr Wang Feng-ting from an illustrious family wrote his poem *Catching the Ghost* to record this incident.

> Yuan Mei (Ch'ing Dynasty)
> From *What Confucius Did Not Talk About*

The Thunder God

Yo Yun-hao and Hsia P'ing-tzu lived as boys in the same village, and when they grew up read with the same tutor, becoming the firmest of friends. Hsia was a clever fellow and had acquired some reputation even at the early age of ten. Yo was not a bit envious, but rather looked up to him, and Hsia in return helped his friend very much with his studies, so that he, too, made considerable progress. This increased Hsia's fame, though try as he would, he could never succeed at the public examinations and, by and by, he sickened and died. His family was so poor they could not find money for his burial whereupon Yo came forward and paid all expenses, besides taking care of his widow and children.

Every peck or bushel he would share with them, the widow trusting entirely to his support; and thus he acquired a good name in the village, though not being a rich man himself, he soon ran through all his own property. 'Alas!' cried he, 'where talents like Hsia's failed, can I expect to succeed? Wealth and rank are matters of destiny, and my present career will only end by my dying like a dog in a ditch. I must try something else.' So he gave up book-learning and went into trade, and in six months he had a trifle of money in hand.

One day when he was resting at an inn in Nanking, he saw a great big fellow walk in and seat himself at no great distance in a very melancholy mood. Yo asked him if he was hungry and, on receiving no answer, pushed some food over towards him. The stranger immediately set to feeding himself by handfuls and in no time the whole had disappeared. Yo ordered another supply, but that was quickly disposed of in like manner; and then he told the landlord to bring a shoulder of pork and a quantity of boiled dumplings. Thus, after eating enough for half a dozen, his appetite was appeased and he turned to thank his benefactor. 'For three years I haven't had such a meal.'

'And why should a fine fellow like you be in such a state of destitution?' inquired Yo, to which the other only replied, 'The judgements of heaven may not be discussed.' Being asked where he lived the stranger replied, 'On land I have no home, on the water no boat; at dawn in the village, at night in the city.'

Yo soon prepared to depart, but his friend would not leave him, declaring that he was in imminent danger, and that he could not forget the late kindness Yo had shown him. So they went along together, and on the way Yo invited the other to eat with him. But this he refused, saying that he only took food occasionally. Yo marvelled more than ever at this, and next day when they were on the river a great storm arose and capsized all their boats, Yo himself being thrown into the water with the others. Suddenly the gale abated and the stranger bore Yo on his back to another boat, plunging at once into the water and bringing back the lost vessel, upon which he placed Yo and bade him remain quietly there. He then returned once more, this time carrying in his arms a part of the cargo, which he replaced in the vessel, and so he went on until it was all restored.

Yo thanked him, saying, 'It was enough to save my life, but you have added to this the restoration of my goods.' Nothing, in fact, had been lost, and now Yo began to regard the stranger as something more than human. The latter here wished to take his leave, but Yo pressed him so much to stay that at last he consented to remain. Then Yo remarked that after all he had lost a gold pin, and immediately the stranger plunged into the water again, rising at length to the surface with the missing article in his mouth and presenting it to Yo with the remark that he was delighted to be able to fulfil his commands. The people on the river were much astonished at what they saw.

Meanwhile Yo went home with his friend and there they lived together, the big man only eating once in ten or twelve days, but then displaying an enormous appetite. One day he spoke of going away, to which Yo would by no means consent. As it was just then about to rain and thunder, he asked him to tell him what the clouds were like, and what thunder was, and how he could get up to the sky and have a look, so as to set his mind at rest on the subject.

'Would you like to have a ramble among the clouds?' asked the stranger, as Yo was lying down to take a nap.

Upon awaking from his nap, Yo felt himself spinning along through the air and not at all as if he was lying on a bed. Opening his eyes he saw he was among the clouds and around him was a fleecy atmosphere. Jumping up in great alarm, he felt giddy as if he had been at sea, and underneath his feet he found a soft, yielding substance unlike the earth. Above him were the stars and this made him think he was dreaming. But looking up he saw that they were set in the sky like seeds in the cup of a lily, varying from the size of the biggest bowl to that of a small basin. On raising his hand he discovered that the large stars were all tightly fixed; but he managed to pick a small one, which he concealed in his sleeve; and then, parting the clouds beneath him, he looked through and saw the sea glittering like silver below. Large cities appeared no bigger than beans – just at this moment, however, he bethought himself that if his foot were to slip, what a tremendous fall he would have. He now beheld two dragons writhing their way along, drawing a cart with a huge vat in it, each movement of their tails sounding like the crack of a bullock-driver's whip. The vat was full of water and numbers of men were employed in ladling it out and sprinkling it on the clouds. These men were astonished at seeing Yo. A big fellow among them called out, 'All right, he's my friend,' and they gave him a ladle to help them throw the water out.

Now it happened to be a very dry season, and when Yo got hold of the ladle he took good care to throw the water so that it should fall on and around his own home. The big stranger then told him that he was an

assistant to the God of Thunder,* and that he had just returned from a
three years' punishment inflicted on him in consequence of some neglect
of his in the matter of rain. He told Yo that they must now part and,
taking the long rope which had been used as reins for the cart, bade Yo
grip it tightly, that he might be let down to earth. Yo was afraid of this,
but on being told there was no danger he did so, and in a moment
whish-h-h-h-h – away he went and found himself safe and sound on
terra firma. He discovered that he had descended outside his native
village, and then the rope was drawn up into the clouds and he saw it no
more.

The drought had been excessive that year, and for three or four miles
round very little rain had fallen, though in Yo's own village the water-
courses were all full. On reaching home he took the star out of his sleeve
and put it on the table. It was dull-looking like an ordinary stone, but at
night it became very brilliant and lighted up the whole house. This made
him value it highly, and he stored it carefully away, bringing it out only
when he had guests, to light them at their wine.

The stone was always thus dazzling bright, until one evening when
his wife was sitting with him doing her hair, the star began to diminish
in brilliancy and to flit about like a fire-fly. Mrs Yo sat gaping with
astonishment when all of a sudden it flitted into her mouth and ran
down her throat. She tried to cough it up, but couldn't, to the very great
amazement of her husband.

That night Yo dreamt that his old friend Hsia appeared before him
and said, 'I am the Shao-wei star. Your friendship is still cherished by
me and now you have brought me back from the sky. Truly our
destinies are knitted together and I will repay your kindness by becoming your son.' Now Yo was thirty years of age but without sons;
after this dream, however, his wife bore him a male child and they called
his name Star. He was extraordinarily clever and at sixteen years of age
took his master's degree.

P'u Sung-ling (Ch'ing Dynasty)
From *Liao Chai Chih I*

* The Thunder God, aided by the Goddess of Lightning, was believed by the
Chinese to be constantly on the watch for wicked people. The idea that a watch-
ful god will wreak vengeance from on high is, of course, an ancient belief
common to many cultures. See, for example, Tylor's *Primitive Culture* (John
Murray, London, 1871, new edition 1920) and *Primitive Religions* by G. T.
Bettany (Part IV of *World Religions*, Ward Lock, 1890).

Dr Tseng's Dream

There was a Fuhkien gentleman named Tseng, who had just taken his doctor's degree. One day he was out walking with several other recently elected doctors, when they heard that at a temple hard by there lived an astrologer, and accordingly the party proceeded thither to get their fortunes told. They went in and sat down, and the astrologer made some very complimentary remarks to Tseng, at which he fanned himself and smiled, saying, 'Have I any chance of ever wearing the dragon robes and the jade girdle?'*

The astrologer immediately put on a serious face, and replied that he would be a Secretary of State during twenty years of national tranquillity. Tseng was much pleased, and began to give himself greater airs than ever. A slight rain coming on, they sought shelter in the priest's quarters, where they found an old bonze,† with sunken eyes and a big nose, sitting upon a mat. He took no notice of the strangers, who, after having bowed to him, stretched themselves upon the couches to chat, not forgetting to congratulate Tseng upon the destiny which had been foretold him. Tseng, too, seemed to think the thing was a matter of certainty, and mentioned the names of several friends he intended to advance, amongst others the old family butler. Roars of laughter greeted this announcement, mingled with the patter-patter of the increasing rain outside.

Tseng then curled himself up for a nap, when suddenly in walked two officials bearing a commission under the Great Seal appointing Tseng to the Grand Secretariat. As soon as Tseng understood their errand, he rushed off at once to pay his respects to the Emperor, who graciously detained him some time in conversation, and then issued instructions that the promotion and dismissal of all officers below the third grade‡

* Such finery indicated rising to the highest offices of State.
† A Buddhist monk.
‡ The official life in China was divided into nine grades.

should be vested in Tseng alone. He was next presented with the dragon robes, the jade girdle, and a horse from the imperial stables, after which he kowtowed before His Majesty and took his leave.

He then went home, but it was no longer the old home of his youth. Painted beams, carved pillars, and a general profusion of luxury and elegance made him wonder where on earth he was until, nervously stroking his beard, he ventured to call out in a low tone. Immediately the responses of numberless attendants echoed through the place like thunder. Presents of costly food were sent to him by all the grandees, and his gate was absolutely blocked up by the crowds of retainers who were constantly coming and going.

When Privy Councillors came to see him he would rush out in haste to receive them; when Under-Secretaries of State visited him he made them a polite bow; but to all below these he would hardly vouchsafe a word. The Governor of Shansi sent him twelve singing-girls, two of whom, Ni-ni and Fairy, he made his favourites.

All day long he had nothing to do but find amusement as best he could, until he bethought himself that formerly a man named Wang had often assisted him with money. Thereupon he memorialized the Throne and obtained official employment for him. Then he recollected that there was another man to whom he owed a long-standing grudge. He at once caused this man, who was in the Government service, to be impeached and stripped of his rank and dignities. Thus he squared accounts with both. One day when out in his chair a drunken man bumped against one of his tablet-bearers.* Tseng had him seized and sent in to the mayor's yamen,† where he died under the bamboo. Owners of land adjoining his would make him a present of the richest portions, fearing the consequences if they did not do so; and thus he became very wealthy, almost on a par with the State itself.

By-and-by, Ni-ni and Fairy died, and Tseng was overwhelmed with grief. Suddenly he remembered that in former years he had seen a

---

* In his translation of this story, Giles describes the Chinese public entourage of officials. 'The retinue of a high mandarin is composed as follows: First, gong-bearers, then banner-men, tablet-bearers (on which tables are inscribed the titles of the official), a large red umbrella, mounted attendants, a box containing a change of clothes, bearers of regalia, a second gong, a small umbrella or sun-shade, a large wooden fan, executioners or lictors from hell, who wear tall hats; a mace (called a "golden melon"), bamboos for bambooing, incense bearers, more attendants, and now the great man himself, followed by a bodyguard of soldiers and a few personal attendants, amounting in all to nearly one hundred persons, many of whom are mere street-rowdies or beggars, hired at a trifling outlay when required to join what might otherwise be an imposing procession.'
† Official's residence.

beautiful girl whom he wished to purchase as a concubine, but want of money had then prevented him from carrying out his intention. Now there was no longer that difficulty and accordingly he sent off two trusty servants to get the girl by force. In a short time she arrived and he found that she had grown more beautiful than ever. And so his cup of happiness was full.

But years rolled on and gradually his fellow officials became estranged, Tseng taking no notice of their behaviour, until at last one of them impeached him to the Throne in a long and bitter memorial. Happily, however, the Emperor still regarded him with favour, and for some time kept the memorial by him unanswered. Then followed a joint memorial from the whole of the Privy Council, including those who had once thronged his doors, and had falsely called him their dear father. The Imperial rescript to this document was 'Banishment to Yunnan,'* his son, who was Governor of P'ing-yang, being also implicated in his guilt.

When Tseng heard the news, he was overcome with fear, but an armed guard was already at his gate and the lictors were forcing their way into his innermost apartments. They tore off his robe and official hat and bound him and his wife with cords. Then they collected together in the hall his gold, his silver, and bank-notes,† to the value of many hundred thousands of taels. His pearls, and jade, and precious stones filled many bushel baskets. His curtains, and screens, and beds, and other articles of furniture were brought out by thousands; while the swaddling-clothes of his infant boy and the shoes of his little girl were lying littered about the steps. It was a sad sight for Tseng; but a worse blow was that of his concubine carried off almost lifeless before his eyes, himself not daring to utter a word. Then all the apartments, storerooms, and treasuries were sealed up; and, with a volley of curses, the soldiers bade Tseng begone and proceeded to leave the place, dragging him with them. The husband and wife prayed that they might be allowed some old cart, but this favour was denied them. After about ten *li*‡ Tseng's wife could barely walk, her feet being swollen and sore. Tseng helped her along as best he could, but another ten *li* reduced him to a state of abject fatigue.

By and by they saw before them a great mountain, the summit of which was lost in the clouds. Fearing they should be made to ascend it, Tseng and his wife stood still and began to weep. The lictors, however, clamoured round them and would permit them no rest. The sun was rapidly sinking and there was no place at hand where they could obtain

---

* The Chinese frequently banished officials to semi-barbarous or wild areas.
† Paper money became quite common around AD 1154 in China.
‡ A *li* is about 550 yards.

shelter for one night. So they continued on their weary way until about half-way up the hill, when his wife's strength was quite exhausted, and she sat down by the roadside. Tseng, too, halted to rest in spite of the soldiers and their abuse. But they had hardly stopped a moment before down came a band of robbers upon them, each with a sharp knife in his hand. The soldiers immediately took to their heels and Tseng fell on his knees before the robbers, crying out, 'I am a poor criminal going into banishment and have nothing to give you. I pray you spare my life.'

But the robbers sternly replied, 'We are all the victims of your crimes and now we want your wicked head.'

Then Tseng began to revile them, saying, 'Dogs! though I am under sentence of banishment I am still an officer of the State.'

But the robbers cursed him again, flourishing a sword over his neck, and the next thing he heard was the noise of his own head as it fell with a thud to the ground. At the same instant two devils stepped forward and seized him each by one hand, compelling him to go with them. After a little while they arrived at a great city where there was a hideously ugly king sitting upon a throne judging between good and evil. Tseng crawled before him on his hands and knees to receive sentence, and the king, after turning over a few pages of his register, thundered out, 'The punishment of a traitor who has brought misfortune on his country: the cauldron of boiling oil!' To this ten thousand devils responded with a cry like a clap of thunder, and one huge monster led Tseng down alongside the cauldron, which was seven feet in height, and surrounded on all sides by blazing fuel, so that it was of a glowing red heat.

Tseng shrieked for mercy, but it was all up with him, for the devil seized him by the hair and the small of his back and pitched him headlong in. Down he fell with a splash, and rose and sank with the bubbling of the oil, which ate through his flesh into his very vitals. He longed to die, but death would not come to him. After about half an hour's boiling, a devil took him out on a pitchfork and threw him down before the Infernal King, who again consulted his notebook and said, 'You relied on your position to treat others with contumely and injustice, for which you must suffer on the Sword-Hill.' Again he was led away by devils to a large hill thickly studded with sharp swords, their points upwards like the shoots of bamboo, with here and there the remains of many miserable wretches who had suffered before him. Tseng again cried for mercy and crouched upon the ground; but a devil bored into him with a poisoned awl until he screamed with pain. He was then seized and flung up high into the air, falling down right on the sword-points, to his most frightful agony. This was repeated several times until he was almost hacked to pieces.

He was then brought once more before the king, who asked what was the amount of his peculations while on earth. Immediately an accountant came forward with an abacus, and said that the whole sum was 3,210,000 taels, whereupon the king replied, 'Let him drink that amount.' Forthwith the devils piled up a great heap of gold and silver and, when they had melted it in a huge crucible, began pouring it into Tseng's mouth. The pain was excruciating as the molten metal ran down his throat into his vitals; but since in life he had never been able to get enough of the dross, it was determined he should feel no lack of it then. He was half a day drinking it and then the king ordered him away to be born again as a woman* in Kan-chou. A few steps brought them to a huge frame, where on an iron axle revolved a mighty wheel many hundred *yojanas*† in circumference, and shining with a brilliant light. The devils flogged Tseng on to the wheel, and he shut his eyes as he stepped up.

Then whiz – and away he went, feet foremost, round with the wheel, until he felt himself tumble off and a cold thrill ran through him, when he opened his eyes and found he was changed into a girl. He saw his father and mother in rags and tatters, and in one corner a beggar's bowl and a staff, and understood the calamity that had befallen him. Day after day he begged about the streets and his inside rumbled for want of food; he had no clothes for his back.

At fourteen years of age he was sold to a gentleman as concubine; and then, though food and clothes were not wanting, he had to put up with the scoldings and floggings of the wife, who one day burnt him with a hot iron. Luckily the gentleman took a fancy to him and treated him well, which kindness Tseng repaid by an irreproachable fidelity. It happened, however, that on one occasion when they were chatting together, burglars broke into the house and killed the gentleman, Tseng having escaped by hiding himself under the bed. Thereupon he was immediately charged by the wife with murder, and on being taken before the authorities was sentenced to die the 'lingering death'.‡ This sentence was at once carried out with tortures more horrible than any in all the Courts of Purgatory, in the middle of which Tseng heard one of his companions call out 'Hello, there! you've got nightmare.'

* As Giles points out, this contingency of rebirth is dreaded by the Chinese male.
† The actual size of a *yojana* is in doubt, but Giles estimates it at from five to nine English miles.
‡ Giles writes that this is a celebrated and dreaded form of ancient torture, reserved for parricide and similar 'awful crimes'. The malefactor is literally chopped to pieces, slowly, so as to prolong his agony. But the sentence is rarely carried out, Giles informs us. Generally, a few gashes are made on the victim's body and he is then decapitated.

Tseng got up and rubbed his eyes, and his friends said, 'It's quite late in the day, and we're all very hungry.' But the old priest smiled, and asked him if the prophecy as to his future was true or not. Tseng bowed and begged him to explain; whereupon the old priest said, 'For those who cultivate virtue, a lily will grow up even in the fiery pit.' Tseng had gone thither full of pride and vainglory; he went home an altered man. From that day he thought no more of becoming a Secretary of State, but retired into the hills, and I know not what became of him after that.

P'u Sung-ling (Ch'ing Dynasty)
From *Liao Chai Chih I*

The Wolf Dream

Mr Pai was a native of Chih-li, and his eldest son was called Chia. The latter had been some two years holding an appointment as magistrate in the south, but because of the great distance between them, his family had heard nothing of him. One day a distant cousin, named Ting, called at the house and Mr Pai, not having seen this gentleman for a long time, treated him with much cordiality. Now Ting was one of those persons who are occasionally employed by the Judge of the Infernal Regions to make arrests on earth; and, as they were chatting together, Mr Pai questioned him about the realms below. Ting told him all kinds of strange things, but Pai did not believe them, answering only by a smile.

Some days afterwards, he had just lain down to sleep when Ting walked in and asked him to go for a stroll. So they went off together, and by and by reached the city. 'There,' said Ting, pointing to a door, 'lives your nephew,' alluding to a son of Mr Pai's elder sister, who was a magistrate in Honan. When Pai expressed his doubts as to the accuracy of this statement, Ting led him in, when, lo and behold! there was his nephew sitting in his court dressed in his official robes. Around him stood the guard. It was impossible to get near him but Ting remarked that his son's residence was not far off, and asked Pai if he would not like to see him too. The latter assenting, they walked along till they came to a large building, which Ting said was the place.

There was a fierce wolf at the entrance, however, and Mr Pai was afraid to go in. But Ting bade him enter. Accordingly they walked in and found that all the employees of the place, some of whom were standing about and others lying down to sleep, were all wolves. The central pathway was piled up with whitening bones and Mr Pai felt horribly alarmed; but Ting kept close to him all the time and at length they got safely in. Pai's son, Chia, was just coming out, and when he saw his father accompanied by Ting, he was overjoyed, and, asking them to sit down, bade the attendants serve some refreshment. Thereupon a great big wolf brought in the carcass of a dead man in his mouth and set it before them, at which Mr Pai rose up in consternation, and asked his son what this meant.

'It's only a little refreshment for you, Father,' replied Chia. But this did not calm Mr Pai's agitation, who would have retired precipitately, had it not been for the crowd of wolves which barred the path. Just as he was at a loss what to do, there was a general stampede among the animals, which scurried away, some under the couches and some under the tables and chairs; and while he was wondering what the cause of this could be, in marched two knights in golden armour who looked sternly at Chia, and, producing a black rope, proceeded to bind him hand and foot. Chia fell down before them, and was changed into a tiger with horrid fangs. Then one of the knights drew a glittering sword and would have cut off its head had not the other cried out, 'Not yet! not yet! that is for the fourth month next year. Let us now only take out its teeth.' Immediately that knight produced a huge mallet, and, with a few blows, scattered the tiger's teeth all over the floor, the tiger roaring so loudly with pain as to shake the very hills and frightening all the wits out of Mr Pai – who woke up with a start.

He found he had been dreaming and at once set off to invite Ting to come and see him; but Ting sent back to say he must beg to be excused. Then Mr Pai, pondering on what he had seen in his dream, dispatched his second son with a letter to Chia, full of warnings and good advice; and lo! when his son arrived, he found that his elder brother had lost all his front teeth, these having been knocked out, as he averred, by a fall he had had from his horse when tipsy. On comparing dates, the day of that fall was found to coincide with the day of his father's dream. The younger brother was greatly amazed at this, and took out their father's letter, which he gave to Chia to read. The latter changed colour but immediately asked his brother what there was to be astonished at in the coincidence of a dream.

Just at that time he was busily engaged in bribing his superiors to put him first on the list for promotion so that he soon forgot all about the circumstance; while the younger, observing what harpies Chia's subordinates were, taking presents from one man and using their influence for another, in one unbroken stream of corruption, sought out his elder brother, and, with tears in his eyes, implored him to put some check upon their rapacity. 'My brother,' replied Chia, 'your life has been passed in an obscure village; you know nothing of our official routine. We are promoted or degraded at the will of our superiors, and not by the voice of the people. He, therefore, who gratifies his superiors is marked out for success, whereas he who consults the wishes of the people is unable to gratify his superiors as well.' Chia's brother saw that his advice was thrown away, and he accordingly returned home and told his father all that had taken place. The old man was much affected, but there was nothing that he could do in the matter, so he devoted himself to assisting the poor, and such acts of charity, daily praying the Gods that the wicked son alone might suffer for his crimes, and not entail misery on his innocent wife and children.

The next year it was reported that Chia had been recommended for a post in the Board of Civil Office, and friends crowded the father's door, offering their congratulations upon the happy event. But the old man sighed and took to his bed, pretending he was too unwell to receive visitors. Before long another message came, informing them that Chia had fallen in with bandits while on his way home, and that he and all his retinue had been killed. Then his father arose and said, 'Verily the Gods are good unto me, for they have visited his sins upon himself alone'; and he immediately proceeded to burn incense and return thanks. Some of his friends would have persuaded him that the report was probably untrue, but the old man had no doubts as to its correctness and made haste to get ready his son's grave.

But Chia was not yet dead. In the fatal fourth moon he had started on his journey and had fallen in with bandits, to whom he had offered all his money and valuables; upon which the latter cried out, 'We have come to avenge the cruel wrongs of many hundreds of victims; do you imagine we want only *that*?' They then cut off his head, and the head of his wicked secretary, and the heads of several of his servants who had been foremost in carrying out his shameful orders, and were now accompanying him to the capital. They then divided the booty between them and made off with all speed.

Chia's soul remained near his body for some time, until at length a high mandarin passing by asked who it was that was lying there dead. One of his servants replied that he had been a magistrate at such and such a place, and that his name was Pai. 'What!' said the mandarin, 'the son of old Mr Pai? It is hard that his father should live to see such sorrow as this. Put his head on again.'* A man stepped forward and placed Chia's head upon his shoulders again, when the mandarin interrupted him, saying, 'A crooked-minded man should not have a straight body: put his head on sideways.' By and by Chia's soul returned to its tenement; and when his wife and children arrived to take away the corpse they found that he was still breathing. Carrying him home, they poured some nourishment down his throat, which he was able to swallow; but there he was at an out-of-the-way place, without the means of continuing his journey. It was some six months before his father heard the real state of the case, and then he sent off the second son to bring his brother home. Chia had indeed come to life again but he was only able to see down his own back and was regarded ever afterwards more as a monstrosity than as a man. Subsequently the nephew, whom old Mr Pai had seen sitting in state surrounded by officials, actually became an Imperial Censor so that every detail of the dream was thus strangely realized.†

P'u Sung-ling (Ch'ing Dynasty)
From *Liao Chai Chih I*

* The Chinese dreaded decapitation, as opposed to strangulation, because the body would appear in the underworld without its head. Families of condemned men with sufficient wealth always, Giles reports, bribed the executioner to sew the head back on after he had done his work.
† The 'dream theme' is a popular one in Chinese literature, and is frequently used. Several other stories and fables in this collection use the dream device. During the Yuan and Ming dynasties, dramatists used the dream idea and Ma Chih-yuan (fl 1230–60) made use of the classic tale of Shen Chi-chi's, 'The Magic Pillow', in his 'Yellow Millet Dream'. There are several other versions of this traditional device: T'ang Hsien-tsu (1550–1617), 'On the Road to Hantan'; Li Kung-tso's 'The Southern Branch' and another dream-tale by P'u Sung-ling, 'A New Version of the Yellow Millet Theme'. For a further description of this traditional Chinese literary device see *Traditional Chinese Tales*, translated by Chi-Chen Wang (Columbia University Press, New York, 1944). In this anthology there is also included Shen Chi-chi's 'The Magic Pillow'.

Black Magic

In his youth, Mr Yu was spirited and gallant, fond of boxing and trials of strength. He was strong enough to raise two heavy bronze vessels and whirl them in the air as fast as wind. During the Chung Chen Era, when he went to the capital for the palace examination, much to his concern, his servant fell ill and had to take to his bed. Since there was a fortune-teller in the market-place who was skilled in determining a man's lease of life, Yu decided to consult him. But before he had uttered a word, the fortune-teller asked, 'Is it about your servant's illness you want to consult me, sir?'

Much astonished, Yu replied that this was so.

'The sick man will come to no harm,' said the fortune-teller. 'You, sir, are the one in danger.'

Yu thereupon asked to have his own fortune told.

The fortune-teller, having consulted his oracles, told him with a look of horror, 'In three days you will be dead.'

Yu was struck speechless for some time.

'I know certain small arts,' observed the fortune-teller. 'Give me ten taels of silver and I will avert this disaster for you.'

But to Yu's way of thinking, if his fate was decreed, no magic art could change it. So without replying, he rose and prepared to leave.

'You begrudge a small outlay,' said the fortune-teller. 'You'll be sorry for it. You'll be sorry for it!'

All Yu's friends were most concerned and advised him to empty his purse and beg for help, but he would not hear of it. The three days slipped quickly by. Yu sat calmly waiting in his hostel, but nothing happened all day. When night fell, he closed the door and trimmed the lamp to sit there alone with a drawn sword at his side.

As the first watch approached its end and he was unscathed, he was thinking of lying down when he heard a rustling by a crack in the window. A quick look showed him a small creature slipping in armed with a spear, who grew to man's size as soon as its feet touched the ground. Seizing his sword, Yu leaped up and struck at it but missed his adversary, who floated up into the air, shrank back to the size of a midget and made for the crack in the window, hoping to escape. Yu slashed again and felled it with one blow. When he brought the lamp, he found a paper figure cut through the middle. This made him afraid to sleep, and he sat up watching. Presently another creature, ugly and fierce as an ogre, crept through the window. No sooner did it reach the ground than he attacked fiercely, cutting it into two. But since both halves went on twitching and he feared it might come back to life, Yu hacked again and again with his sword, producing a dull thud each time. And when he examined it closely, he found this was a clay image smashed into pieces. So now he moved his seat near to the window and kept his eye fixed on the crack.

After a long time, he heard a noise like an ox wheezing outside as something pressed against the lattice so hard that the whole house shook and seemed about to fall. To avoid being crushed, Yu decided to go out and fight. He unbolted the door with a clatter and darted out. His eyes fell on a monstrous giant as tall as the eaves. The dim light of the moon revealed its coal-black face and glittering yellow eyes. Stripped to the waist and barefooted, it had a bow in one hand and arrows at its waist. As Yu stared in consternation, the ogre bent its bow. Yu struck the arrow to the ground with his sword; but before he could attack, the ogre took aim again. Yu leaped hastily aside to avoid the shot and the arrow pierced the wall, which clanged and quivered. In a passion, the ogre drew its sabre and whirled it like the wind to smash down on Yu; but the latter darted nimbly forward so that the sabre hit a rock in the yard, cleaving it asunder. Slipping between the ogre's legs, Yu slashed at its ankles, drawing from them a strange clanging. More enraged than ever, the ogre roared like thunder and wheeled round brandishing its sabre again. Once more Yu ducked and darted forward. The sabre swung down to slice off the lower part of his garment, but meanwhile he had reached the ogre's armpit. He belaboured it hard causing the same strange clanging, till the ogre fell and ceased to move. Yu hit out wildly; his blows produced a muffled sound like the beating of a wooden clapper. When he brought the light, he saw it was a life-size wooden figure with a bow and arrows strapped to its waist and a fierce painted face – where his sword had struck there was blood.

Yu sat up till dawn by his lamp, understanding now that these monsters had been sent by the fortune-teller to kill him and thereby manifest his own magic powers. The next day he told this to all his friends and together they went to find the fortune-teller. But the latter, seeing Yu in the distance, suddenly vanished.

Someone said, 'This trick of invisibility can be counteracted by the use of dog's blood.'

Following this advice, Yu went again, prepared. The fortune-teller made himself invisible as before. But Yu promptly sprinkled the place where the man had been with dog's blood, and there stood the fortune-teller like an ogre, his face all bespattered with dog's blood, his eyes glaring wildly. Yu seized him and handed him over to the authorities, who had him put to death.

P'u Sung-ling (Ch'ing Dynasty)
From *Liao Chai Chih I*

The Old Scholar's Reincarnation

There lived in Foochow, the capital of Fukien Province, during the reign of Hung Chih in the Ming dynasty an old scholar, who was very learned and excellent as an essayist. In spite of frequent attempts, he failed to pass the civil service examinations, and because of his unpractical ways sank deeper and deeper into poverty. He had a son, who was of no account with books and made his living as a farm labourer.

When the scholar reached the age of seventy, he died in great unhappiness. On the day of his death, he assembled his literary works and wrote a poem as epilogue, instructing his wife to take good care of them. He was so poor when he died, that his pupils, five in all, had to make a collection to pay the expenses of his burial. One student in particular, a wealthy man and very sentimental, expressed deep grief, weeping bitterly and following the remains to the grave. From time to time he sent gifts to the widow and the son to relieve them in their distress.

Some fifteen years later a brilliant young scholar coming from an ordinary family made his appearance south of the Yangtze River, passing successfully and rapidly the civil service examinations one after the other and becoming imperial academician within the remarkably short period of five years. He was appointed imperial examiner for the province of Fukien, and distinguished himself by his meticulous care and impartiality in selecting the papers of the candidates who attended the examinations, while his own essays, masterpieces of the day, were read avidly throughout the region.

On the fifteenth day of the ninth moon the highest local authorities, including the governor and the chief justice, assembled at a banquet to do him honour, the day being his birthday. The gathering was a distinguished one, as the guest of honour was both an academician and provincial examiner and the other guests the most prominent men of Foochow. He was much envied and toasted, being regarded as almost a demigod, not so much because he was the man of the hour, as because he had become one at so young an age.

Tired out by the festivities and somewhat overcome by the innumerable cups of wine which he was obliged to drain, he retired finally to his houseboat, giving orders to permit no visitors to come on board. After some hours of profound slumber, he woke up near midnight feeling much refreshed. The moon was shining brightly through the windows and one could amost believe that it was broad daylight. Gazing at the picturesque bank of the river he conceived the notion to take a stroll on shore. He changed into simple, everyday clothes, and, accompanied by his page, he landed and commenced his walk under the moon, having no particular destination in mind.

For several *li* he wandered along and noted with some new interest the familiar hills, woods, creeks and ravines. Suddenly he heard heart-rending lamentations coming from a nearby hamlet and, much distressed, he followed the sound of weeping till he came to a humble cottage, without even a simple hedge around it. He told his page to knock and open the primitive door. They entered and saw by the light of a lantern a white-haired woman of more than eighty years of age offering sacrifices of wild herbs and porridge to her deceased husband, and weeping as if her heart would break.

The imperial examiner bowed profoundly to the old lady and inquired for the reason of her great sorrow. She thanked him, arranged a seat for him on a broken chair, and related through her tears the cause of her grief.

'It was my intention, sir, to offer sacrifices earlier today to my departed husband, but my son, who left for a distant place, has delayed his return, so I am obliged to make the sacrifice at night. I have failed, however, to find any wine for the ceremony, hence my particular chagrin, although you, sir, must know that it is against the rules and rites to weep at night.'

'Who was your husband?' asked the examiner, 'how long has he been dead? And if wine is missing for the sacrifice, why not postpone the ceremony till tomorrow?'

'My husband was an aged scholar, rich in talent but poor in luck,' she replied. 'He died twenty years ago, and today is the anniversary of his demise. We were a very happy couple, and although I have little or nothing to offer to his memory, I could not postpone the sacrifice due on this day.'

The examiner was struck by the fact that the date of death of the old scholar coincided with that of his birth, exactly twenty years ago. The old lady looked wan and tired, but her language was highly cultured. He felt the greatest pity and sympathy for her.

'If your lamented husband was a great scholar,' he remarked, 'he must have left behind him numerous writings and manuscripts; may I be permitted to have a look at them?'

The old lady nodded, mused for a moment and finally confided the following story to the examiner.

'I was his wife for nearly fifty years and can bear witness to his industry and devotion to learning, whether it be in the heat of summer or the cold of winter. If the jar contained no rice or the kitchen chimney produced no smoke, that was of little moment to him. His compositions reached hundreds of volumes, and all his papers written for the civil service examinations were collected into a separate volume. He often took these papers out and read them after he was past sixty. Whenever he did so, he would sigh and tears would roll down his cheeks. Fearing that his sorrow might ruin his health, I hid the book to prevent him from reading it any more. A month before his death, he lit a fire and swore to burn the book, but then he fondled it and hesitated to carry out his resolution. "The child of my heart's labour during a life-time," he said to me, "I cannot bear to destroy by fire. I shall have it buried with me as my companion in death." Then he would softly sigh to himself repeatedly. On the night of his death, he asked to see the book again, and wrote a poem at the end. "Put it away carefully: someone will appreciate it." Then he smiled and continued, "The contents of my book are too profound for profane eyes. Unless I returned from the other world, who would be able to recognize their excellence? I am ashamed of nothing in my life, and I shall reap my reward after death. In another generation our family will become very illustrious, thus vindicating all poor but worthy scholars." So saying, and with a loud laugh, he died. It is now twenty years, but with the exception of a few of his students, who made copies of the book and read it, no one else has ever referred to the work.'

After the young academician had heard the remarkable story, he asked to see the book. The very first essay was word for word what he wrote when he took the first examination. Amazed, he ran over the entire contents and found therein every one of the essays which secured for him the higher degrees, his successful palace examination, his admission to the Imperial Academy, and even the subjects he gave to the candidates for their theses at the recent provincial examination. On the last page of the book he found the Farewell Poem:

> *In this poor hut I have spent seventy years in vain.*
> *When I return, I shall not be the same frustrated, wretched person.*
> *You will fulfil what I failed to achieve*
> *And find in this book the line of our identity.*

After perusing the poem the academician realized the whole situation. He nodded, sighed deeply, and looking up at the shabby roof and the crumbling walls, felt at home in the surroundings. He demanded where the old bed was. There it stood in the corner with its worn-out mat and old bed-clothes covered with dust, while the old lady's sleeping place was on some straw. He could not restrain from weeping, which astonished her.

'Why do you give way to tears?' she asked. 'Is it that you are also a student of my late husband and shocked at the misery that meets your eyes?'

'No,' he replied, 'it is because I am he of whom he speaks as the one who would return. Is it not Fate that has brought me here tonight?'

'When my husband died,' she observed softly, 'my heart nearly broke. But then he said something about coming back, so I bit him on the leg and stained the spot with blood from my finger as a secret mark. Do you, sir, bear such a clue on your body?'

The academician removed his boot and exposed the leg: the mark left by the teeth was very distinct and red in colour.

The old lady wept copiously, while he, greatly saddened, tried his best to comfort her.

'Madam,' he declared, 'you need worry no more. Your lamented husband studied diligently during a life-time and received no recognition in his old age, expecting to receive his reward through me. My success and glory is the fruit of his intellectual labour. If I ignore my efforts, which were really his, then my youthful success would indeed be a strange antic of fortune. No; I shall glorify the house of my previous personality, thus fulfilling his ambitions and giving encouragement to all aged scholars, besides providing for your future comfort.'

He asked whither the son had gone.

'Since the death of my husband,' confessed the old lady, 'my son and I have had difficulty in maintaining ourselves. Fortunately, some former pupils of his come to visit us sometimes, and on the anniversaries offer sacrifices to his spirit. Today one of them failed to appear because he has just obtained the master's degree, so I sent my son to inquire.'

On asking for the student's name, the examiner remembered it as the one he had chosen to head the successful candidates. The other four or five students mentioned by the old lady were also among the examinees who pleased him very much.

Soon it was dawn and the son returned, followed by an old man with rice wine, money and other things. With dishevelled hair and cotton garments, the son looked as rustic as any simple peasant. The old lady introduced him to the distinguished guest, who asked why he was late in coming home. He explained that their scholar friend and several of his fellow successful examinees had gone to present their felicitations on the examiner's birthday but failed to find him either in his official residence or on his houseboat.

'Is the old man who came with you the servant of the successful scholar?' asked the examiner.

'Yes, sir,' the son replied. 'Return to your master and invite him to meet me here,' said the guest to the servant. The old man left in a hurry.

In the meantime the old lady explained to the son the significance of the visit of the examiner, and he wanted to greet the latter as his father.

'No,' said the guest, 'that cannot be, for it has to do with my previous existence.'

Not long after the scholar friend in question arrived together with a few other successful candidates, and after hearing the whole story from the mouth of their examiner, all prostrated themselves before him.

'Our illustrious teacher and master during two existences!' they exclaimed. 'Such a case has never been known in human history.'

Later the magistrate came, then the prefect and other high officials made their appearance. They likewise were all amazed at the account related to them.

In the next few days the examiner occupied himself with sacrifices before the tomb of the old scholar, planting a tree in memory of the occasion. Invitations were sent out to friends and relatives of the family to attend a feast, when gifts were distributed to all. Those who had been particularly attentive to the old lady received double portions. For the old widow and her son a comfortable house with adjoining fields and servants was provided, so that they could pass their days in ease, while all the provincial officials from the governor down presented them with suitable gifts. Mother and son were now well off, and the latter took to himself a wife. The news of the strange affair spread like wild fire throughout the province, and many an old and indigent scholar throughout south China felt wonderfully encouraged by it.

The imperial examiner was obliged by official duties to return soon after to Peking, but time and again he revisited the place. The former farm labourer became the father of five sons and five daughters. The boys turned out to be good scholars, three of whom succeeded in passing the metropolitan examinations. Generation after generation distinguished itself, and the family flourished as one of the most celebrated of Fukien Province.

Sha Chang-pai (Ch'ing Dynasty)

Smearing the Ghost's Face with Ink

According to Liu Hsiang-wan, an old scholar was staying with one of his relatives when his host's son-in-law, a young rogue, arrived without warning. Since they were incompatible and neither wanted to share a room with the other, the old scholar was moved to another room. For some reason which he could not fathom, the son-in-law looked at him rather oddly and smiled.

This new room seemed quite pleasant and clean, with brushes, inkstone and books set ready for use. And by lamplight the scholar started writing a letter home. Suddenly beside the lamp there appeared a woman, no great beauty, but possessed of considerable charm. Though the old man knew this was a ghost, he was not afraid. Indicating the lamp he said, 'Since you're here, make yourself useful and trim my lamp.' Instead the woman put out the light and stepped forward to stand over him. Very angry, the scholar quickly rubbed his fingers in the ink on the ink-stone and slapped the woman's face, smearing both cheeks with ink. 'I'll know you by this mark,' he said. 'Tomorrow I'll find your corpse, cut it up and burn it.' Then with a screech the ghost fled.

The next day he related this to his host, who confessed, 'A maid-servant did die in that room and often appears at night to trouble men. So we only entertain guests there in the daytime. No one has ever spent a night there. Yesterday, however, we had nowhere else to put you; and we thought since you are elderly and a great scholar, the ghost probably would not come. We did not expect it to show itself again.' Then the scholar realized why the young man had laughed up his sleeve at him.

This ghost often walked in the moonlight through the courtyard. Later, when some of the household came across it by chance, the ghost would cover its face with its hands and flee. Once they managed to look at it closely, and saw that its face was still smeared with ink.

Chi Yun (Ch'ing Dynasty)
From *Notes of the Yueh-wei Hermitage*

The Country of the Cannibals

At Chiao-chou there lived a man named Hsu, who gained his living by trading across the sea. On one occasion he was carried far out of his course by a violent tempest and reached a country of high hills and dense jungle, where, after making fast his boat and taking provisions with him, he landed, hoping to meet with some of the inhabitants. He then saw that the rocks were covered with large holes, like the cells of bees, and hearing the sound of voices from within he stopped in front of one of them and peeped in.

To his infinite horror he beheld two hideous beings, with thick rows of horrid fangs and eyes that glared like lamps, engaged in tearing to pieces and devouring some raw deer's flesh. Turning round, he would have fled instantly from the spot had not the cannibals already espied him and leaving their food, they seized him and dragged him in. There-upon ensued a chattering between them, resembling the noise of birds or beasts, and they proceeded to pull off Hsu's clothes as if about to eat him. But Hsu, who was frightened almost to death, offered them the food he had in his wallet, which they ate up with great relish, and looked inside for more. Hsu waved his hand to show it was all finished. Then they angrily seized him again and he cried out, 'I have a saucepan in my boat and can cook you some.' The cannibals did not understand what he said but, by dint of gesticulating freely, they at length seemed to have an idea of what he meant. Having taken him down to the shore to fetch the saucepan, they returned with him to the cave where he lighted a fire and cooked the remainder of the deer, with the flavour of which they appeared to be mightily pleased. At night they rolled a big stone to the mouth of the cave, fearing lest he should try to escape. Hsu himself lay down at a distance from them deeply in doubt as to whether his life would be spared.

At daybreak the cannibals went out, leaving the entrance blocked, and by and by came back with a deer, which they gave to Hsu to cook. Hsu flayed the carcass, and from a remote corner of the cave took some water and prepared a large quantity, which was no sooner ready than several other cannibals arrived to join in the feast. When they had finished all there was they made signs that Hsu's saucepan was too small; and three or four days afterwards they brought him a large one, of the same shape as those in common use amongst men, subsequently furnishing him with constant supplies of wolf and deer, of which they always invited him to partake. By degrees they began to treat him kindly and not to shut him up when they went out. And Hsu, too, gradually learnt to understand and even to speak a little of their language, which pleased them so much that they finally gave him a cannibal woman for his wife. Hsu was horribly afraid of her, but, as she treated him with great consideration, always reserving titbits of food for him, they lived very happily together.

One day all the cannibals got up early in the morning and, having adorned themselves with strings of fine pearls, they went forth as if to meet some honoured guest, giving orders to Hsu to cook an extra quantity of meat that day. 'It is the birthday of our King,' said Hsu's wife to him, and then, running out, she informed the other cannibals that her husband had no pearls. So each gave five from his own string and Hsu's wife added ten to these, making in all fifty, which she threaded on a hempen fibre and hung around his neck, each pearl being worth over a hundred ounces of silver. Then they went away and as soon as Hsu had finished his cooking his wife appeared and invited him to come and receive the King. So off they went to a huge cavern, covering about a mow * of ground, in which was a huge stone smoothed away

---

* About one sixth of an acre. Giles wrote that at the turn of the century landed property was still measured 'according to the amount of grain that could be sown thereon'.

at the top like a table with stone seats at the four sides. At the upper end was a dais, over which was spread a leopard's skin, the other seats having only deer-skins. Within the cavern some twenty or thirty cannibals ranged themselves on the seats.

After a short interval a great wind began to stir up the dust, and they all rushed out to meet a creature very much resembling themselves, which hurried into the cave and, squatting down cross-legged, cocked its head and looked about like a cormorant. The other cannibals then filed in and took up their positions right and left of the dais, where they stood gazing up at the King with their arms folded before them in the form of a cross. The King counted them one by one and asked if they were all present. When they replied in the affirmative, he looked at Hsu and inquired who he was. Thereupon Hsu's wife stepped forward and said he was her husband, and the others all loudly extolled his skill in cookery, two of them running out and bringing back some cooked meat, which they set before the King. His Majesty swallowed it by handfuls and found it so nice that he gave orders to be supplied regularly. Then turning to Hsu he asked him why his string of beads was so short. 'He has but recently arrived among us,' replied the cannibals, 'and hasn't got a complete set.' The King then drew ten pearls from the string round his own neck and bestowed them upon Hsu. Each was as big as the top of one's finger and as round as a bullet. Hsu's wife threaded them for him and hung them round his neck. Hsu himself crossed his arms and thanked the King in the language of the country, after which His Majesty went off in a gust of wind as rapidly as a bird can fly. The cannibals then sat down and finished what was left of the banquet.

Four years afterwards Hsu's wife gave birth to a triplet of two boys and one girl, all of whom were ordinary human beings and not at all like the mother, at which the other cannibals were delighted and would often play with them and caress them.* Three years passed away and the children could walk about, after which their father taught them to speak his own tongue; and in their early babblings their human origin was manifested. The boys, as mere children, could climb about on the mountains as easily as though walking upon a level road and between them and their father there grew up a mutual feeling of attachment.

One day the mother had gone out with the girl and one of the boys, and was absent for a long time. A strong north wind was blowing and Hsu, filled with thoughts of his old home, led his other son down with

---

* Intense fondness for children seems a special trait of the Chinese character, and Giles (during the turn-of-the-century violence) advised that one baby 'would do far more to ensure the safety of a foreign traveller in China than all the usual paraphernalia of pocket pistols and revolvers'.

him to the beach where lay the boat in which he had formerly reached this country. He then proposed to the boy that they should go away together. Having explained to him that they could not inform his mother, father and son stepped on board, and, after a voyage of only twenty-four hours arrived safely at Chiao-chou. On reaching home Hsu found that his wife had married again, so he sold two of his pearls for an enormous sum of money and set up a splendid establishment. His son was called Piao and at fourteen or fifteen years of age the boy could lift a weight of 3,000 catties [4,000 lb]. He was extremely fond of athletics of all kinds, and thus attracted the notice of the Commander-in-Chief, who gave him a commission as sub-lieutenant. Just at that time there happened to be some trouble on the frontier and young Piao, having covered himself with glory, was made a colonel at the age of eighteen.

About that time, another merchant was driven by stress of weather to the country of the cannibals, and had hardly stepped ashore before he observed a young man whom he knew at once to be of Chinese origin. The young man asked him whence he came, and finally took him into a cave hid away in a dark valley and concealed by the dense jungle. There he bade him remain, and in a little while he returned with some deer's flesh, which he gave the merchant to eat, saying at the same time that his own father was a Chiao-chou man. The merchant now knew that the young man was Hsu's son, he himself being acquainted with Hsu as a trader in the same line of business. 'Why, he's an old friend of mine,' cried the latter. 'His other son is now a colonel.' The young man did not know what was meant by a *colonel*, so the merchant told him it was the title of a Chinese mandarin. 'And what is a *mandarin*?' asked the youth. 'A mandarin,' replied the merchant, 'is one who goes out with a chair and horses; who at home sits upon a dais in the hall; whose summons is answered by a hundred voices; who is looked at only with sidelong eyes and in whose presence all people stand aslant – this is to be a mandarin.'

The young man was deeply touched at this recital, and at length the merchant said to him, 'Since your honoured father is at Chiao-chou, why do you remain here?'

'Indeed,' replied the youth, 'I have often indulged the same feeling. But my mother is not a Chinese woman, and, apart from the difference of her language and appearance, I fear that if the other cannibals found it out they would do us some mischief.' He then took his leave, being in rather a disturbed state of mind, and bade the merchant wait until the wind should prove favourable, when he promised to come and see him off and charge him with a letter to his father and brother. Six months the merchant remained in that cave, occasionally taking a peep at the cannibals passing backwards and forwards, but not daring to leave his retreat.

As soon as the monsoon set in the young man arrived and urged him to hurry away, begging him, also, not to forget the letter to his father. So the merchant sailed away and soon reached Chiao-chou where he visited the colonel and told him the whole story. Piao was much affected and wished to go in search of those members of the family, but his father feared the dangers he would encounter and advised him not to think of such a thing. However, Piao was not to be deterred, and having imparted his scheme to the Commander-in-Chief, he took with him two soldiers and set off. Adverse winds prevailed at that time, and they beat about for half a moon, until they were out of sight of all land, could not see a foot before them, and had completely lost their reckoning. Just then a mighty sea arose and capsized their boat, tossing Piao into the water where he floated about for some time at the will of the waves until suddenly somebody dragged him out and carried him into a house.

Then he saw that his rescuer was to all appearances a cannibal. Accordingly he addressed him in the language of the country and told him whither he himself was bound. 'It is my native place,' replied the cannibal in astonishment. 'But you will excuse my saying that you are now 8000 *li* out of your course. This is the way to the country of the Poisonous Dragons, and not your route at all.' He then went off to find a boat for Piao, and, himself swimming in the water behind, pushed it along like an arrow from a bow, so quickly that by the next day they had traversed the whole distance.

On the shore Piao observed a young man walking up and down and evidently watching him. Knowing that no human beings dwelt there he guessed at once that he was his brother. Approaching more closely he saw that he was right, and seizing the young man's hand, he asked after his mother and sister. On hearing that they were well, he would have gone directly to see them; but the younger one begged him not to do so and ran away himself to fetch them. Meanwhile, Piao turned to thank the cannibal who had brought him there, but he, too, had disappeared. In a few minutes his mother and sister arrived, and, on seeing Piao, they could not restrain their tears. Piao then laid his scheme before them, and when they said they feared people would ill-treat them, he replied, 'In China I hold a high position, and people will not dare to show you disrespect.' Thus they determined to go. The wind, however, was against them, and mother and son were at a loss what to do when suddenly the sail bellied out towards the south and a rustling sound was heard. 'Heaven helps us, my mother!' cried Piao, full of joy; and, hurrying on board at once, in three days they had reached their destination.

As they landed the people fled right and left in fear, Piao having divided his own clothes amongst the party. When they arrived at the house, and his mother saw Hsu, she began to berate him soundly for running away without her. Hsu hastened to acknowledge his error, and then all the family and servants were introduced to her, each one being in mortal dread of such a singular personage. Piao now bade his mother learn to talk Chinese, and gave her any quantity of fine clothes and rich meats, to the infinite delight of the old lady. She and her daughter both dressed in man's clothes, and by the end of a few months were able to understand what was said to them. The brother, named Pao [Leopard], and the sister, Yeh [Night], were both clever enough, and immensely strong into the bargain. Piao was ashamed that Pao could not read and set to work to teach him. The youngster was so quick that he learnt the Sacred Books * and histories by merely reading them once over. However, he would not enter upon a literary career, loving better to draw a strong bow or ride a spirited horse, and finally taking the highest military degree. He married the daughter of a post-captain. But his sister had some trouble in getting a husband because of her being the child of a cannibal woman. At length a sergeant named Yuan, who was under her brother's command and had become a widower, consented to take her as his wife. She could draw a hundred-catty bow and shoot birds at a hundred paces without ever missing. Whenever Yuan went on a campaign she went with him, and his subsequent rise to high rank was chiefly due to her. At thirty-four years of age Pao got a command; and in his great battles his mother, clad in armour and grasping a spear, would fight by his side to the terror of all their adversaries; and when he himself received the dignity of an hereditary title, he memorialized the Throne to grant his mother the title of 'lady'.

P'u Sung-ling (Ch'ing Dynasty)
From *Liao Chai Chih I*

* The *Sacred Books* form the unvarying core of Chinese education. They are (1) the *Four Books*, composed of the teachings of Confucius and Mencius; and (2) the *Five Canons* or, the Canons of Changes, History, Poetry, the Rites, and the Spring and Autumn classics.

The Wonderful Stone

In the prefecture of Shun-t'ien there lived a man named Hsing Yun-fei, who was an amateur mineralogist and would pay any price for a good specimen. One day as he was fishing in the river something caught his net. Diving down he brought up a stone about a foot in diameter, beautifully carved on all sides to resemble clustering hills and peaks. He was quite as pleased with this as if he had found some precious stone; and having had an elegant sandalwood stand made for it, he set his prize upon the table.

Whenever it was about to rain, clouds, which from a distance looked like new cottonwool, would come forth from each of the holes or grottoes on the stone and appear to close them up. By and by, an influential personage called at the house and begged to see the stone, immediately seizing it and handing it over to a lusty servant, at the same time whipping his horse and riding away. Hsing was in despair, but all he could do was to mourn the loss of his stone and indulge his anger against the thief. Meanwhile, the servant, who had carried off the stone on his back, stopped to rest at a bridge when all of a sudden his hand slipped and the stone fell into the water. His master was extremely put out at this and gave him a sound beating. He subsequently hired several divers, who tried every means in their power to recover the stone, but were quite unable to find it. He then went away, having first published a notice of reward, and by these means many were tempted to seek for the stone.

Soon after, Hsing himself came to the spot, and as he mournfully approached the bank, lo! the water became clear, and he could see the stone lying at the bottom. Taking off his clothes, he quickly jumped in and brought it out, together with the sandalwood stand, which was still with it. He carried it off home but, being no longer desirous of showing it to people, he had an inner room cleaned and put it in there. Some time afterwards an old man knocked at the door and asked to be allowed to see the stone, whereupon Hsing replied that he had lost it a long time ago.

'Isn't that it in the inner room?' said the old man, smiling.

'Oh, walk in and see for yourself if you don't believe me,' answered Hsing, and the old man did walk in, and there was the stone on the table. This took Hsing very much aback. The old man then laid his hand upon the stone and said, 'This is an old family relic of mine. I lost it many months since. How does it come to be here? I pray you now restore it to me.'

Hsing didn't know what to say, but declared he was the owner of the stone, upon which the old man remarked, 'If it is really yours, what evidence can you bring to prove it?' Hsing made no reply, and the old man continued, 'To show you that I know this stone, I may mention that it has altogether ninety-two grottoes, and that in the largest of these are five words:

A STONE FROM HEAVEN ABOVE.

Hsing looked and found that there were actually some small characters, no larger than grains of rice, which by straining his eyes a little he managed to read; also, that the number of grottoes was as the old man had said. However, he would not give him the stone.

The old man laughed and asked, 'Pray, what right have you to keep other people's things?' He then bowed and went away, Hsing escorting him as far as the door. But when he returned to the room, the stone had disappeared. In a great fright, he ran after the old man, who had walked slowly and was not far off, and seizing his sleeve entreated him to give back the stone. 'Do you think,' said the latter, 'that I could conceal a stone a foot in diameter in my sleeve?' But Hsing knew that he must be super-human and led him back to the house, where he threw himself on his knees and begged that he might have the stone.

'Is it yours or mine?' asked the old man.

'Of course it is yours,' replied Hsing, 'though I hope you will consent to deny yourself the pleasure of keeping it.'

'In that case,' said the old man, 'it is back again,' and going into the inner room they found the stone in its old place.

'The jewels of this world,' observed Hsing's visitor, 'should be given to those who know how to take care of them. This stone can choose its own master, and I am very pleased that it should remain with you. At the same time I must inform you that it was in too great a hurry to come into the world of mortals and has not yet been freed from all contingent calamities. I had better take it away with me, and three years hence you shall have it again. If, however, you insist on keeping it, then your span of life will be shortened by three years, that your terms of existence may harmonize together. Are you willing?' Hsing said he was; whereupon the old man with his fingers closed up three of the stone's grottoes, which yielded to his touch like mud. When this was done, he turned to Hsing and told him that the grottoes on that stone represented the years of his life. Then he took his leave, firmly refusing to remain any longer, and not disclosing his name.

More than a year after this Hsing had occasion to go away on business, and in the night a thief broke in and carried off the stone, taking nothing else at all. When Hsing came home he was dreadfully grieved, as if his whole object in life was gone. He made all possible inquiries and efforts to get it back but without the slightest result. Some time passed away, when one day going into a temple Hsing noticed a man selling stones, and amongst the rest he saw his old friend. Of course he immediately wanted to regain possession of it but, as the stone-seller would not consent, he shouldered the stone and went off to the nearest mandarin. The stone-seller was then asked what proof he could give that the stone was his and he replied that the number of grottoes was eighty-nine. Hsing inquired if that was all he had to say, and when the other acknowledged that it was, he himself told the magistrate what were the characters inscribed within, also calling attention to the finger marks at the closed-up grottoes. He therefore gained his case, and the mandarin would have bambooed the stone-seller, had he not declared that he bought it in the market for twenty ounces of silver – whereupon he was dismissed.

A high official next offered Hsing one hundred ounces of silver for it, but he refused to sell it even for ten thousand, which so enraged the would-be purchaser that he worked up a case against Hsing,* and got him put in prison. Hsing was thereby compelled to pawn a great deal of his property. Then the official sent someone to try if the affair could not be managed through his son, to which Hsing, on hearing of the attempt, steadily refused to consent, saying that he and the stone could not be parted even in death. His wife and son, however, laid their heads together and sent the stone to the high official. Hsing only heard of it when he arrived home from the prison. He cursed his wife and beat his son, and frequently tried to make away with himself, though luckily his servants always managed to prevent him from succeeding.

At night he dreamt that a noble-looking personage appeared to him and said, 'My name is Shih Ch'ing-hsu [Stone from Heaven]. Do not grieve. I purposely quitted you for a year and more; but next year on the twentieth of the eighth moon, at dawn, come to the Hai-tai Gate and buy me back for two strings of cash.' Hsing was overjoyed at this

* This was a common form of revenge in China. It was easily accomplished when the prosecutor was a man of wealth or power.

dream, and carefully took down the day mentioned. Meanwhile, the stone was at the official's private house, but as the cloud manifestations ceased, the stone was less and less prized; and the following year when the official was disgraced for maladministration and subsequently died, Hsing met some of his servants at the Hai-tai Gate going off to sell the stone and purchased it back from them for two strings of cash.

Hsing lived till he was eighty-nine and then having prepared the necessaries for his interment, bade his son bury the stone with him,* which was accordingly done. Six months later robbers broke into the vault and made off with the stone. His son tried in vain to secure their capture. However, a few days afterwards he was travelling with his servants when suddenly two men rushed forth dripping with perspiration, and looking up into the air, acknowledged their crime, saying, 'Mr Hsing, please don't torment us thus! We took the stone and sold it for only four ounces of silver.' Hsing's son and his servants then seized these men and took them before the magistrate, where they at once acknowledged their guilt. Asking what had become of the stone, they said they had sold it to a member of the magistrate's family; and when it was produced, that official took such a fancy to it that he gave it to one of his servants and bade him place it in the treasury. Thereupon the stone slipped out of the servant's hand and broke into a hundred pieces, to the great astonishment of all present. The magistrate now had the thieves bambooed and sent them away; but Hsing's son picked up the broken pieces of the stone and buried them in his father's grave.

P'u Sung-ling (Ch'ing Dynasty)
From *Liao Chai Chih I*

---

* Giles reports that valuables of some kind or other 'are often placed in the coffins of wealthy Chinese. Women are almost always provided with a certain quantity of jewels with which to adorn themselves in the realms below'.

Miss Lien-hsiang, the Fox Girl

There was a young man named Sang Tzu-ming, a native of I-chou, who had been left an orphan when quite young. He lived near the Saffron Market, and kept very much to himself, only going out twice a day for his meals to a neighbour's close by, and sitting quietly at home all the rest of his time. One day his neighbour called, and asked him in joke if he wasn't afraid of devil-foxes, so much alone as he was.

'Oh,' replied Sang, laughing, 'what has the Superior Man * to fear from devil-foxes. If they come as men, I have here a sharp sword for them; and if as women, why, I shall open the door and ask them to walk in.'

The neighbour went away, and having arranged with a friend of his, they got a young lady of their acquaintance to climb over Sang's wall with the help of a ladder, and knock at the door. Sang peered through, and called out, 'Who's there?' to which the girl answered, 'A devil!' Sang was so dreadfully frightened that his teeth chattered in his head. The girl then ran away, and next morning when his neighbour came to see him, Sang told him what had happened, and said he meant to return to his native home. The neighbour then clapped his hands, and said to

* The *Chuntzu*, or Superior Man, is a description used constantly by Confucius throughout his writings to indicate the ideal man, whose life is in harmony with the cosmic principles of Yin and Yang. Giles translates this term to mean perfect probity, learning and refinement: in short, the perfect gentleman. But Confucius seemed to imply a far more philosophical meaning, as can be clearly seen in his use of the word throughout the classic of changes, the *I Ching*. The *Chuntzu* is frequently held up as an ideal in the *I Ching*, a book absorbed in the metaphysical flux and cosmic underpinnings of nature and the universe. A closer parallel than Giles's 'gentleman' would perhaps be Thomas à Kempis's perfect man, the Christ figure we are all urged to imitate in his *Imitation of Christ*. For a further description of the *Chuntzu* and his relationship to Chinese philosophy see the *I Ching*, a new edition based on the James Legge translation, edited and arranged by Raymond Van Over (New American Library, New York, 1971), p 20.

Sang, 'Why didn't you ask her in?' Whereupon Sang perceived that he had been tricked, and went on quietly again as before.

Some six months afterwards, a young lady knocked at his door; and Sang, thinking his friends were at their old tricks, opened it at once, and asked her to walk in. She did so; and he beheld to his astonishment a perfect Helen for beauty.* Asking her whence she came, she replied that her name was Lien-hsiang, and that she lived not very far off, adding that she had long been anxious to make his acquaintance. After that she used to drop in every now and again for a chat; but one evening when Sang was sitting alone expecting her, another young lady suddenly walked in. Thinking it was Lien-hsiang, Sang got up to meet her, but found that the newcomer was somebody else. She was about fifteen or sixteen years of age, wore very full sleeves, and dressed her hair after the fashion of unmarried girls, being otherwise very stylish-looking and refined, and apparently hesitating whether to go on or go back.

Sang, in a great state of alarm, took her for a fox; but the young lady said, 'My name is Li, and I am of a respectable family. Hearing of your virtue and talent, I hope to be accorded the honour of your acquaintance.' Sang laughed, and took her by the hand, which he found was as cold as ice; and when he asked the reason, she told him that she had always been delicate, and that it was very chilly outside. She then remarked that she intended to visit him pretty frequently, and hoped it would not inconvenience him; so he explained that no one came to see him except another young lady, and that not very often.

'When she comes, I'll go,' replied the young lady, 'and only drop in when she's not here.' She then gave him an embroidered slipper, saying that she had worn it, and that whenever he shook it she would know that he wanted to see her, cautioning him at the same time never to shake it before strangers. Taking it in his hand he beheld a very tiny little shoe almost as fine-pointed as an awl, with which he was much pleased; and next evening, when nobody was present, he produced the shoe and shook it, whereupon the young lady immediately walked in. Henceforth, whenever he brought it out, the young lady responded to his wishes and appeared before him. This seemed so strange that at last he asked her to give him some explanation; but she only laughed, and said it was mere coincidence.

One evening after this Lien-hsiang came, and said in alarm to Sang, 'Whatever has made you look so melancholy?' Sang replied that he did not know, and by and by she took her leave, saying they would not meet again for some ten days. During this period Miss Li visited Sang every day, and on one occasion asked him where his other friend was. Sang

* Literally, 'a young lady whose beauty would overthrow a kingdom'.

told her, and then she laughed and said, 'What is your opinion of me as compared with Lien-hsiang?'

'You are both of you perfection,' replied he, 'but you are a little *colder* of the two.' Miss Li didn't much like this, and cried out, '*Both of us perfection* is what you say to *me*. Then she must be a downright Cynthia,* and I am no match for her.' Somewhat out of temper, she reckoned that Lien-hsiang's ten days had expired, and said she would have a peep at her, making Sang promise to keep it all secret. The next evening Lien-hsiang came, and while they were talking she suddenly exclaimed, 'Oh, dear! how much worse you seem to have become in the last ten days. You must have encountered something bad.' Sang asked her why so, to which she answered, 'First of all your appearance and then your pulse is very thready.† You've got the devil-disease.'

The following evening when Miss Li came, Sang asked her what she thought of Lien-hsiang. 'Oh,' said she, 'there's no question about her beauty, but she's a fox. When she went away I followed her to her hole on the hill-side.' Sang, however, attributed this remark to jealousy, and took no notice of it. But the next evening when Lien-hsiang came, he observed, 'I don't believe it myself, but someone has told me you are a fox.' Lien-hsiang asked who had said so, to which Sang replied that he was only joking. Then she begged him to explain what difference there was between a fox and an ordinary person.

* Literally, the 'Lady of the Moon'. From an ancient tale involving the beautiful wife of a legendary chieftain, Hou I, who was supposed to have lived around 2500 BC. Ch'ang-ngo was believed to have stolen the elixir of immortality from her husband and fled with it to the moon.

The elixir of immortality was, however, most often associated with Taoist priests, who are believed by some to possess an elixir of immortality in the form of a precious liquor. Others believed that the 'elixir' should not be taken literally, but that it symbolizes virtuous conduct of one's life – by which method alone one can achieve immortality.

† Many volumes have been written by the Chinese on the subject of the body's pulses. Chinese doctors claim to distinguish as many as twenty-four different kinds of pulses, whereas Western medicine recognizes only a few. The thready pulse mentioned here is one that Western medicine also uses. The Chinese, however, utilize both wrists, where they claim to recognize different qualities. Unlike Giles, who reports that the Chinese recognize only twenty-four pulses, Felix Mann claims they work with twenty-seven. In any event, this system is the foundation for the ancient Chinese medicine known as acupuncture. It is still practised in China today alongside more orthodox, Western-type medical techniques. Two valuable books on acupuncture generally available today are: *Acupuncture: Cure of Many Diseases* by Felix Mann, with a Foreword by Aldous Huxley (Pan Books Ltd, London, 1973); and the Chinese classic on acupuncture, *The Yellow Emperor's Classic of Internal Medicine*, translated by Ilza Veith (University of California Press, Los Angeles, London, 1970).

'Well,' answered Sang, 'foxes frighten people to death, and, therefore, they are very much dreaded.'

'Don't you believe that!' cried Lien-hsiang; 'and now tell me who has been saying this of me.' Sang declared at first that it was only a joke of his, but by and by yielded to her and let out the whole story.

'Of course I saw how changed you were,' said Lien-hsiang; 'she is surely not a human being to be able to cause such a rapid alteration in you. Say nothing. Tomorrow I'll watch her as she watched me.'

The following evening Miss Li came in, and they had hardly interchanged half a dozen sentences when a cough was heard outside the window, and Miss Li ran away. Lien-hsiang then entered and said to Sang, 'You are lost! She is a devil, and if you do not at once forbid her coming here, you will soon be on the road to the other world.' 'All jealousy,' thought Sang, saying nothing, as Lien-hsiang continued, 'I know that you don't like to be rude to her; but I, for my part, cannot see you sacrificed, and tomorrow I will bring you some medicine to expel the poison from your system. Happily, the disease has not yet taken firm hold of you, and in ten days you will be well again.'

The next evening she produced a knife and chopped up some medicine for Sang, which made him feel better; but, although he was very grateful to her, he still persisted in disbelieving that he had the devil-disease. After some days he recovered and Lien-hsiang left him, warning him to have no more to do with Miss Li. Sang pretended that he would follow her advice, and closed the door and trimmed his lamp. He then took out the slipper, and on shaking it Miss Li appeared, somewhat cross at having been kept away for several days. 'She merely attended on me these few nights while I was ill,' said Sang, 'don't be angry.' At this Miss Li brightened up a little; but by and by Sang told her that people said she was a devil. 'It's that nasty fox,' cried Miss Li, after a pause, 'putting these things into your head. If you don't break with her, I won't come here again.' She then began to sob and cry, and Sang had some trouble in pacifying her.

Next evening Lien-hsiang came and found out that Miss Li had been there again; whereupon she was very angry with Sang, and told him he would certainly die.

'Why need you be so jealous?' said Sang, laughing; at which she only got more enraged, and replied, 'When you were nearly dying the other day and I saved you, if I had not been jealous, where would you have been now?' Sang pretended he was only joking, and said that Miss Li had told him his recent illness was entirely owing to the machinations of a fox; to which she replied, 'It's true enough what you say, only you don't see *whose* machinations. However, if anything happens to you, I should never clear myself even had I a hundred mouths; we will, there-fore, part. A hundred days hence I shall see you on your bed.' Sang could not persuade her to stay, and away she went; and from that time Miss Li became a regular visitor.

Two months passed away, and Sang began to experience a feeling of great lassitude, which he tried at first to shake off, but by and by he became very thin, and could only take thick gruel. He then thought about going back to his native place; however, he could not bear to leave Miss Li, and in a few more days he was so weak that he was unable to get up. His friend next door, seeing how ill he was, daily sent in his boy with food and drink; and now Sang began for the first time to suspect Miss Li. So he said to her, 'I am sorry I didn't listen to Lien-hsiang before I got as bad as this.' He then closed his eyes and kept them shut for some time; and when he opened them again Miss Li had dis-appeared. Their acquaintanceship was thus at an end, and Sang lay all emaciated as he was upon his bed in his solitary room longing for the return of Lien-hsiang.

One day, while he was still thinking about her, some one drew aside the screen and walked in. It was Lien-hsiang and, approaching the bed, she said with a smile, 'Was I then talking such nonsense?' Sang struggled a long time to speak; and, at length, confessing he had been wrong, implored her to save him. 'When the disease has reached such a pitch as this,' replied Lien-hsiang, 'there is very little to be done. I merely came to bid you farewell, and to clear up your doubts about my jealousy.' In great tribulation, Sang asked her to take something she would find under his pillow and destroy it; and she accordingly drew forth the slipper, which she proceeded to examine by the light of the lamp, turning it over and over. All at once Miss Li walked in, but when she saw Lien-hsiang she turned back as though she would run away which Lien-hsiang instantly prevented by placing herself in the door-way. Sang then began to reproach her, and Miss Li could make no reply; whereupon Lien-hsiang said, 'At last we meet. Formerly you attributed this gentleman's illness to me; what have you to say now?' Miss Li bent her head in acknowledgment of her guilt, and Lien-hsiang continued, 'How is it that a nice girl like you can thus turn love into hate?' Here Miss Li threw herself on the ground in a flood of tears and begged for mercy; and Lien-hsiang, raising her up, inquired of her as to her past life. 'I am a daughter of a petty official named Li, and I died young, leaving the web of my destiny incomplete, like the silkworm that perishes in the spring. To be the partner of this gentleman was my ardent wish; but I had never any intention of causing his death.'

'I have heard,' remarked Lien-hsiang, 'that the advantage devils obtain by killing people is that their victims are ever with them after death. Is this so?'

'It is not,' replied Miss Li. 'The companionship of two devils gives no pleasure to either. Were it otherwise, I should not have wanted for friends in the realms below. But tell me, how do foxes manage not to kill people?'

'You allude to such foxes as suck the breath out of people?' replied Lien-hsiang. 'I am not of that class. Some foxes are harmless; no devils are, because of the dominance of the Yin* in their compositions.'

Sang now knew that these two girls were really a fox and a devil; however, from being long accustomed to their society, he was not in the least alarmed. His breathing had dwindled to a mere thread, and at length he uttered a cry of pain. Lien-hsiang looked round and said, 'How shall we cure him?' upon which Miss Li blushed deeply and drew back. Then Lien-hsiang added, 'If he does get well, I'm afraid you will be dreadfully jealous.' Miss Li drew herself up, and replied, 'Could a physician be found to wipe away the wrong I have done to this gentleman, I would bury my head in the ground. How should I look the world in the face?'

Lien-hsiang here opened a bag and drew forth some drugs, saying, 'I have been looking forward to this day. When I left this gentleman I proceeded to gather my simples, as it would take three months for the medicine to be got ready; but then, should the poison have brought any one even to death's door, this medicine is able to call him back. The only condition is that it be administered by the very hand which wrought the ill.' Miss Li did as she was told, and put the pills Lien-hsiang gave her one after another into Sang's mouth. They burnt his inside like fire, but soon vitality began to return, and Lien-hsiang cried out, 'He is cured!' Just at this moment Miss Li heard the cock crow and vanished,† Lien-

---

* Yin is the female principle. The male principle, Yang, constitutes the alternating element of these two primeval forces underlying all phenomena. Nothing short of a book would be adequate to discuss the Chinese philosophy of alternating change (see the reference to the *I Ching* on page 75).

† The note on page 76 referred to a 'young lady whose beauty would overthrow a kingdom'. Such cultural parallels are always intriguing and the reader undoubtedly recognizes the connection with Helen of Troy. The same can be said here, where the spirit's retreat at the cock's crow reminds one of *Hamlet*.

BERNARDO: It was about to speak, when the cock crew.
HORATIO: And then it started like a guilty thing.
Upon a fearful summons. I have heard,
The cock, that is the trumpet to the morn,
Doth with his lofty and shrill-sounding throat
Awake the God of Day; and at his warning,
Whether in sea or fire, in earth or air,
The extravagant and erring spirit hies
To his confine.

hsiang remaining behind in attendance on the invalid, who was unable to feed himself. She bolted the outside door and pretended that Sang had returned to his native place, so as to prevent visitors from calling. Day and night she took care of him, and every evening Miss Li came in to render assistance, regarding Lien-hsiang as an elder sister, and being treated by her with great consideration and kindness.

Three months afterwards Sang was as strong and well as ever he had been, and then for several evenings Miss Li ceased to visit them, only staying a few moments when she did come, and seeming very uneasy in her mind. One evening Sang ran after her and carried her back in his arms, finding her no heavier than so much straw; and then, being obliged to stay, she curled herself up and lay down, to all appearance in a state of unconsciousness, and by and by she was gone. For many days they heard nothing of her, and Sang was so anxious that she should come back that he often took out her slipper and shook it. 'I don't wonder at your missing her,' said Lien-hsiang, 'I do myself very much indeed.' 'Formerly,' observed Sang, 'when I shook the slipper she invariably came. I thought it very strange, but I never suspected her of being a devil. And now, alas! all I can do is to sit and think about her with this slipper in my hand.' He then burst into a flood of tears.

Now a young lady named Yen-erh, belonging to the wealthy Chang family, and about fifteen years of age, had died suddenly, without any apparent cause, and had come to life again in the night, when she got up and wished to go out. Her family barred the door and would not hear of her doing so; upon which she said, 'I am the spirit daughter of a petty magistrate. A Mr Sang has been very kind to me, and I have left my slipper at his house. I am really a spirit! What is the use of keeping me in?' There being some reason for what she said, they asked her why she had come there, but she only looked up and down without being able to give any explanation. Someone here observed that Mr Sang had already gone home, but the young lady utterly refused to believe them.

The family was much disturbed at all this, and when Sang's neighbour heard the story, he jumped over the wall, and peeping through, beheld Sang sitting there chatting with a pretty-looking girl. As he went in, there was some commotion, during which Sang's visitor had disappeared, and when his neighbour asked the meaning of it all, Sang replied, laughing, 'Why, I told you if any ladies came I should ask them in.' His friend then repeated what Miss Yen-erh had said and Sang, unbolting his door, was about to go and have a peep at her, but unfortunately had no means of so doing.

Meanwhile Mrs Chang, hearing that he had not gone away, was more lost in astonishment than ever, and sent an old woman-servant to get back the slipper. Sang immediately gave it to her, and Miss Yen-erh was delighted to recover it, though when she came to try it on it was too small for her by a good inch. In considerable alarm, she seized a mirror to look at herself and suddenly became aware that she had come to life again in some one else's body. She therefore told all to her mother, and finally succeeded in convincing her, crying all the time because she was so changed for the worse as regarded personal appearance from what she had been before. And whenever she happened to see Lien-hsiang, she was very much disconcerted, declaring that she had been much better off as a devil than now as a human being. She would sit and weep over the slipper, no one being able to comfort her; and finally, covering herself up with bed-clothes, she lay all stark and stiff, positively refusing to take any nourishment. Her body swelled up, and for seven days she refused all food, but did not die. Then the swelling began to subside and an intense hunger to come upon her which made her once more think about eating. Then she was troubled with a severe irritation, and her skin peeled entirely away. When she got up in the morning she found that the shoes had fallen off. On trying to put them on again, she discovered that they did not fit her any longer; and then she went back to her former pair, which were now exactly of the right size and shape. In an ecstasy of joy, she grasped her mirror, and saw that her features had also changed back to what they had formerly been, so she washed and dressed herself and went in to visit her mother. Every one who met her was much astonished, and when Lien-hsiang heard the strange story, she tried to persuade Mr Sang to make her an offer of marriage. But the young lady was rich and Sang was poor, and he did not see his way clearly.

However, on Mrs Chang's birthday, when she completed her cycle,* Sang went along with the others to wish her many happy returns of the day, and when the old lady knew who was coming, she bade Yen-erh take a peep at him from behind the curtain. Sang arrived last of all; and immediately out rushed Miss Yen-erh and seized his sleeve, and said she would go back with him. Her mother scolded her well for this, and she ran in abashed, but Sang, who had looked at her closely, began to weep, and threw himself at the feet of Mrs Chang, who raised him up without saying anything unkind. Sang then took his leave, and got his uncle to act as medium between them, the result being that an auspicious day was fixed upon for the wedding.

At the appointed time Sang proceeded to the house to fetch her. When he returned he found that, instead of his former poor-looking

* The Chinese cycle is sixty years and the birthday of any person who completes this cycle is a very auspicious occasion.

furniture, beautiful carpets were laid down from the very door and thousands of coloured lanterns were hung about in elegant designs. Lien-hsiang assisted the bride to enter, and took off her veil, finding her the same bright girl as ever. She also joined them while drinking the wedding cup,* and inquired of her friend as to her recent transmigration. Yen-erh related as follows: 'Overwhelmed with grief, I began to shrink from myself as some unclean thing; and, after separating from you that day, I would not return any more to my grave. So I wandered about at random, and whenever I saw a living being, I envied its happy state. By day I remained among trees and shrubs, but at night I used to roam about anywhere. And once I came to the house of the Chang family, where, seeing a young girl lying upon the bed, I took possession of her mortal coil, unknowing that she would be restored to life again.'

When Lien-hsiang heard this she was for some time lost in thought, and a month or two afterwards she became very ill. She refused all medical aid and gradually got worse and worse, to the great grief of Mr Sang and his wife, who stood weeping at her bedside. Suddenly she opened her eyes, and said, 'You wish to live; I am willing to die. If fate so ordains it, we shall meet again ten years hence.' As she uttered these words, her spirit passed away and all that remained was the dead body of a fox. Sang, however, insisted on burying it with all the proper ceremonies.

Now Sang's wife had no children, but one day a servant came in and said, 'There is an old woman outside who has got a little girl for sale.' Sang's wife gave orders that she should be shown in, and no sooner had she set eyes on the girl than she cried out, 'Why, she's the image of Lien-hsiang!' Sang then looked at her and found to his astonishment that she was really very like his old friend. The old woman said she was fourteen years old. When asked what her price was, she declared that her only wish was to get the girl comfortably settled, and enough to keep herself alive, and ensure not being thrown out into the kennel at death. So Sang gave a good price for her;† and his wife, taking the girl's hand, led her into a room by themselves. Then, chucking her under the chin, she asked her, smiling, 'Do you know me?' The girl said she did not; after which she told Mrs Sang that her name was Wei, and that her father, who had been a pickle-merchant at Hsu-ch'eng, had died three

* A Chinese wedding requires the bride and bridegroom to drink wine together out of two cups joined by a red string, signifying the imaginary bond of destiny that determines the marriage long before the two set eyes upon each other.
† The children of poor or unlucky Chinese were frequently sold or bartered. A bill of sale was needed to prove the child was not stolen or kidnapped. A regular kidnapping trade flourished even though it was considered a capital crime, punishable by instant decapitation.

years before. Mrs Sang then calculated that Lien-hsiang had been dead just ten years; and, looking at the girl, who resembled her so exactly in every trait, at length patted her on the head, saying, 'Ah, my sister, you promised to visit us again in ten years, and you have not played us false.' The girl here seemed to wake up as if from a dream and, uttering an exclamation of surprise, fixed a steady gaze upon Sang's wife. Sang himself laughed, and said, 'Just like the return of an old familiar swallow.'

'Now I understand,' cried the girl, in tears. 'I recollect my mother saying that when I was born I was able to speak, and that, thinking it an inauspicious manifestation, they gave me dog's blood to drink, so that I should forget all about my previous state of existence. Is it all a dream, or are you not the Miss Li who was so ashamed of being a devil?' Thus they chatted of their existence in a former life, with alternate tears and smiles; but when it came to the day for worshipping at the tombs, Yen-erh explained that she and her husband were in the habit of annually visiting and mourning over her grave. The girl replied that she would accompany them; and when they got there they found the whole place in disorder, and the coffin wood all warped.

'Lien-hsiang and I,' said Yen-erh to her husband, 'have been attached to each other in two states of existence. Let us not be separated, but bury my bones here with hers.' Sang consented, and opening Miss Li's tomb took out the bones and buried them with those of Lien-hsiang, while friends and relatives, who had heard the strange story, gathered round the grave in gala dress to the number of many hundreds.

I learnt the above when travelling through I-chou, where I was detained at an inn by rain, and read a biography of Mr Sang written by a comrade of his named Wang Tzu-chang. It was lent me by a Mr Liu Tzu-ching, a relative of Sang's, and was quite a long account. This is merely an outline of it.

P'u Sung-ling (Ch'ing Dynasty)
From *Liao Chai Chih I*

The Lo-ch'a Country and the Sea-market*

Once upon a time there was a young man, named Ma Chun, who was also known as Lung-mei. He was the son of a trader and a youth of surpassing beauty. His manners were courteous, and he loved nothing better than singing and playing. He used to associate with actors, and with an embroidered handkerchief round his head the effect was that of a beautiful woman. Hence he acquired the sobriquet of the Beauty. At fourteen years of age he graduated and began to make a name for himself; but his father, who was growing old and wished to retire from business, said to him, 'My boy, book-learning will never fill your belly or put a coat on your back; you had much better stick to the old thing.' Accordingly, Ma from that time occupied himself with scales and weights, with principal and interest, and such matters.

He made a voyage across the sea, and was carried away by a typhoon. After being tossed about for many days and nights he arrived at a country where the people were hideously ugly. When these people saw Ma, they thought he was a devil and all ran screeching away. Ma was somewhat alarmed at this, but finding that it was they who were frightened at him, he quickly turned their fear to his own advantage. If he came across people eating and drinking he would rush upon them, and when they fled away for fear, he would regale himself upon what they had left.

By and by, he went to a village among the hills, and there the people had at any rate some facial resemblance to ordinary men. But they were all in rags and tatters like beggars. So Ma sat down to rest under a tree, and the villagers, not daring to come near him, contented themselves with looking at him from a distance. They soon found, however, that he did not want to eat them, and by degrees approached a little closer to him. Ma, smiling, began to talk, and although their language was

* 'Sea-market' is generally understood in the sense of a mirage, or similar phenomenon.

different, yet he was able to make himself tolerably intelligible, and told them whence he had come. The villagers were much pleased, and spread the news that the stranger was not a man-eater. Nevertheless, the very ugliest of all would only take a look and be off again; they would not come near him. Those who did go up to him were not very much unlike his own countrymen, the Chinese. They brought him plenty of food and wine. Ma asked them what they were afraid of. They replied, 'We had heard from our forefathers that 26,000 *li* to the west there is a country called China. We had heard that the people of that land were the most extraordinary in appearance you can possibly imagine. Hitherto it has been hearsay; we can now believe it.' He then asked them how it was they were so poor. They answered, 'You see, in our country everything depends not on literary talent, but on beauty. The most beautiful are made ministers of state; the next handsomest are made judges and magistrates; and the third class in looks are employed in the palace of the king. Thus these are enabled out of their pay to provide for their wives and families. But we, from our very birth, are regarded by our parents as inauspicious, and are left to perish, some of us being occasionally preserved by more humane parents to prevent the extinction of the family.' Ma asked the name of their country, and they told him it was Lo-ch'a, and also that the capital city was some thirty *li* to the north. He begged them to take him there, and next day at cock-crow he started thitherwards in their company, arriving just about dawn.

The walls of the city were made of black stone, as black as ink, and the city gate-houses were about a hundred feet high. Red stones were used for tiles, and picking up a broken piece Ma found that it marked his finger-nail like vermilion. They arrived just when the Court was rising, and saw all the equipages of the officials. The village people pointed out one who they said was Prime Minister. His ears drooped forward in flaps; he had three nostrils, and his eye-lashes were just like bamboo screens hanging in front of his eyes. Then several came out on horseback, and they said these were the privy councillors. So they went on, telling him the rank of all the ugly uncouth fellows he saw. The lower they got down in the official scale the less hideous the officials were. By and by Ma went back, the people in the streets marvelling very much to see him, and tumbling helter-skelter one over another as if they had met a goblin. The villagers shouted out to reassure them, and then they stood at a distance to look at him. When he got back, there was not a man, woman, or child in the whole nation but knew that there was a strange man at the village; and the gentry and officials became very desirous of seeing him. However, if he went to any of their houses the porter always slammed the door in his face, and the master, mistress, and family, in general, would only peep at, and speak to him through the cracks. Not a single one dared receive him face to face; but, finally, the village people, at a loss what to do, bethought themselves of a man who had been sent by a former king on official business among strange nations. 'He,' said they, 'having seen many kinds of men, will not be afraid of you.'

So they went to his house, where they were received in a very friendly way. He seemed to be about eighty or ninety years of age; his eyeballs protruded, and his beard curled up like a hedgehog. He said, 'In my youth I was sent by the king amongst many nations, but I never went to China. I am now one hundred and twenty years of age, and that I should be permitted to see a native of your country is a fact which it will be my duty to report to the Throne. For ten years and more I have not been to Court, but have remained here in seclusion; yet I will now make an effort on your behalf.' Then followed a banquet, and when the wine had already circulated pretty freely, some dozen singing girls came in and sang and danced before them. The girls all wore white embroidered turbans, and long scarlet robes which trailed on the ground. The words they uttered were unintelligible, and the tunes they played perfectly hideous. The host, however, seemed to enjoy it very much, and said to Ma, 'Have you music in China?' He replied that they had, and the old man asked for a specimen. Ma hummed him a tune, beating time on the table, with which he was very much pleased, declaring that his guest had the voice of a phoenix and the notes of a dragon, such as he had never heard before.

The next day he presented a memorial to the Throne, and the king at once commanded Ma to appear before him. Several of the ministers, however, represented that his appearance was so hideous it might frighten His Majesty, and the king accordingly desisted from his intention. The old man returned and told Ma, being quite upset about it. They remained together some time until they had drunk themselves tipsy. Then Ma, seizing a sword, began to attitudinize, smearing his face all over with coal-dust. He acted the part of Chang Fei,* at which his host was so delighted that he begged him to appear before the Prime Minister in the character of Chang Fei. Ma replied, 'I don't mind a little amateur acting, but how can I play the hypocrite for my own personal advantage?' On being pressed he consented, and the old man prepared a great feast, and asked some of the high officials to be present, telling Ma to paint himself as before. When the guests had arrived, Ma was brought out to see them; whereupon they all exclaimed, 'Ai-yah! how is it he was so ugly before and is now so beautiful?' By and by,

* A famous general in the wars of the Three Kingdoms.

when they were all taking wine together, Ma began to sing them a most bewitching song, and they got so excited over it that next day they recommended him to the king. The king sent a special summons for him to appear, and asked him many questions about the government of China, to all of which Ma replied in detail, eliciting sighs of admiration from His Majesty. He was honoured with a banquet in the royal guest-pavilion, and when the king had made himself tipsy he said to him, 'I hear you are a very skilful musician. Will you be good enough to let me hear you?' Ma then got up and began to attitudinize, singing a plaintive air like the girls with the turbans. The king was charmed, and at once made him a privy councillor, giving him a private banquet, and bestowing other marks of royal favour.

As time went on his fellow officials found out the secret of his painted face, and whenever he was among them they were always whispering together, besides which they avoided being near him as much as possible. Thus Ma was left to himself, and found his position anything but pleasant in consequence. So he memorialized the Throne, asking to be allowed to retire from office, but his request was refused. He then said his health was bad, and he got three months' sick leave, during which he packed up his valuables and went back to the village.

The villagers on his arrival went down on their knees to him, and he distributed gold and jewels amongst his old friends. They were very glad to see him, and said, 'Your kindness shall be repaid when we go to the sea-market; we will bring you some pearls and things.' Ma asked them where that was. They said it was at the bottom of the sea where the mermaids * kept their treasures, and that as many as twelve nations were accustomed to go thither to trade. Also that it was frequented by spirits, and that to get there it was necessary to pass through red vapours and great waves.

'Dear sir,' they said, 'do not yourself risk this great danger, but let us take your money and purchase these rare pearls for you. The season is now at hand.' Ma asked them how they knew this. They said, 'Whenever we see red birds flying backwards and forwards over the sea, we know that within seven days the market will open.' He asked when they were going to start, that he might accompany them, but they begged him not to think of doing so. He replied, 'I am a sailor: how can I be afraid of wind and waves?' Very soon after this people came with merchandise to forward and so Ma packed up and went on board the vessel that was going.

This vessel held some tens of people, was flat-bottomed, with a railing all round and, rowed by ten men, it cut through the water like an arrow.

* Pearls were believed to be the tears of Chinese mermaids.

After a voyage of three days they saw afar off faint outlines of towers and minarets, and crowds of trading vessels. They soon arrived at the city, the walls of which were made of bricks as long as a man's body, the tops of its buildings being lost in the Milky Way. Having made fast their boat, they went in, and saw laid out in the market rare pearls and wondrous precious stones of dazzling beauty, such as are quite unknown amongst men. Then they saw a young man come forth riding upon a beautiful steed. The people of the market stood back to let him pass, saying he was the third son of the king. But when the prince saw Ma, he exclaimed, 'This is no foreigner,' and immediately an attendant drew near and asked his name and country. Ma made a bow, and standing at one side told his name and family. The prince smiled, and said, 'For you to have honoured our country thus is no small piece of good luck.' He then gave him a horse and begged him to follow.

They went out of the city gate and down to the sea-shore, whereupon their horses plunged into the water. Ma was terribly frightened and screamed out but the sea opened dry before them and formed a wall of water on either side. In a little time they reached the king's palace, the beams of which were made of tortoiseshell and the tiles of fishes' scales. The four walls were of crystal and dazzled the eye like mirrors. They got down off their horses and went in, and Ma was introduced to the king. The young prince said, 'Sire, I have been to the market, and have got a gentleman from China.' Whereupon Ma made obeisance before the king, who addressed him as follows: 'Sir, from a talented scholar like yourself I venture to ask for a few stanzas upon our sea-market. Pray do not refuse.'

Ma made a k'o-t'ou and undertook the king's command. Using an ink-slab of crystal, a brush of dragon's beard, paper as white as snow, and ink scented like the larkspur,* Ma immediately threw off some thousand odd verses, which he laid at the feet of the king. When His Majesty saw them, he said, 'Sir, your genius does honour to these marine nations of ours.' Then, summoning the members of the royal family, the king gave a great feast in the Coloured Cloud pavilion; and, when the wine had circulated freely, seizing a great goblet in his hand, the king rose and said before all the guests, 'It is a thousand pities, sir, that you are not married. What say you to entering the bonds of wedlock?'

Ma rose blushing and stammered out his thanks; upon which the king, looking round, spoke a few words to the attendants, and in a few moments in came a bevy of Court ladies supporting the king's daughter, whose ornaments went tinkle, tinkle, as she walked along. Immediately the nuptial drums and trumpets began to sound forth and bride and

* Chinese ink was usually highly scented.

bridegroom worshipped Heaven and Earth together. Stealing a glance, Ma saw that the princess was endowed with a fairy-like loveliness. When the ceremony was over she retired, and by and by the wine party broke up. Then came several beautifully dressed waiting-maids, who with painted candles escorted Ma within. The bridal couch was made of coral adorned with eight kinds of precious stones, and the curtains were thickly hung with pearls as big as acorns.

Next day at dawn a crowd of young slave-girls trooped into the room to offer their services; whereupon Ma got up and went off to Court to pay his respects to the king. He was then duly received as a royal son-in-law and made an officer of state.

The fame of Ma's poetical talents spread far and wide, and the kings of the various seas sent officers to congratulate him, vying with each other in their invitations to him. Ma dressed himself in gorgeous clothes, and went forth riding on a superb steed, with a mounted body-guard all splendidly armed. There were musicians on horseback and musicians in chariots, and in three days he had visited every one of the marine kingdoms, making his name known in all directions.

In the palace there was a jade tree, about as big round as a man could clasp. Its roots were as clear as glass, and up the middle ran, as it were, a stick of pale yellow. The branches were the size of one's arm; the leaves like white jade, as thick as a copper cash. The foliage was dense, and beneath its shade the ladies of the palace were wont to sit and sing. The flowers which covered the tree resembled grapes, and if a single petal fell to the earth it made a ringing sound. Taking one up, it would be found to be exactly like carved cornelian, very bright and pretty to look at. From time to time a wonderful bird came and sang there. Its feathers were of a golden hue, and its tail as long as its body. Its notes were like the tinkling of jade, very plaintive and touching to listen to. When Ma heard this bird sing, it called up in him recollections of his old home, and accordingly he said to the princess, 'I have now been away from my own country for three years, separated from my father and mother. Thinking of them my tears flow and the perspiration runs down my back. Can you return with me?' His wife replied, 'The way of immortals is not that of men. I am unable to do what you ask, but I cannot allow the feelings of husband and wife to break the tie of parent and child. Let us devise some plan.' When Ma heard this he wept bitterly, and the princess sighed and said, 'We cannot both stay or both go.'

The next day the king said to him, 'I hear that you are pining after your old home. Will tomorrow suit you for taking leave?' Ma thanked the king for his great kindness, which he declared he could never forget, and promised to return very shortly. That evening the princess and Ma talked over their wine of their approaching separation. Ma said they would soon meet again; but his wife averred that their married life was at an end. Then he wept afresh, but the princess said, 'Like a filial son you are going home to your parents. In the meetings and separations of this life, a hundred years seem but a single day; why, then, should we give way to tears like children? I will be true to you; do you be faithful to me; and then, though separated, we shall be united in spirit, a happy pair. Is it necessary to live side by side in order to grow old together? If you break our contract, your next marriage will not be a propitious one; but if loneliness * overtakes you, then choose a concubine. There is one point more of which I would speak, with reference to our married life. I am about to become a mother and I pray you give me a name for your child.' To this Ma replied, 'If a girl, I would have her called Lung-kung; if a boy, then name him Fu-hai.'† The princess asked for some token of remembrance, and Ma gave her a pair of jade lilies that he had got during his stay in the marine kingdom. She added, 'On the eighth of the fourth moon, three years hence, when you once more steer your course for this country, I will give you up your child.' She next packed a leather bag full of jewels and handed it to Ma, saying, 'Take care of this; it will be a provision for many generations.'

When the day began to break a splendid farewell feast was given him by the king, and Ma bade them all adieu. The princess, in a car drawn by snow-white sheep, escorted him to the boundary of the marine kingdom, where he dismounted and stepped ashore. 'Farewell!' cried the princess, as her returning car bore her rapidly away, and the sea, closing over her, snatched her from her husband's sight.

Ma returned to his home across the ocean. Some had thought him long since dead and gone; all marvelled at his story. Happily his father and mother were yet alive, though his former wife had married another man; and so he understood why the princess had pledged him to constancy, for she already knew that this had taken place. His father wished him to take another wife, but he would not. He only took a concubine. Then, after the three years had passed away, he started across the sea on his return journey, when lo! he beheld, riding on the wave-crests and splashing about the water in playing, two young children. On going near, one of them seized hold of him and sprang into his arms; upon which the elder cried until he, too, was taken up. They were a boy and girl, both very lovely, and wearing embroidered caps adorned with jade lilies. On the back of one of them was a worked case, in which Ma found the following letter:

* Literally, 'If you have no one to cook your food'.
† *Fu-hai* and *Lung-kung* mean, literally, 'Happy Sea' and 'Dragon Palace'.

'I presume my father- and mother-in-law are well. Three years have passed away and destiny still keeps us apart. Across the great ocean, the letter-bird would find no path.* I have been with you in my dreams until I am quite worn out. Does the blue sky look down upon any grief like mine? Yet Ch'ang-ngo† lives solitary in the moon, and Chih Nu‡ laments that she cannot cross the Silver River. Who am I that I should expect happiness to be mine? Truly this thought turns my tears into joy. Two months after your departure I had twins, who can already prattle away in the language of childhood, at one moment snatching a date, at another a pear. Had they no mother, they would still live. These I now send to you, with the jade lilies you gave me in their hats, in token of the sender. When you take them upon your knee, think that I am standing by your side. I know that you have kept your promise to me, and I am happy. I shall take no second husband, even unto death. All thoughts of dress and finery are gone from me; my looking-glass sees no new fashions; my face has long been unpowdered, my eyebrows unblacked. You are my Ulysses, I am your Penelope;§ though not actually leading a married life, how can it be said that we are not husband and wife. Your father and mother will take their grandchildren upon their knees, though they have never set eyes upon the bride. Alas! there is something wrong in this. Next year your mother will enter upon the long night. I shall be there by the side of the grave, as is becoming in her daughter-in-law. From this time forth our daughter will be well; later on she will be able to grasp her mother's hand. Our boy, when he grows up, may possibly be able to come to and fro. Adieu, dear husband, adieu, though I am leaving much unsaid.'

Ma read the letter over and over again, his tears flowing all the time. His two children clung round his neck, and begged him to take them home. 'Ah, my children,' said he, 'where is your home?' Then they all wept bitterly, and Ma, looking at the great ocean stretching away to meet the sky, lovely and pathless, embraced his children, and proceeded sorrowfully to return. Knowing, too, that his mother could not last long, he prepared everything necessary for the ceremony of interment, and planted a hundred young pine-trees at her grave.¶

The following year the old lady did die and her coffin was borne to its

* This refers to an ancient legend where letters were conveyed by a bird.
† See the note on page 77.
‡ *Chih Nu* is the name of a star in the constellation Lyra, the 'Spinning Damsel', and legend holds that it travels an annual transit across the Milky Way.
§ Herbert Giles, the translator of this tale, notes that these are, of course, only the equivalents of the Chinese names in the text.
¶ Trees were used to keep off the dreaded wind, which was believed to disturb the rest of the departed.

last resting-place, when lo! there was the princess standing by the side of the grave. The lookers-on were much alarmed, but in a moment there was a flash of lightning, followed by a clap of thunder and a squall of rain, and she was gone. It was then noticed that many of the young pine-trees which had died were one and all brought to life. Subsequently, Fu-hai went in search of the mother for whom he pined so much, and after some days' absence returned. Lung-king, being a girl, could not accompany him, but she mourned much in secret. One dark day her mother entered and bade her dry her eyes, saying, 'My child, you must get married. Why these tears?' She then gave her a tree of coral eight feet in height, some Baroos camphor, one hundred valuable pearls, and two boxes inlaid with gold and precious stones, as her dowry. Ma having found out she was there, rushed in, and, seizing her hand, began to weep for joy, when suddenly a violent peal of thunder rent the building, and the princess had vanished.*

P'u Sung-ling (Ch'ing Dynasty)
From *Liao Chai Chih I*

* Episodes from this story were woven together to form the Japanese tale of 'Urashima, the fisher-lad who was beloved of the Sea King's daughter'. See W. G. Aston's *Japanese Literature*, 1899.

2 Parables and Fables

Chuang Tzu

Dream and Reality

Once upon a time I dreamt I was a butterfly, fluttering hither and thither, to all intents and purposes a butterfly. I was conscious only of following my fancies (as a butterfly), and was unconscious of my individuality as a man. Suddenly, I awakened; and there I lay, myself again. I do not know whether I was then dreaming I was a butterfly or whether I am now a butterfly dreaming that it is a man. Between a man and a butterfly there is necessarily a barrier; and the transition is called *metempsychosis*.

The Bird Killed by Kindness

A sea-gull alighted in a suburb of the capital of Lu. The Marquis of Lu welcomed it and feasted it in the temple hall, ordering the best music and grandest sacrifices for it. But the bird remained in a daze, looking quite wretched, not daring to swallow a morsel of meat or a single cup of wine. And after three days it died.

This was entertaining the sea-gull as the Marquis of Lu liked to be entertained, not as a sea-gull likes to be entertained.

Independence

Chuang Tzu was one day fishing, when the Prince of Ch'u sent two high officials to interview him, saying that his Highness would be glad of Chuang Tzu's assistance in the administration of his government. The latter quietly fished on, and without looking round, replied, 'I have heard that in the State of Ch'u there is a sacred tortoise, which has been dead three thousand years, and which the prince keeps packed up in a box on the altar in his ancestral shrine. Now do you think that tortoise would rather be dead and have its remains thus honoured, or be alive and wagging its tail in the mud?' The two officials answered that no doubt it would rather be alive and wagging its tail in the mud; whereupon Chuang Tzu cried out, 'Begone! I too elect to remain wagging my tail in the mud.'

P'u Sung-ling
The Stream of Cash

A certain gentleman's servant was one day in his master's garden, when he beheld a stream of cash * flowing by, two or three feet in breadth and of about the same depth. He immediately seized two large handfuls, and then threw himself down on the top of the stream in order to try and secure the rest. However, when he got up he found that it had all flowed

* See 'The Talking Eye Pupils' (the note on page 29) for description of 'streams of cash'.

away from under him, none being left except what he had got in his two hands.

['Ah!' says the commentator, 'money is properly a circulating medium, and is not intended for a man to lie upon and keep all to himself.']

Playing at Hanging

A number of wild young fellows were one day out walking when they saw a young lady approach, riding on a pony. One of them said to the others, 'I'll back myself to make that girl laugh', and a supper was at once staked by both sides on the result. Our hero then ran out in front of the pony, and kept on shouting, 'I'm going to die! I'm going to die!' at the same time pulling out from over the top of a wall a stalk of millet, to which he attached his own waistband, and, tying the latter round his neck, made a pretence of hanging himself. The young lady did laugh as she passed by, to the great amusement of the assembled company; but as, when she was already gone some distance off, their friend did not move, the others laughed louder than ever. However, on going up to him they saw that his tongue protruded, and that his eyes were glazed; he was, in fact, quite dead.

The Wine Insect

A Mr Lin of Ch'ang-shan was extremely fat, and so fond of wine* that he would often finish a pitcher by himself. However, he owned about fifty acres of land, half of which was covered with millet, and being well

* The wine of the ordinary man in China was made from distilled rice.

off, he did not consider that his drinking would bring him into trouble. One day a foreign Buddhist priest saw him, and remarked that he appeared to be suffering from some extraordinary complaint. Mr Lin said nothing was the matter with him; whereupon the priest asked him if he often got drunk. Lin acknowledged that he did; and the priest told him that he was afflicted by the wine insect. 'Dear me!' cried Lin, in great alarm, 'do you think you could cure me?' The priest declared there would be no difficulty in doing so; but when Lin asked him what drugs he intended to use, the priest said he should not use any at all. He then made Lin lie down in the sun; and tying his hands and feet together, he placed a stoup of good wine about half a foot from his head. By and by, Lin felt a deadly thirst coming on; and the flavour of the wine passing through his nostrils seemed to set his vitals on fire. Just then he experienced a tickling sensation in his throat, and something ran out of his mouth and jumped into the wine. On being released from his bonds, he saw that it was an insect about three inches in length, which wriggled about in the wine like a tadpole, and had mouth and eyes all complete. Lin was overjoyed, and offered money to the priest, who refused to take it, saying, all he wanted was the insect, which he explained to Lin was the essence of wine, and which, on being stirred up in water, would turn it into wine. Lin tried this, and found it was so; and ever afterwards he detested the sight of wine.

Lieh Tzu

How the Fool Moved Mountains

Taihang and Wangwu Mountains are some seven hundred *li* around, and hundreds of thousands of feet high.

North of these mountains lived an old man of nearly ninety, who was called the Fool. His house faced these mountains, and he found it very inconvenient to have to make a detour each time he went out and came back; so one day he summoned his family to discuss the matter.

'Suppose we work together to level the mountains?' he suggested. 'Then we can open a road southward to the bank of the Han River.'

To this they all agreed. Only his wife was dubious.

'You haven't the strength to level even a small hill,' she objected. 'How can you move these two mountains? Besides, where will you dump all the earth and rocks?'

'We'll dump them in the sea,' was the reply.

Then the Fool set out with his son and grandson, the three of them carrying poles. They dug up stones and earth, and carried them in baskets to the sea. A neighbour of theirs named Ching was a widow with a son of seven or eight, and this boy went with them to help them. It took them several months to make one trip.

A man living at the river bend, who was called the Wise Man, laughed at their efforts and did his best to stop them.

'Enough of this folly!' he cried. 'How stupid this is! Old and weak as you are, you won't be able to remove even a fraction of the mountains. How can you dispose of so much earth and stones?'

The Fool heaved a long sigh.

'How dull and dense you are!' he said. 'You haven't even the sense of the widow's young son. Though I shall die, I shall leave behind me my son, and my son's son, and so on from generation to generation. Since these mountains can't grow any larger, why shouldn't we be able to level them?'

Then the Wise Man had nothing to say.

Presenting Doves

It was the custom in Hantan to catch doves to present to the prince on New Year's Day, for this pleased him so much that he gave rich rewards. Someone asked the prince the reason for this custom.

'I free the doves at New Year to show my kindness,' he said.

'Since your subjects know you want doves to set free, they all set about catching them,' objected the other. 'And the result is that many doves are killed. If you really want to save the doves, you had better forbid people to catch them. As things are, you catch them to free them, and your kindness cannot make up for the damage you do.'

The prince agreed with him.

Dream and Reality

A man of the State of Cheng was one day gathering fuel, when he came across a startled deer, which he pursued and killed. Fearing lest any one should see him, he hastily concealed the carcass in a ditch and covered it with plantain leaves, rejoicing excessively at his good fortune. By and by, he forgot the place where he had put it and thinking he must have been dreaming, he set off towards home, humming over the affair on his way.

Meanwhile, a man who had overheard his words, acted upon them, and went and got the deer. The latter, when he reached his house, told his wife, saying, 'A woodman dreamt he had got a deer, but did not know where it was. Now I have got the deer so his dream was a reality.' 'It is you,' replied his wife, 'who have been dreaming you saw a woodman. Did he get the deer? And is there really such a person? It is you who have got the deer: how, then, can his dream be a reality?' 'It is true,' assented the husband, 'that I have got the deer. It is therefore of little importance whether the woodman dreamt the deer or I dreamt the woodman.'

Now when the woodman reached his home, he became much annoyed at the loss of the deer; and in the night he actually dreamt where the deer then was, and who had got it. So next morning he proceeded to the place indicated in his dream – and there it was. He then took legal steps to recover possession; and when the case came on, the magistrate delivered the following judgment: 'The plaintiff began with a real deer and an alleged dream. He now comes forward with a real dream and an alleged deer. The defendant really got the deer which plaintiff said he dreamt, and is now trying to keep it; while, according to his wife, both the woodman and the deer are but the figments of a dream, so that no one got the deer at all. However, here is a deer, which you had better divide between you.'

When the Prince of Cheng heard this story, he cried out, 'The magistrate himself must have dreamt the case!' So he inquired of his prime minister, who replied, 'Only the Yellow Emperor and Confucius could distinguish dream from reality, and they are unfortunately dead. I advise, therefore, that the magistrate's decision be confirmed.'

Han Fei Tzu

Why Tseng Shen Killed the Pig

One day, when Tseng Shen's wife was going to the market, their son cried and clamoured to go with her.

'Go back now!' she wheedled him. 'When I get home, we'll kill the pig for you.'

Upon her return, she found Tseng Shen about to kill the pig. She hastily stopped him.

'I didn't really mean it,' she protested. 'I just said that to keep the boy quiet.'

'How can you deceive a child like that?' asked Tseng Shen. 'Children know nothing to begin with, but they copy their parents and learn from them. When you cheat the boy, you are teaching him to lie. If a mother deceives her child, he will not trust her, and that is no way to bring him up.'

So he killed the pig after all.

The Crumbling Wall

There was once a rich man in the state of Sung. After a downpour of rain his wall began to crumble.

'If you don't mend that wall,' warned his son, 'a thief will get in.'

An old neighbour gave the same advice.

That night, indeed, a great deal of money was stolen. Then the rich man commended his son's intelligence, but suspected his old neighbour of being the thief.

Ivory Chopsticks

When King Chou ordered chopsticks made of ivory, Chi Tzu was most perturbed. For he feared that once the king had ivory chopsticks he would not be content with earthenware, but would want cups of rhinoceros horn and jade; and instead of beans and vegetables, he would insist on such delicacies as elephant's tail and baby leopard. He would hardly be willing either to wear rough homespun or live under a thatched roof, but would demand silks and splendid mansions.

'It is fear of what this will lead to,' said Chi Tzu, 'that upsets me.'

Five years later, indeed, King Chou had a garden filled with meat, tortured his subjects with hot irons, and caroused in a lake of wine. And so he lost his kingdom.

Liu Chi
Outsides

At Hangchow there lived a costermonger who understood how to keep oranges a whole year without letting them spoil. His fruit was always fresh-looking, firm as jade, and of a beautiful golden hue; but inside – dry as an old cocoon.

One day I asked him, saying, 'Are your oranges for altar or sacrificial purposes, or for show at banquets? Or do you make this outside display merely to cheat the foolish, as cheat them you most outrageously do.' 'Sir,' replied the orangeman, 'I have carried on this trade now for many years. It is my source of livelihood. I sell; the world buys. And I have yet to learn that you are the only honest man about, and that I am the only cheat. Perhaps it never struck you in this light. The baton-bearers of today, seated on their tiger skins, pose as the martial guardians of the State; but what are they compared with the captains of old? The broad-brimmed, long-robed Ministers of today pose as pillars of the constitution; but have they the wisdom of our ancient counsellors? Evil-doers arise, and none can subdue them. The people are in misery, and none can relieve them. Clerks are corrupt, and none can restrain them. Laws decay, and none can renew them. Our officials eat the bread of the State and know no shame. They sit in lofty halls, ride fine steeds, drink themselves drunk with wine, and batten on the richest fare. Which of them puts on an awe-inspiring look, a dignified mien? – all gold and gems without, but dry cocoons within. You pay, sir, no heed to these things, while you are very particular about my oranges.'

I had no answer to make. Was he really out of conceit with the age, or only quizzing me in defence of his fruit?

Yen Tzu
The Conceited Coachman

One day Yen Tzu, prime minister of the state of Chi, went out in his carriage. His coachman's wife, from her gate, saw her husband looking thoroughly smug and conceited under the great carriage awning as he drove his four horses.

When the coachman went home, his wife told him she wanted to leave him.

Her husband asked her why.

'Yen Tzu is prime minister of Chi,' she replied. 'He is famed throughout the states. But I saw him out today, deep in thought and not giving himself any airs. You are only a coachman, yet you look so conceited and pleased with yourself. That's why I want to leave you.'

After this, her husband behaved more modestly. When Yen Tzu, surprised, inquired the reason for this change, the coachman told him the truth. Then Yen Tzu recommended him for an official post.

Warring States Anecdotes
The Fox who Profited by the Tiger's Might

While hunting for prey, the tiger caught a fox.

'You can't eat *me*,' said the fox. 'The Emperor of Heaven has appointed me king of the beasts. If you eat me, you'll be disobeying his orders. If you don't believe me, follow me. You'll soon see whether the other animals run away at the sight of me or not.'

Agreeing to this, the tiger accompanied him; and when all the beasts saw them coming they dashed away. Not realizing that they were afraid of him, the tiger thought they were afraid of the fox.

Ying Shao
The Reflection of the Bow

My grandfather, who was magistrate of the district of Chi, once invited his secretary, Tu Hsuan, to drink with him during the midsummer festival. A red bow which was hanging on the north wall cast a reflection in the cup just like a snake; but although Tu Hsuan was frightened he dared not refuse to drink. Then he had a severe pain in his stomach, and could not eat, so that he grew very thin. Though he tried all manner of drugs, he could find no cure.

Later my grandfather called on him on some business, and asked him how he had contracted this illness.

'Through fear of the snake which I swallowed,' Tu Hsuan told him.

After going home my grandfather thought this over, then turned and saw the bow, and understood what had happened. He sent a subordinate with a carriage to escort Tu Hsuan to his house and set wine in the same place, so that once more a snake appeared in the cup.

'This is simply a reflection of that bow on the wall,' he told his secretary.

At once Tu Hsuan felt better and, greatly relieved, recovered.

Ch'u-p'ing
The Fisherman's Reply

When Ch'u-p'ing was dismissed, he wandered away to the banks of a river, and there poured forth his soul in verse. His colour changed. His body wasted to a skeleton.

One day a fisherman accosted him, saying, 'Are you not his Excellency the Prime Minister? What has brought you to this pass?'

'The world,' replied Ch'u-p'ing, 'is foul; and I alone am clean. There they are all drunk, while I alone am sober. So I am dismissed.'

'Ah!' said the fisherman, 'the true sage does not quarrel with his environment, but adapts himself to it. If, as you say, the world is foul, why not leap into the tide and make it clean? If all men are drunk, why not drink with them, and teach them to avoid excess? Of what avail are these subtle thoughts, these lofty schemes, which end only in disgrace?'

'I have heard,' rejoined Ch'u-p'ing, 'that the bather fresh from the bath will shake the dust from his hat and clothes. How should he allow his pure body to be soiled with the corruption of earth? I am willing to find a grave in the bellies of the fishes that swim in this stream: I will not let my purity be defiled by the filth and corruption of the world.'

The fisherman laughed, and keeping time with his oar, sculled off, singing:

My tassel I'll wash if the water is sweet;
If the water is dirty 'twill do for my feet.

Ma Chung-hsi
An Ungrateful Wolf

Chao Chien-tsu was hunting in a valley in the state of Chungshan. The beaters and guides led the way, while hunting dogs and falcons and their keepers followed in the rear. Numerous birds noted for their flight and beasts for their ferocity fell victim to the mighty hunter's arrows. A wolf, finding itself in the path of the great hunter, stood up on its hind legs like a man and gave a long howl. Chao, mounting his chariot and picking up his famous long bow, let fly an arrow, which hit the animal in one of its front legs. Giving a yelp it ran for dear life. Infuriated, Chao gave chase in his chariot, creating a noise like rumbling thunder and raising such a cloud of dust that one could see nothing beyond ten feet.

It happened that Mr Tungkuo, a believer in Motzu's philosophy of universal love was stumbling through the valley, accompanied by a lame mule loaded with a bag of books, on his way northward to seek some official preferment. When he saw the cloud of dust in the distance and heard the approaching tumult, he was much frightened.

The wolf appeared before him. Leaning its head forward, it asked: 'Are you not charitably inclined towards all living creatures?' It continued: 'In the olden days, Mao Pao, you will recall, liberated a captured turtle and was ultimately ferried across the water by his grateful debtor, while the Marquis of Sui protected a snake from harm and received as reward a wonderful pearl. Neither a turtle nor a snake is as intelligent as a wolf. In my emergency why not conceal me in your bag and save my life? If I should happily escape the present danger I would not fail to follow the example of the turtle and the snake in return for the good turn you do me today in saving my hide.'

'Huh,' replied the disciple of Motzu, 'how foolish of you, a common wolf, to get in the way of a noble hunter, and how am I to expect any reward from you when your very life is in the balance? Nevertheless, as a follower of the philosophy of universal love, it is my bounden duty to save you, come what danger may.'

He emptied the bag of its contents, and started to replace them with the wolf. He met with much difficulty with the task, what with the dangling leg and the thick bushy tail. Three times he failed, in spite of his conscientious efforts.

The hunters were rapidly approaching and the wolf became highly impatient.

'Sir,' he cried, 'when one desires to save the drowning from the water or the inmates of a house which has caught fire, one has no time for bowing and scraping, nor does one beat the gong in order to escape from robbers and bandits. Hurry up with your job.'

He huddled himself into a heap and assisted as best he could the scholar, who was trying to tie his legs together. He bent his head as far as possible to the tail, which he quickly drooped, adopted the posture of a porcupine, curbed himself like a snail and held his breath like a turtle, so as to facilitate the task. Following the suggestions of the wolf, the scholar finally succeeded in cramming him in the bag, which, after having been tied up, was replaced on the back of the mule. Then he waited on one side of the road for the hunters to pass.

Chao Chien-tsu soon arrived in his chariot and not seeing any sign of the wolf, was exceedingly wroth. He struck with his mighty sword the pole of his chariot, cutting off the tip, and swore a terrible oath.

'Let this be a warning to anyone attempting to conceal from me the whereabouts of the wolf,' he shouted.

The scholar approached the hunter and fell on his knees. 'I am but an ignorant scholar, on my way to a distant place to seek official appointment,' he pleaded. 'I have myself missed the way, still less am I in a position to show the trail of the wolf to Your Honour's dogs and falcons.

'However,' he continued, 'your servant has heard it said that it is easy to lose a sheep on the highway because of the many crossroads. A sheep is a gentle animal which even a little boy can manage, yet a strayed one cannot be found on account of the numerous turnings in the highway. A wolf differs entirely from a sheep, and in this valley there are innumerable bypaths for even a sheep to escape. When you seek for the wolf on the main road, may the action not be compared to climbing a tree to capture the eluding fish, or to waiting behind the tree trunk for a hare to break its neck on it? Moreover, the chase is a profession of the huntsmen: would it not be wiser for you to seek their advice than to threaten a chance wayfarer? I confess that I am ignorant, yet I know well the nature of the wolf. It is a cruel and rapacious beast and has for its wicked partner the ferocious hyena. If it were within my power I should certainly render you my feeble assistance, why should I conceal the truth from you?'

Chao made no response, but turned his chariot and proceeded on his way.

The scholar, touching the mule with his whip, also hurriedly resumed his journey. In a few minutes the hunting party disappeared from view, nor could one hear any sound of it.

The wolf, realizing that there existed no more peril, commenced to stir in the bag. 'Sir,' he called out, 'please note that you must now free me from the bag, untie the rope from my legs and remove the arrow from my foreleg, otherwise I shall soon die.'

No sooner had the scholar done what was requested of him than the wolf commenced to show its ugly fangs. 'When I was pursued by the hunters,' he snarled, 'they were hot on my heels and I was grateful to you for delivering me from them. However, I am now terribly hungry, and if my hunger is not satisfied I shall surely die. Now as I look at it, it would be preferable to have been killed by the hunters and made a sacrifice in an aristocratic house, to perishing from hunger at the roadside and being devoured by wild beasts. You, sir, are a faithful follower of Motzu, and your guiding principle is to save the world even at the cost of your own life. Such being the case, you surely would not mind sacrificing yourself in order to deliver my poor life.'

Thereupon the wretched beast opened wide its mouth, exposing its sharp and powerful teeth, and stretched its claws to attack Mr Tungkuo, who defended himself the best he could with his bare hands, retreating gradually, so as to place the mule between himself and the wolf. Thus the two circled around the mule, the wolf being unable to seize hold of his prey, until both were breathless and exhausted. They faced each other with the mule between them, trying to recover some strength.

'You are an ungrateful beast,' complained the man.

'Not at all,' retorted the wolf, 'it is not that I am ungrateful, but you men were created for us to devour.'

The deadlock continued until the sun began to set, and the scholar feared that the fall of night might bring other wolves, making certain his own death.

'According to human custom,' he remarked to the wolf, 'when two persons argue over a question without result, they decide by asking the opinion of three elderly ones. Let us follow this procedure as we walk along. If all three of them declare that you are justified in devouring me, I am prepared to submit. If not, then you must let me go.'

The wolf accepted the proposal, and the two continued on their way. For quite a while they met no one on the road and the wolf was becoming ravenous. Suddenly he saw an old tree by the side of the road, and he proposed to the scholar to put the question to it.

'Plants have no intelligence,' objected the man, 'what's the use of asking a tree?'

'Just try,' insisted the wolf. 'Perhaps you'll get a reply.'

The follower of Motzu bowed to the tree and gave an account of their dispute, ending by demanding to know if the wolf was entitled to devour him. To his amazement a voice issued from inside the trunk.

'I am,' it said, 'an apricot tree. When the farmer planted me it cost him just a small kernel. In a year or so I commenced to put forth buds, after two years to grow small fruit, and at the end of ten years it required the two arms of a man to encircle my trunk. I am now twenty years old. The farmer, his wife and children, as well as friends and servants have eaten greedily the fruit that I produced and sold the kernels for a profit. It is obvious that I have greatly benefited the farmer. After I grew aged, I naturally bloomed and produced less, much to the displeasure of the farmer, who chopped my twigs, sawed off my branches, and is even trying to tear away my trunk as wood for which he will receive from the joiner a handsome price. Old and decrepit as I am, I cannot escape death from the axe and the saw. Compared to my fate, in what way is the wolf so indebted to you as to justify your hope in escaping death from him? It seems to me he has every reason to devour you.'

The wolf, delighted with the verdict given by the apricot tree, commenced once more to attack his deliverer.

'Wait a moment,' expostulated the scholar. 'You are violating our agreement, for so far only the apricot tree has given an opinion and we should have that of three parties.'

They again proceeded on their way, the wolf growing more and more irritated, when they caught sight of an old ox sunning itself behind the crumbling wall of a farmyard. The wolf wanted to obtain its opinion on their disagreement.

'No,' objected the scholar, 'we made a serious mistake in consulting the fool apricot tree, whose ridiculous views nearly ruined my life. An ox is only a stupid animal, what's the sense in demanding its opinion?'

'Do as I say, or you die anyway,' was the brutal rejoinder.

The potential victim could do nothing but salute the stolid ox and repeat his story.

Knitting its brow as if in deep thought, rolling its eyes and licking its nose, the ox slowly opened its mouth.

'The apricot tree was right in its assertions,' he declared. 'Take my own case: I am now old and shrivelled up and yet I was once young and vigorous. The farmer, my master, sold only a kitchen knife and with the price bought me. When I was young I helped other oxen in ploughing the fields, and when they grew old and feeble and I became stronger, I shouldered all the labour. If my master wanted to go anywhere, it was I that pulled the cart, seeking out the best part of the road so as to travel faster. When he worked alone in the field, and I was released from the yoke, I spent my time in ridding the field of weeds and brambles. I was like the farmer's right hand: he depended on me for his food and clothes. The weddings in the family took place only through my laborious efforts, the taxes were paid with my hard work, and the barn was full due to my contribution. I was easily satisfied – I asked only for a shelter and a place to sleep, like the horse and the dog.

'Formerly,' the ox went on, 'the farmer had hardly any rice stored up; now there is a large annual yield. He was as poor as a church mouse; now he struts about proudly in the village. In former days the wine jars were empty and covered with dust, my master suffered from thirst, and during half his life he never had a taste of good liquor. Now he makes different brews, drinks freely, and carries himself as the cock of the walk. He wore the short clothes of a day labourer, his friends and companions were only weeds and stones and he did not know how to bow or read like a gentleman. Now he owns a rabbit warren, he wears a broad-brimmed straw hat, he boasts of a broad, handsome belt and appears in an elegant gown: in short, every grain of rice and every fibre of cotton have come from me. But he takes advantage of my age and debility, and drives me out into the open field, where the biting wind hurts my tired eyes and the icy rays of the winter sun almost freeze my shadow. My bony structure looks like a bald and bleak mound, my tears fall like the rain, my saliva drips from my mouth in a steady stream, my legs are cramped and cannot be lifted, while not only the hair but my very skin is falling away – skin which is covered with sores and bruises.

'But worst of all, my master has a jealous and cruel wife. "Every part of an ox has some value," she murmurs day and night into the ears of my master. "The flesh can be eaten as meat, the skin turned into leather, and the bones employed to make various useful articles. You," she says, pointing to her son, "you have learned your trade at the shop of the butcher. Why don't you sharpen your knife and get yourself ready for the job?"

'From what I have heard, it is evident that something harmful to me is being plotted and I have no notion as to where and when I shall suddenly be slain. I have rendered invaluable services to the farmer and his family, but they are utterly ungrateful, so before long I shall meet with disaster. Compared to my cruel fate, what claim have you on the wolf to expect leniency from his claws and jaws?'

Just as the wolf made another attempt to seize the scholar, the latter perceived an elderly gentleman approaching from a distance, supporting himself with a walking stick. He was neatly dressed, had snow-white hair and eyebrows and was of the philosopher type.

'Please wait a minute,' appealed the poor scholar to his aggressor, feeling somewhat relieved at the sight of the new arrival. He turned away from the wolf and advanced towards the old gentleman, falling on his knees and commencing to weep.

'Sir,' he begged, 'say only a word, and you'll save me from a cruel death.'

The newcomer demanded an explanation.

'This wretched wolf,' repeated the scholar, 'was in danger of being killed by hunters, when he supplicated my help. I succeeded in saving his life at my own peril, yet he insists on devouring me. To prolong my life for even a short while, I made him agree to leave the decision of the dispute to three elders. The first was an apricot tree, which, having little common sense, almost caused my death by his stupid reply. The second arbiter was an ox, which, being only a stolid and unintelligent animal, did no better. I am, indeed, fortunate in meeting you, sir. Perhaps it is the will of Heaven that I, a scholar, should be spared my life. A word of wisdom from you would be sufficient to save the situation.'

Prostrating himself on the ground, he awaited the response of the old gentleman.

While listening to the story the white-haired gentleman sighed several times. 'You wolf,' cried he, as he struck the beast with his stick, 'you are in the wrong. When one has received a favour and shows himself ungrateful, such behaviour would certainly land him in misfortune. Confucius taught to the contrary. If a man does not forget a good turn done to him, he declared, one can be sure that he will become famous as a filial son. This axiom is true even in the case of tigers and wolves, wild beasts though they are. You seem to be an exception to the rule, so with you the happy relation between father and son is obviously something unknown and non-existent. Away with you, you ungrateful beast, or I'll kill you with my staff.'

'Venerable sir,' argued the wolf, 'you see only one side of the question and not the other. Please listen to me and let me explain. When the scholar tried to save me, he tied my legs and sewed me in his bag. He then thrust his books therein, so that I was terribly cramped and could hardly breathe. Making a long-winded discourse to the hunter, his real intention was to suffocate me in his bag in order to profit himself out of my death. Why should I not kill him?'

The old man glanced at Mr Tungkuo, admitting that if what the wolf complained was true, the scholar was perhaps also in the wrong.

The scholar denied the accusation and swore that his entire action was motivated by pity for the wolf. The latter, in its turn, employed much sophistry to establish his case.

'Neither of you,' the old gentleman finally asserted, 'has convinced me with your biased statements. Only circumstantial evidence will satisfy me.' Turning to the wolf, he added, 'Let me judge for myself if you were really, as you claim, uncomfortable in the bag, by getting into it once more.'

The wolf willingly accepted the proposal and allowed himself to be bound a second time and pushed into the bag, which the scholar tied as before and lay onto the back of the mule. As soon as it was done, the old man whispered to the scholar, asking if he had a knife, and if he did, to plunge it into the wolf.

'Would it not hurt the wolf?' demanded the scholar.

'You are a fool to hesitate to kill so ungrateful and dangerous a beast,' responded the old gentleman, 'though you mean to be kind-hearted. To jump into a well to save a man who has fallen therein, or to divest oneself of clothes to use them to resuscitate your freezing neighbour, may be profitable and acceptable to the other, but how about certain death for yourself? You seem to wish to follow such examples. Remember, however, that when charity borders on stupidity, it is no longer a virtue for the wise.'

He broke into great laughter, which was joined by the scholar. Then the two of them stuck the knife into the bag and, having killed the wolf and thrown its carcass to the roadside, proceeded each on his way.

3 Morality and Justice

The King

A certain Governor of Hunan province dispatched a magistrate to the capital in charge of a treasure of 600,000 ounces of silver. On the road, the magistrate encountered a rainstorm so violent that night descended upon him before he could reach the next refuge station and he was forced to take cover in an old temple nearby.

When morning came he discovered in horror that the treasure had disappeared. Unable to fix the guilt on any one person, he returned to the Governor who refused to believe his story and would have had him severely punished had not all of his attendants stoutly corroborated his statements. The Governor, however, told the magistrate to return and find the missing silver or he would be dealt with harshly.

When the magistrate reached the temple he found an extraordinary-looking blind man who informed him that he could read people's thoughts. The blind man immediately told the magistrate that he had come there about money. He admitted this was so and recounted his misfortune. After listening patiently, the blind man suddenly called for sedan-chairs and then climbing into one said, 'Follow me,' which the magistrate and all his retinue accordingly did.

If the blind man said 'east', they went east, or if 'north', they went north. They journeyed for five days far into the hills until they suddenly beheld a large city. They entered the gates, and proceeded on for a short distance when suddenly the blind man cried, 'Stop.' Alighting from his chair, he pointed to a lofty door facing the west. He told the magistrate to knock and make what inquiries were necessary. He then bowed and silently took his leave.

The magistrate obeyed his instructions. A man dressed in an ancient style came out in reply to his summons. When the magistrate informed him why he had come, he replied that if he would wait a few days he would personally assist him in the matter. The man then conducted the magistrate within and, giving him a room to himself, provided him regularly with food and drink.

One day the magistrate chanced to stroll around to the back of the building, and there he found a beautiful garden with dense avenues of pine trees and smooth lawns of fine grass. After wandering about for some time among the arbours and ornamental buildings, the magistrate came to a lofty kiosk. Mounting the steep steps he saw a number of human skins hanging on the wall before him, each with its eyes, nose, ears, mouth and heart intact.* Horrified, he beat a hasty retreat to his quarters. Convinced that he was about to leave his own skin in this strange, out-of-the-way place, he gave himself up for lost. After a moment's reflection, however, he decided he would gain nothing by trying to escape and made up his mind to wait.

On the following day the same man came to fetch him, saying he could now have an audience. The magistrate replied that he was ready and his conductor then mounted a fiery steed, leaving him to follow on foot.

By and by, they reached a door where crowds of official servants stood on either side preserving the utmost silence and decorum. The man dismounted and led the magistrate inside; and after passing through another door they came into the presence of a King who wore a cap decorated with pearls and an embroidered sash and who sat on a great throne facing the south. The magistrate rushed forward and prostrated himself on the ground. The King asked him if he was the Hunan official who had been charged with the conveyance of treasure.

On his answering the affirmative, the King said, 'The money is all here. It's a mere trifle, but I have no objection to receiving it as a present from the Governor.'

The magistrate then burst into tears and declared that his term of grace had already expired and that he would be punished if he went back empty handed, especially as he would have no evidence to substantiate his story.

'That is easy enough,' replied the King, and putting a thick letter into his hands bade him give it to the Governor, assuring him that this would prevent him from getting into any trouble. The King also provided him with a rich escort; and the magistrate, who dared not argue the point further, sorrowfully accepted the letter and took his departure.

* This corresponds with our five senses, the heart taking the place of the brain, and being regarded by Chinese doctors as the seat not only of intelligence and the passions, but also of all sensation.

The road he travelled was not that by which he had come, and when the hills ended his escort left him and turned back. In a few days, he reached Ch'ang-sha and respectfully informed the Governor what had taken place. The Governor thought he was telling more lies, and in a great rage bade the attendants to bind him hand and foot. The magistrate then drew the letter forth from his coat. When the Governor broke the seal and saw its contents his face turned deadly pale.

Without looking at the magistrate, the Governor gave orders that he was free to go, and that the loss of the treasure was of no great importance. He turned to his aides and issued instructions to make up the amount in one way or another and forward it immediately to the capital.

Hastily, the Governor left the room and went to his home. There, in secret, he opened the thick letter again. From it fell an abundance of long, black hair. The Governor knew it was his wife's hair, for one morning some time ago she had awakened to find all her hair gone. This event had thrown the entire household into dismay and fear. Trembling now, the Governor read the note that accompanied the returned hair.

'Ever since you first entered into public life, your career has been one of thievery and avarice. The 600,000 ounces of silver are safely stored in my treasury. Make good this sum from your own accumulated extortions. The officer you charged with the treasure is innocent; he must not be wrongly punished. On a former occasion I took your wife's hair as a gentle warning. If you now disobey my injunctions, it will not be long before I have your skin. Herewith I return the hair as an evidence of what I say.'

Shortly after this, the Governor fell ill and died. His family divulged the contents of the letter, and sent some of his subordinates to search for the secret mountain city, but they found only range upon range of inaccessible mountains with no path or road.

P'u Sung-ling (Ch'ing Dynasty)
From *Liao Chai Chih I*

Quest of the Filial Son

Chou Fang-yung, better known as Chou the Filial Son, was a native of Huating. His father, Wen-jung, went to Hupeh as an official when he was a young man, and returned home to get married at the age of twenty-eight. The next year Fang-yung was born, and the following year his father again proceeded to Hupeh.

It was only after five years that Wen-jung came home once more to pay a visit to his parents, leaving after a stay of a few months. Fang-yung was then five years old, and afterwards could recall only a little of the voice and looks of his father, for after eight years an official notice received at Huating brought news of Wen-jung's death at his post in Kueichou, Hupeh. This took place on the seventeenth day of the ninth moon of the fifty-eighth year during the reign of Emperor Chien Lung. The boy was then thirteen years old, his grandparents being still alive.

The family was left penniless, and it was through the spinning and weaving of his hard-working mother that the boy and his grandparents were supported. The Chou family had few male members, and friends and relatives sighed deeply when they received the obituary announcement. It being impossible for any of the Chous to go to fetch the remains, the funeral ceremony could only be held by invoking the soul of the dead to return to its home, so the obsequies were incomplete and very unsatisfactory.

Then the grandparents also died, and on their death-bed appealed to young Fang-yung to fulfil his duties as a filial son by bringing home his dead father, so that they could rest in peace in purgatory. The young man wept bitterly and engraved their words on his heart.

The thought of bringing home the remains of his father never left him, but sickness and death caused the family to become poorer than ever. What he made from his pen was hardly sufficient to keep his mother and himself alive, let alone permit of his embarking on a long trip. For several years he made repeated attempts to proceed on the journey, but in the end he was compelled to admit defeat.

At one of the seasonal sacrificial ceremonies in memory of the ancestors, he was deeply stirred by the bitter lamentations of his mother, and looking at himself, already a grown man and capable of sustaining hardships on a long journey, he made a resolution then and there. 'How can I consider myself a man, when my father's remains are still abroad?' he declared with a deep sense of shame.

He gave up eating meats and wore only coarse clothes, putting aside what was thus saved for the provision of his mother during his planned absence.

'If I do not find the remains of my father, I swear not to return home,' he declared as he offered incense before the ancestral shrine. He said to himself that the trip being long and expensive, it was not possible for a poor man like him to undertake it empty and single-handed. It would be much facilitated by his going to Peking and joining the suite of some official appointed to serve in Hupeh Province. Therefore, in the seventeenth year of the reign of Chia Ching, he took passage on a tribute-rice-bearing boat for the capital.

Fang-yung had been employed as a tutor and during his spare hours learned to paint orchids and bamboos, and made good progress in the art of calligraphy. He continued his pursuit of the two accomplishments on the boat, besides learning to draft official letters and memoranda, with the belief that these attainments would be helpful to him on his trip to Hupeh.

Arriving at Peking, he stopped at a small inn, and made calls on metropolitan officials from his home town, to whom he related his ambition. They sympathized deeply with him on his project and promised to secure for him a post as clerk to some official going to Hupeh. Wuchang, the provincial capital of Hupeh, they assured him, was an important city and a transit centre, hundreds of officials from their native province travelling annually in that direction, and if one did not insist on a large salary, it was a simple matter to secure an appointment. But for some reason or other no such opportunity came to Chou even after a long wait.

'My purpose,' he ruminated, 'is to find the remains of my father, and if I wait for a good appointment it may require a long time. If I could reach Hupeh, I should be satisfied even if I had to go as a merchant's assistant or as a servant.' His fellow townsmen thought compassionately of his ambition, but failed to find for him the humble position he wanted. He decided to proceed on his journey, begging his way.

His stay at Peking had lasted already some six months, and he had to pawn his belongings to pay expenses. The innkeeper demanded urgently the settlement of the bill: it was in the twelfth moon near the end of the year, when bills must be liquidated.

One Mr Keng, a neighbour of his in Huating, was then visiting the capital, so Chou approached him, asking for some financial assistance to make it possible for him to leave Peking. His friend promised to do something after the New Year.

When Fang-yung called on him again as instructed, he was shown into an ante-room, where he found some other fellow townsmen, among them an old Mr Tai, who had been his father's colleague at Kueichou. Falling on his knees Fang-yung begged him to tell where the coffin was temporarily deposited, as was customary with people who died far away from home. The host entering the room at the moment repeated the whole story of the young man's case to Mr Tai.

'So you are the son of Wen-jung,' observed the old gentleman. 'You are a filial child indeed to think of going to Hupeh to bring back your father's remains, but Peking and Kueichou are separated by several thousand *li* of sand and water, and you appear to me to be but a penniless scholar. How are you to undertake the trip on an empty stomach? That is the first difficulty. During two years, the city of Kueichou was ravaged by the disorders of the White Lily Secret Society, nearly all the houses were destroyed by fire and the present population consists almost entirely of refugees. Your father's coffin, among many others', was buried in the midst of these troubles. How are you to identify the grave after the years of war and conflagration? That is the second difficulty. As an orphan it is your duty to look after the welfare of your mother, whereas the course of the Yangtze River above Ichang is most dangerous, and the slightest accident would turn you into food for the fishes and turtles. While you may sacrifice your life in favour of filial piety, how about your widow mother, who is watching at the gate for your early return? This is the third difficulty.

'My advice to you, therefore,' the old man continued, 'is to return to your home and fulfil your other duties of a son. I have been for many years an official in Hupeh, and I meet many friends coming from time to time from Kueichou. I will seek for information from them, and if I learn of something definite, I will transmit it to you, and it will not be too late then for you to start on your pilgrimage.'

The only response on the part of Chou was prolonged weeping.

The host then mentioned the young man's intention to beg his way to his destination.

'Folly, oh, what folly!' commented Mr Tai. 'Nevertheless, it is a kind of folly difficult to refrain from admiring. Since you are so determined in your filial ambitions, I'll help you as far as I can. The chief constable at Kueichou now is an old friend of mine, and I'll write a letter of introduction to him for you. He is a highly honourable person, and will not take advantage of you in any way.'

That day Mr Keng, the host, proposed to those present to make up a purse for the young man, and all contributed something, which would enable him to buy a few necessities for the trip. The next day old Mr Tai brought his letter of introduction and also an itinerary of the trip.

'From Hankow westward the itinerary goes into detail, so you need have no fear of losing your way,' he declared. He himself had asked the government to transfer him to a post nearer home on account of his aged parents, but he expressed the hope of seeing Fang-yung later in their native town, together with other words of encouragement.

In the same inn was a man from Nanking by the name of Chang, who had been doorkeeper to a county magistrate and was familiar with many government offices on the way between Peking and Nanking. He was at the time also destitute, and he proposed to Chou to travel together to Nanking first.

'You are good at calligraphy and painting,' he explained, 'but you have few friends to approach. I have many friends, but no gifts with which to approach them. Why not let us two cooperate? At Nanking you will find many ships bound for Wuchang-Hankow and you can arrive there in a few days.'

Thus the two indigent men started on their journey southward, ekeing out expenses from friends and on the scrolls and paintings. When they reached the Linhuai Customs Barrier, Chang went to look up a friend, leaving Chou alone in the inn, feeling very depressed. It flashed across his mind that a fellow townsman was teaching in a neighbouring city: why not pay him a visit and obtain some information from him as to the roads leading direct to Hupeh?

Ever since the young man left Peking on his arduous overland journey, he suffered much from the hardships of travel, being exposed to the sun, wind, rain and frost, as well as from hunger and changes of climate, so that his health deteriorated seriously. Thus, when he arrived at an inn after spending four days in a small boat and about halfway to the teacher's town, he broke down with high fever. His thirst was unquenchable and he was confined to his bed. It was early summer; the plague was raging in the region and people were dying like flies. The innkeeper was frightened with the sick stranger on hand, and decided to move him to a temple, which was without any priest. Sick travellers were left there simply to die.

Chou appealed to the innkeeper, saying: 'I don't blame you for wishing to get rid of me, a sick and solitary traveller. However, though I am very ill, my mind is quite clear, and I feel sure that, given proper medicaments, I shall recover. I have an important mission which I simply must fulfil, so please call the headman of the street that I may confide my affairs to him.'

Upon the headman's arrival, Chou explained the main purpose of his journey to Hupeh and why he was going to visit his teacher friend, showing at the same time the letter of introduction from Mr Tai, besides two pieces of silver from his bag.

'Please take charge of the letter, as I am afraid of losing it during my illness,' he requested of the headman, 'my life depends on it. As to the money, please use it for curing my illness, and in case I die, for my burial. If anyone from Huating should pass through here, show him the letter and he will surely take my coffin home.'

The headman was very much impressed by the content of the letter, and secured for him the service of a neighbouring physician, who happened to be a student of Chou's teacher friend.

'Why, my patient is a noted filial son and related to my teacher,' he exclaimed. 'I'll do my best to cure him, and you people must not neglect him.'

A crowd had gathered together by that time, and the innkeeper was persuaded not to expel his guest. Meanwhile, the doctor took very good care of Chou, coming to see him two or three times a day. After a week his temperature became normal, and in a fortnight he was fully recovered. Unfortunately, in his haste to resume his journey, he shaved his head in a draught, and got a relapse. His ailment continued off and on for some weeks, and it was already the beginning of the sixth moon when, moneyless and almost clotheless, he walked the rest of the way to see Mr Shih, his teacher friend.

Mr Shih, seeing the ravages of his visitor's illness and the desperation of his condition, advised the latter strongly to abandon his quest. His own second son was proceeding to Nanking for the examinations, and the two, he urged, could go in the same boat; from Nanking he could easily return to his home. Moreover, he tried to dissuade Chou on the ground that filial piety obligated no one to seek his dead father at the cost of leaving his mother to starve.

However, the young man refused to deviate from his set purpose, so Mr Shih told him to make a few scrolls and paintings, and had them sent to his well-off students, together with his own letters appealing for their patronage. In this way some twenty taels of silver was raised, with which Chou bought some clothes and started for Hupeh again.

The country he had to traverse before reaching Hankow, his next stop, was mountainous, wild and uninhabited. The only means of conveyance was by bamboo sedan-chairs, but the cost was prohibitive to our lone traveller. Due to the luxuriant vegetation and summer heat, the area was covered with a pall of unhealthful miasma, hiding even the sun.

The roads, if they could be called such, were infested with robbers, while inns were few and far between.

In short clothes and hemp sandals, Chou would cover some ten miles or so daily, and where he found no inn or shelter, would sleep on the ground or under trees; in rainy weather he would be soaked to the skin. Once sleeping under the eaves of a mountain cabin, he was awakened by something in his dreams: a black and white snake went down the nape of his neck and crawled out of his sleeve! On another occasion, walking at night he perceived what he believed was a pair of lanterns. He called out. No human voice answered, but a tiger jumped on to the road in front of him. Only by throwing himself into a ditch did he escape the king of beasts.

Owing to the heavy rains the mountain paths were flooded, so his bare feet were often cut by the sharp stones, leading to much bleeding. At this time he was travelling in the company of some pedlars who sold straw helmets. A few of them stopped to rest, while others pressed forward to the next village. It was not long before two of them rushed back in sorry shape, because the party had encountered a dozen bandits who had robbed them of the little they had. One of their comrades was killed and the others scattered, they having fled back to warn those who were resting. Under the circumstances, Chou and the others remained where they were till some more travellers came along before they ventured to continue on their journey. Such painful and dangerous experiences were many and frequent, and by the time he reached Hankow the cold weather had already commenced.

Mr Tai's itinerary was, indeed, very conscientiously compiled and gave full particulars as to the best routes to be followed from Hankow westward, the distances between cities, places where the travellers must trans-ship, and hotels and inns to spend the nights on the way. Chou booked a seat on a passenger boat, but on account of the floods the boat had to follow a roundabout route, by the Tung-t'ing Lake. He felt miserable on the boat, not being able to eat or sleep. But when questioned by his fellow passengers he did not reveal his objective.

By the time he arrived at Ichang he was once more penniless. Selling all available personal articles of any value, he raked together a thousand small cash and resumed his ascent of the Yangtze River. That night he dreamed that his father spoke to him in a warning way: 'Tomorrow the gorges begin; be careful.'

Sure enough, the rapids were unusually perilous, and late in the next day the boat ran into a rock in midstream and all on board were only short of being drowned. Ultimately, the boat arrived at Kueichou, on the first day of the ninth moon.

From Ichang upwards the rapids succeeded one another like rungs of a ladder and the town of Kueichou, located near the upper end of the Yangtze gorges, occupied a point of high vantage. When one listened to the crowing of cocks and barking of dogs in the town from a distance down the river, one would believe it to be up in the clouds. The city walls and their battlements were built in the early years of the Ming dynasty, but were razed to the ground during the years of rebellion led by Chang Hsien-chung. The wooden barriers set up later around the key points of the city were again burned down in recent riots. Reconstruction of the town had just been commenced, some headway had been made in the rehabilitation of the refugees, and gradually the town was picking up prosperity.

No sooner had Chou lodged himself in an inn near the magistracy than he went and called on the chief constable with the letter of introduction from Mr Tai. The officer read the letter over and over again, and was astounded at the contents.

'Ever since the war with the rebels, the lay-out of the town and its population have entirely changed,' he said mournfully. 'Few people know anything about events which occurred here ten years, still less of twenty years, ago. Even the cemeteries and family graveyards of the local people have been turned into fields and ponds; how is one to trace the coffin of a stranger? However, young man, since you are already here, rest up a little while and then we may go together to outside the city limits, where you can wrap up a piece of sod, invoke the spirit of your lamented father and return to your home. In this way you will have fulfilled more than the usual obligations of a filial son. It would be an utterly vain attempt, I am afraid, to find the actual remains of your beloved father.'

Absolutely undaunted, Chou insisted upon making thorough inquiries. The chief constable had to accede to his request, and every policeman, every temple and other depositaries of coffins were questioned about the matter, but nothing materialized.

One day an aged constable from the country who used to come to the town to serve for a certain period turned up at the magistracy. He was asked if he remembered the Magistrate Huang from Chekian Province and one of his secretaries who died in office and the replies to both questions were in the affirmative.

'Of course I know,' replied the veteran constable. 'I was captain of the county police that year when Magistrate Huang arrived with three secretaries, one of whom was Mr Chou. The latter was already ill on reaching Kueichou and a boy-servant looked after him. One day the boy sent for me, and when I went to the house I found Mr Chou already dead, the medicine cup still in the boy's hand. One of his colleagues attended to the funeral and burial, as the magistrate and the third secretary had gone on a visit to the provincial capital. Although twenty years have elapsed, I can still remember a little the looks of this Mr Chou.'

Young Chou, who was there listening to the details of his father's death, was overwhelmed with sorrow and at the same time with contentment. He eagerly asked if the old man recalled the place of burial. The latter believed that it was in a cemetery outside the East Gate, a little to the left, but after all those years of devastation, he seriously doubted if the tomb could be located.

'Now that we possess some inkling of the tomb,' observed the chief constable, 'you might as well move your lodging as near to it as possible. There is the Taiping Temple outside the East Gate, where you can stay. Tomorrow I'll send Captain Hsu to guide you in finding the grave.'

The following day Chou, accompanied by the guide, went to a rising ground overgrown with weeds, half a mile outside the East Gate, where travelling merchants and strangers in the old days used to be buried. In spite of assiduous search and reading of all the tombstones meeting his eyes, he failed to identify his object. At twilight of the third day he was still engaged in his search.

Here in an area of a square mile human bones were as plentiful as weeds. 'If necessary, I'll devote half a month's time to locate the tomb,' he thought to himself. 'If I should fail, after having travelled so many thousand miles, there can be but one ending – I shall jump into the river.'

At that very moment he saw a stone tablet some ten yards away, jutting out of the ground to about half its height. Hurrying over and pulling it out of the earth, he discovered three vertical lines of characters engraved on the stone, the middle one stating unmistakably that the departed was Chou Wen-jung of Huating County, Sungkiang Prefecture, the line on the right the date of his death, and the one on the left that the stone was erected by his friends and colleagues. Chou was both overjoyed and heart-broken at the discovery and could hardly raise himself from the ground. He wanted to spend the night on the grave, but the old guide dragged him away, saying that the place was infested with wild beasts that attacked people often in broad daylight.

The chief constable felt very happy when informed of the turn of events. 'Now that you have found the remains,' he advised the young man, 'you should be completely satisfied. I don't think it's practical to convey them back home, for the voyage is long and costly, requiring at least two hundred taels. Besides, why disturb them, after they have been interred so long? You can well follow the example of the noted scholars of the Sung dynasty, who frequently had their parents buried in separate localities.'

But the young man was obdurate, and there was no way of diverting him from his purpose.

The matter was reported to the magistrate, who sympathized with the young man's aspiration, sent the local headman to assist him in unearthing and gathering the bones.

Equipped with two jars, one yellow bag, oil and ordinary wrapping paper, pieces of silk, string, writing implements and so on, the party went to the grave on the ninth day of the ninth moon to carry out their pious task. After appropriate sacrifices the coffin, half decomposed, was opened, and the skeleton appeared. Chou was so moved by the sight that he took out a knife and removed a piece of flesh from his arm to seal up the jaw of his dead father. After dressing the wound with some earth and cloth, he fell down on his knees, picked up the bones one after the other, wrapped them separately and noted down their particulars on the wrapping paper. The packages were then solemnly and respectfully placed in the yellow bag, which was further protected with heavy cloth. Then he took rubbings of the engraved characters on the tombstone, to be taken home as evidence of his find. As a final act, the tombstone was carefully buried in its original spot.

Now Kueichou was noted for its landscape, with its lovely hills rising from the river bank, and outside the East Gate the scenery was specially pretty. It being the tradition for the people to visit the elevated spots on the 'Double Ninths', many townspeople were enjoying themselves in the vicinity of the cemetery, and when they heard of what was happening, they came in crowds to watch the ceremony, expressing their admiration and amazement.

Chou returned to his temple lodging with his precious packages and commenced to plan his return trip, hoping to cover expenses by selling specimens of his calligraphy and painting. But it was difficult to raise sufficient funds in this way for the purpose. Fortunately through a chance acquaintance he was introduced to a General Chang, also from Sungkiang, who promised his help.

The following day the chief constable called and congratulated his young friend, reporting that at a dinner the previous night, where were gathered all the local officials, General Chang mentioned Chou's financial difficulty to the magistrate, who declared at once that if such a filial son failed in his mission due to shortage of funds, he as magistrate would be the first one to be thoroughly ashamed. Thereupon he contributed five taels of silver to a fund to assist Chou. Others followed suit, and in a few minutes more than twenty taels were raised, besides a gift of ten strings of cash from the general. The latter would also commandeer a boat to convey the young man and his belongings to Hankow, starting within three days.

Calling on the magistrate to present his heartfelt thanks, Chou was requested to copy for him in ancient script several pages of the *Classic on Filial Piety*, so that he would always treasure the handwriting as coming from a remarkable young man and pass it on to his children for their edification. The magistrate gave him an official communication addressed to the Magistrate of Huating, containing a full account of Chou's visit to Kueichou and its successful termination.

Wearing the white hat and white clothes of mourning, Chou embarked in triumph for his trip down the river, his departure being witnessed by hundreds of the residents who crowded the streets and the river bank. This happened on the twenty-sixth day of the ninth moon in the eighteenth year of the Chia Ching period. The boat arrived in a few days at Hankow, the wind being favourable and the current very swift.

At Hankow Chou trans-shipped, joining the boatmen in their daily offer of incense to the Deity of the Golden Dragon, and in a fortnight reached his home. His mother, though impatient and worried at his lengthy absence, was as healthy as ever.

The bones were first deposited in a temple together with the paper rubbings from the tombstone, and then buried properly in their ancestral graveyard.

Having delivered the official communication from Kueichou to the local magistrate, Chou was invited to the latter's office, where he was highly commended for his virtues. Later the affair was reported even to the Throne, and the Chou family was duly honoured.

Chien Yung (Ch'ing Dynasty)

The Tiger of Chao-ch'eng

At Chao-ch'eng there lived an old woman more than seventy years of age, who had an only son. One day he went up to the hills and was eaten by a tiger, at which his mother was so overwhelmed with grief that she hardly wished to live. With tears and lamentations she ran and told her story to the magistrate of the place, who laughed and asked her how she thought the law could be brought to bear on a tiger. But the old woman would not be comforted, and at length the magistrate lost his temper and bade her begone. Of this, however, she took no notice. Then the magistrate, in compassion for her great age and unwilling to resort to extremities, promised her that he would have the tiger arrested. Even then she would not go until the warrant had been actually issued. The magistrate, at a loss what to do, asked his attendants which of them would undertake the job.*

Upon this one of them, Li Neng, who happened to be gloriously drunk, stepped forward and said that he would, whereupon the warrant was immediately issued and the old woman went away.

When our friend, Li Neng, got sober, he was sorry for what he had done. But reflecting that the whole thing was a mere trick of his master's to get rid of the old woman's importunities, he did not trouble himself much about it, handing in the warrant as if the arrest had been made.

'Not so,' cried the magistrate, 'you said you could do this, and now I shall not let you off.' Li Neng was at his wits' end, and begged that he might be allowed to impress the hunters of the district.† This was conceded. So collecting together these men, he proceeded to spend a day and night among the hills in the hope of catching a tiger, and thus making a show of having fulfilled his duty.

A month passed away, during which he received several hundred blows with the bamboo,‡ and at length, he betook himself in despair to the Ch'eng-huang temple in the eastern suburb, where, falling on his knees, he prayed and wept by turns. By and by, a tiger walked in, and

* In old China, government officials, from the highest to the lowest, were entitled to a small (and completely inadequate) fee for their work – which most of them turned down on the grounds of the official being 'unworthy'. The money was returned to the treasury and the official made his income out of a complicated and pervasive system of graft, bribery, and favours. Herbert Giles reported that some of this imaginative graft occurred in the giving of warrants where jailers, for a fee, allowed their prisoners to remain at large until called for trial; clerks took bribes to use their influence, and the various warrants issued by a magistrate were taken up by clerks who thought to make some quick or easy money on its issuance. In some cases, Giles tells us, a clerk would not even issue a warrant, and for a small bribe would report back that the party was 'not at home', or, for a larger bribe, say that the wanted person 'had absconded'.

† Anyone was liable to be 'impressed' into the service of the government at any time. Those so 'impressed' into official service received a fee so small that it was insufficient, in most cases, to defray even their expenses.

‡ Constables and petty officials were liable to be bambooed at intervals of three or five days until their mission had been successfully concluded. In the case of theft the responsible official might even be called upon to make its value good from his own pocket.

Li Neng, in a great fright, thought he was going to be eaten alive. But the tiger took no notice of anything, remaining seated in the doorway. Li Neng then addressed the animal as follows: 'O tiger, if thou didst slay that old woman's son, suffer me to bind thee with this cord.' And drawing a rope from his pocket, he threw it over the animal's neck. The tiger drooped his ears, and allowing itself to be bound, followed Li Neng to the magistrate's office.

The magistrate then asked it, 'Did you eat the old woman's son?' to which the tiger replied by nodding its head. Whereupon the magistrate rejoined, 'That murderers should suffer death has ever been the law. Besides, this old woman had but one son, and by killing him you took from her the sole support of her declining years. But if now you will be as a son to her, your crime shall be pardoned.' The tiger again nodded assent, and accordingly the magistrate gave orders that he should be released, at which the old woman was highly incensed, thinking that the tiger ought to have paid with his life for the destruction of her son.

Next morning, however, when she opened the door of her cottage, there lay a dead deer before it and the old woman by selling the flesh and skin, was able to purchase food. From that day, this became a common event, and sometimes the tiger would even bring her money and valuables, so that she became quite rich and was much better cared for than she had been even by her own son. Consequently, she became very well-disposed to the tiger, which often came and slept in the verandah, remaining for a whole day at a time, and giving no cause of fear either to man or beast.

In a few years the old woman died, upon which the tiger walked in and roared its lamentations in the funeral hall. With all the money she had saved, however, she was able to have a splendid funeral. While her relatives were standing round the grave, out rushed a tiger and sent them all running away in fear. But the tiger merely went up to the mound, and after roaring like a thunder-peal, disappeared again. Then the people of that place built a shrine in honour of the Faithful Tiger, and it remains there to this day.

P'u Sung-ling (Ch'ing Dynasty)
From *Liao Chai Chih I*

The Loyal City Clerk

The family of the City Clerk Yen Ying-yuan came originally from Shaohsing in Chekiang Province. Four generations before him, his great-grandfather moved to Tungchou, near Peking, where he settled. Ying-yuan started out in life as a petty official, attached to one of the imperial granaries. In the fourteenth year of the reign of Chung Cheng, the last emperor of the Ming dynasty, he was transferred to the post of city clerk of Kiangyin, near Nanking.

Soon after his arrival a band of pirates, massing a hundred junks, took advantage of the favourable wind and tide to sail up the Yangtze River with the object of pillaging the city. The magistrate happened to be away taking charge of a neighbouring county, while the assistant magistrate was a timid and nervous person. The people, left without a leader, ran hither and thither, not knowing what to do in the face of the unexpected raid. Thereupon Ying-yuan seized his sword, mounted his horse and galloped to the market-place.

'Come on, you men,' he shouted, 'follow me. We'll kill the pirates and save our homes.'

Almost instantly a thousand men followed him. They had no banners, and he led them to a bamboo shop.

'The situation is desperate,' he appealed to the proprietor. 'Let every man have a bamboo pole: I shall be responsible for the payment.'

The thousand stalwart men stood on the river bank, their poles and banners standing out like a forest, which together with the men formed a formidable rampart. Ying-yuan on horseback dashed forward and backward along the line, shooting incessantly at the pirates and killing one with every arrow. The pirates were so overawed by the defence that they set sail and departed.

When the incident was reported to the governor, our hero was promoted and granted the honour of having a tall yellow awning and a huge flag to precede him whenever he appeared in public, besides having the streets cleared of people. As both were rare privileges, he enjoyed in consequence much respect among the townsmen. Later he was nominated to a still higher post in Kwangtung, but on account of his mother's illness he was unable to accept the appointment.

The Ming dynasty fell soon after and he moved to Sandy Hill to the east of Kiangyin. It was already the second year of the Manchu dynasty, and the Manchu Prince Yu came south with his armies. No sooner had they crossed the Yangtze River than Nanking surrendered, the hurriedly enthroned Prince Hungkuang was captured and many high officials ran away.

The Manchu Prince Yu dispatched part of his troops to attack other cities of the south-east, of which most of the magistrates either surrendered or fled. Though some local officials loyal to the Ming dynasty entrenched themselves in their walled cities, trying to put up some resistance, nearly all such places were easily captured, some in a few hours, others within a week or ten days, so that south of Nanking more than a hundred large towns were occupied by the new masters within a month. The rather small city of Kiangyin, however, singularly put up a desperate defence, which lasted more than eighty days, due largely to the able leadership and clever strategy of Yen Ying-yuan.

When the Manchu government issued an imperial decree commanding the people to shave their heads and grow queues, a Kiangyin scholar by the name of Hsu Yung-teh hung up on the first day of the intercalary sixth moon the portrait of the founder of the Ming dynasty in the Confucian temple and led the townsmen to it. They wept bitterly as they prostrated themselves before the imperial portrait.

As many as ten thousand of the citizens gathered together and elected the assistant magistrate Chen Ming-hsuan as leader of the defence. Chen, however, declined the honour, suggesting that Yen Ying-yuan, the former city clerk, was superior to him in wisdom and courage and should undertake the important task. A deputation rode that night to Yen's retreat to acclaim and welcome him. Without hesitation he discarded his long gown and, accompanied by some forty of his relations and domestics, returned with the deputation to Kiangyin.

At the time the city had a garrison of less than a thousand men, a population of ten thousand families and no funds in the treasury to pay the troops. As soon as he arrived, Yen commenced to study his resources, repair the city walls and towers and conscript one man from each household as wall guard, the remaining males to perform other military duties. He took immediate delivery of the gunpowder, muskets and other fire-arms manufactured by the previous intendant, and had them safely stored in the wall towers. The wealthy families were requested to contribute their silver or, as alternatives, grains, cloth, and other commodities. Chen Pi, a leading citizen, contributed at once twenty-five thousand taels of silver, while others competed with one another in giving their share.

Within a short period the city authorities had collected three hundred barrels of gunpowder, thousands of catties of iron shots and balls, a hundred cannons, a thousand muskets, a large sum of cash, besides provisions of all kinds, salt, iron, straw and so on. The plan of defence was quickly drawn up, officers being detailed to guard the various city gates. All these preparations were just completed when the city was closely besieged.

The attacking armies were a hundred thousand strong, divided into hundreds of camps, and the encirclement was many lines in depth. The besiegers shot upward with their bows and arrows and wounded quite a number of the defenders on the city walls, who retaliated with gunfire and archery and, owing to their more favourable position, succeeded in inflicting great damage on the enemy. The besiegers then brought up heavy guns and made breaches in the walls, which Ying-yuan caused to be rapidly repaired with heavy planks riveted together by iron bands and with unused coffins filled with earth. When the wall on the northern side was pierced, his men rolled a huge boulder to fill up the gap, finishing the job in a night.

Soon the defenders found themselves short of a supply of arrows: Ying-yuan ordered that figures of straw be made and, on a moonless night, these were set up on the ramparts, each with a lantern by its side. The real soldiers commenced to create a tremendous hubbub with their drums, as if they intended to drop down from the walls for an assault. The bewildered besiegers shot wildly at the figures with their arrows, and in this manner thousands of the missiles were collected by the defenders. Making an unexpected sortie at night, when the wind was blowing in a favourable direction, Yen's soldiers set fire to the enemy's camps, creating a panic in the dark, so that the enemy lost thousands of men and withdrew a mile from the walls.

One day the commander of the attacking forces, Liu Liang-tso, escorted by a squadron of cavalry, approached the city.

'Mr Yen is an old friend of mine,' he yelled at the guards on the wall. 'Tell him that I should like to speak to him.' Ying-yuan appeared as requested.

Now Liu had been one of the four former garrison commanders of the Ming dynasty south of the Yangtze River and ennobled with the rank of an earl, but surrendered to the new Manchu government and was made a general.

'The Pretender to the Ming throne exists no more,' he shouted at

Yen Ying-yuan, 'and there is no longer any ruler south of the River. If you submit promptly, you are assured of rank and wealth.'

'I am only a city clerk of the Ming dynasty,' replied Ying-yuan proudly, 'and yet I know what is right and what is wrong. You were placed in charge of the defence of a large territory and held great responsibilities, yet you have not only failed in your mission, but even degraded yourself further by fighting for the enemy. How can you have the cheek to face the patriots of our city?'

Abashed, Liu slunk away.

Ying-yuan was very tall of stature and swarthy in complexion, possessing a small beard. Severe by nature, he enforced rigid discipline among his soldiers. Those who violated rules and orders were visited without fail by canings, piercing the ears with arrows and other corporal punishments, but on the other hand he thought lightly of personal wealth, was prompt and just in making rewards, and personally looked after the wounded soldiers. When they died, he provided them with good coffins, sacrificed to their spirits and manifested deep sorrow. When he addressed them he employed the expression 'brethren' – never by name.

The assistant magistrate was also kind, generous and fatherly in his attitude to the defenders. When he made a tour of the city walls, he would pat the soldiers on their backs, sympathize with them in their hardships and even drop tears over their fate. Both leaders won the hearts of the army, and the men were only too willing to give up their lives for the cause.

A Manchu duke under Prince Yu, who had captured many important cities of the south-east, now arrived to assist in the siege. Two Ming officers, who had also surrendered to the Manchus, were sent hand-cuffed to kneel before the walls and appeal to Yen Ying-yuan to submit.

'You disgraceful men,' he cried. 'Why don't you die after your capture? Stop prattling, get away!'

The duke had announced that if Ying-yuan only executed two men who advocated the defence of the city, he would raise the siege. 'I'd rather that you behead me than that any of my men should be punished with death,' replied Ying-yuan vigorously. He told the duke to betake himself elsewhere.

The Mid-Autumn Festival came and money was distributed to the soldiers and civilians to celebrate it. The entire population mounted the walls and ate and drank to their hearts' content. Hsu, the scholar who started the resistance campaign, composed a special song, which was sung with gusto by those with good voices, and the music interspersed with the sound of trumpets and the tinkling of drinking vessels lasted for three nights.

The duke realized now that the defenders had no intention whatever to surrender, doubled his efforts of attack. Fully armoured men were dispatched to scale the walls with the help of ladders, but they encountered the blows of broadswords and battle-axes from above, producing loud clanking sounds and blunting and cracking the weapons of the attackers. The incessant uproar of gunfire and explosions continued day and night and could be heard at a great distance, causing the earth itself to tremble. More and more numerous became the deaths within the city, and the weeping and wailing of those left behind was heard in every lane and street.

However, Yen Ying-yuan remained as composed as ever and mounted stoically the city walls every day. One morning there was a heavy downpour of rain, and at noon a bright red streak was seen shooting in the direction of the western part of the town. The wall in that vicinity collapsed, and the enemy soldiers poured into the city through the smoke, mist and rain. Ying-yuan at the head of a hundred men continued the defence in the narrow streets and killed a thousand of the invaders. He and his men then rushed to one of the city gates but, finding it closed, were unable to get out. Convinced that there existed no way of escape for him, he jumped into a pond, but the water hardly reached his neck.

The turncoat Liu Liang-tso had given orders to his soldiers to capture Yen Ying-yuan alive, whatever the cost, so in the end he was caught. Liu sat with his legs crossed on the floor of a temple hall, and when Ying-yuan appeared, jumped up and pretended to weep.

'What is there to bewail?' said Ying-yuan with a laugh. 'I am ready to die.'

When he was brought before the duke, he refused to kneel down. A soldier pierced his leg with a spear, and he fell to the ground. At night they pushed him violently into a temple, where the monks heard him crying: 'Kill me quickly! Kill me quickly!' And soon there reigned silence.

The attack and defence of the city lasted 81 days: the number of the besiegers was 250,000, of which 67,000 were killed during the siege and 7,000 in street fighting. In the city nearly the whole populace – between 50,000 and 60,000 – died in the defence. The corpses were piled up high and the lanes and streets were choked with them, yet not a single man surrendered. The assistant magistrate dismounted when the city fell, and was attacked in front of the Intendant's Office. He was grievously wounded, but though dying remained upright against a wall, sword in hand. It was reported that his entire family killed themselves by jumping into a burning house.

Shao Chang-heng (Ch'ing Dynasty)

On an Old Battlefield

Vast, vast – a limitless extent of flat sand, without a human being in sight; girdled by a stream and dotted with hills; where in the dismal twilight the wind moans at the setting sun. Shrubs gone: grass withered: all chill as the hoar-frost of early morn. The birds of the air fly past: the beasts of the field shun the spot; for it is, as I was informed by the keeper, the site of an old battlefield. 'Many a time and oft,' said he, 'has an army been overthrown on this spot; and the voices of the dead may frequently be heard weeping and wailing in the darkness of the night.'

Oh, sorrow! oh, ye Ch'ins, ye Hans, ye dynasties now passed away! I have heard that when the Ch'is and the We'is gathered at the frontier, and when the Ch'ins and the Hans collected their levies, many were the weary leagues they trod, many were the years of privation and exposure they endured. Grazing their horses by day, fording the river by night, the endless earth beneath, the boundless sky above, they knew not the day of their return; their bodies all the time exposed to the pitiless steel, with many other unspeakable woes.

Again, since the Ch'in and the Han dynasties, countless troubles have occurred within the boundaries of the empire, desolating the Middle Kingdom. No age has been free from these. In the olden days, barbarians and Chinese alike meekly followed their Imperial guide. But the place of right was usurped by might; the rude soldier cast aside the obligations of morality, and the rule of reason lost its sway.

Alas! methinks I see them now, the bitter wind enveloping them in dust, the Tartar warriors in ambuscade. Our general makes light of the foe. He would give battle upon the very threshold of his camp. Banners wave over the plain; the river closes in the battle array. All is order, though hearts may beat. Discipline is everything: life is of no account.

And now the cruel spear does its work, the startled sand blinds the combatants locked fast in the death struggle; while hill and vale and stream groan beneath the flash and crash of arms. By and by, the chill cold shades of night fall upon them, knee-deep in snow, beards stiff with ice. The hardy vulture seeks its nest; the strength of the war-horse is broken. Clothes are of no avail; hands frost-bitten, flesh cracked. Even nature lends her aid to the Tartars, contributing a deadly blast, the better to complete the work of slaughter begun. Ambulance wagons block the way; our men succumb to flank attacks. Their officers have surrendered; their general is dead. The river is choked with corpses to its topmost banks: the fosses of the Great Wall are swimming over with blood. All distinctions are obliterated in that heap of rotting bones . . .

Faintly and more faintly beats the drum. Strength exhausted, arrows spent, bow-strings snapped, swords shattered, the two armies fall upon one another in the supreme struggle for life or death. To yield is to become the barbarian's slave; to fight is to mingle our bones with the desert sand . . .

No sound of bird now breaks from the hushed hillside. All is still, save the wind whistling through the long night. Ghosts of the dead wander hither and thither in the gloom: spirits from the nether world collect under the dark clouds. The sun rises and shines coldly over the trampled grass, while the fading moon still twinkles upon the frost-flakes scattered around. What sight more horrible than this!

I have heard that Li Mu led the soldiers of Chao to victory over their Tartar foes, clearing the country for miles, and utterly routing the Huns. The Hans, on the other hand, exhausted in vain the resources of the empire. They had not the man, and their numbers availed them naught.

The Chows, too, drove back the barbarous hordes of the north; and having garrisoned the country, returned safely home. Then they offered thanks to the Gods, and gave themselves up to the universal enjoyment which peace alone can bring.

The Ch'ins built the Great Wall, stretching far away to the sea. Yet the poison-breath of war decimated the people, and mile upon mile ran with their red blood.

The Hans beat down the Huns, and seized Yin-shan. But their corpses lay pillowed over the plain, and the gain was not equal to the loss.

O high Heaven! which of these but has father and mother, who bore them about in childhood, fearing only lest maturity should never come? Which of these but has brothers, dear to them as themselves? Which of these but has a wife, bound by the closest ties? They owe no thanks for life, for what have they done to deserve death? They may be alive or dead – the family knows it not. And if one brings the news, they listen, half doubting, half believing, while the heart overflows with grief.

Sleeping and waking, they seem to see the lost one's form. Sacrifices are made ready and libations poured, with tearful eyes strained towards the far horizon; heaven and earth, nay, the very trees and plants, all seeming to sympathize with their sorrow. And when, in response to prayers and libations, these wanderers return not, where shall their spirits find repose? Verily there shall be a famine over the land, and the people be scattered abroad. Alas! such is life, and such it has ever been. What resource then is left but to keep within our frontier lines?

Li Hua (T'ang Dynasty)

Taking Revenge

Hsiang Kao, otherwise called Ch'u-tan, was a T'ai-yuan man, and deeply attached to his half-brother Sheng. Sheng himself was desperately enamoured of a young lady named Po-ssu, who was also very fond of him, but the mother wanted too much money for her daughter. Now a rich young fellow named Chuang thought he should like to get Po-ssu for himself and proposed to buy her as a concubine.

'No, no,' said Po-ssu to her mother, 'I prefer being Sheng's wife to becoming Chuang's concubine.' So her mother consented, and informed Sheng, who had only recently buried his first wife. Sheng was delighted and made preparations to take her over to his own house.

When Chuang heard this he was infuriated against Sheng for thus depriving him of Po-ssu and chancing to meet him out one day, set to and abused him roundly. Sheng answered back, and then Chuang ordered his attendants to fall upon Sheng and beat him well, which they did, leaving him lifeless on the ground.

When Hsiang heard what had taken place he ran out and found his brother lying dead upon the ground. Overcome with grief, he proceeded to the magistrate's and accused Chuang of murder – but the latter had bribed so heavily that nothing came of the accusation. This worked Hsiang to frenzy and he determined to assassinate Chuang on the high road. He daily concealed himself, with a sharp knife about him, among the bushes on the hillside, waiting for Chuang to pass. By degrees, this plan of his became known far and wide, and accordingly Chuang never went out except with a strong bodyguard, besides which he engaged at a high price the services of a very skilful archer, named Chiao T'ung, so that Hsiang had no means of carrying out his intention. But Hsiang continued to lie in wait day after day; and on one occasion it began to rain heavily, and in a short time Hsiang was wet through to the skin. Then the wind got up, a hailstorm followed, and by and by Hsiang was quite numbed with the cold.

On the top of the hill there was a small temple wherein lived a Taoist priest, whom Hsiang knew from the latter having occasionally begged alms in the village, and to whom he had often given a meal. This priest, seeing how wet he was, gave him some other clothes and told him to put them on. But no sooner had he done so than he crouched down like a dog, and found that he had been changed into a tiger, and that the priest had vanished. It now occurred to him to seize this opportunity of revenging himself upon his enemy and away he went to his old ambush, where lo and behold! he found his own body lying stiff and stark. Fearing lest it should become food for birds of prey, he guarded it carefully, until at length one day Chuang passed by. Out rushed the tiger and sprang upon Chuang, biting his head off and swallowing it upon the spot, at which Chiao T'ung, the archer, turned round and shot the animal through the heart.

Just at that moment Hsiang awakened as though from a dream. It was some time before he could crawl home, where he arrived to the great delight of his family, who didn't know what had become of him. Hsiang said not a word, lying quietly on the bed until some of his people came in to congratulate him on the death of his great enemy Chuang. Hsiang then cried out, 'I was that tiger', and proceeded to relate the whole story, which thus got about until it reached the ears of Chuang's son, who immediately set out to work to bring his father's murderer to justice. The magistrate, however, did not consider this wild story as sufficient evidence against him, and thereupon dismissed the case.

P'u Sung-ling (Ch'ing Dynasty)
From *Liao Chai Chih I*

The Lost Brother

In Honan there lived a man named Chang, who originally came from Shantung. His wife had been seized and carried off by the soldiery during the period when Ching Nan's troops were overrunning the latter province;* and as he was frequently in Honan on business, he finally settled there and married a Honan wife, by whom he had a son named Na. By and by, this wife died and he took another, who bore him a son named Ch'eng. The last-mentioned lady was from the Niu family and a very malicious woman. So jealous was she of Na, that she treated him like a slave or a beast of the field, giving him only the coarsest food and making him cut a large bundle of wood every day, in default of which she would beat and abuse him in a most shameful manner. On the other hand, she secretly reserved all the tit-bits for Ch'eng, and also sent him to school. As Ch'eng grew up and began to understand the meaning of filial piety and fraternal love, he could not bear to see this treatment of his elder brother, and spoke privately to his mother about it. But she would pay no heed to what he said.

One day, when Na was on the hills performing his task, a violent storm came on and he took shelter under a cliff. However, by the time it was over the sun had set and he began to feel very hungry. So, shouldering his bundle, he wended his way home where his stepmother, displeased with the small quantity of wood he had brought, refused to give him anything to eat. Quite overcome with hunger, Na went in and lay down. When Ch'eng came back from school and saw the state he was in, he asked him if he was ill. Na replied that he was only hungry and then told his brother the whole story; whereupon Ch'eng coloured up and went away, returning shortly with some cakes, which he offered to Na.

'Where did you get them?' asked Na. 'Oh,' replied Ch'eng, 'I stole some flour and got a neighbour's wife to make them for me. Eat away, and don't talk.' Na ate them up but begged his brother not to do this

* AD 1400.

again, as he might get himself into trouble. 'I shan't die,' added he, 'if I only get one meal a day.'

'You are not strong,' rejoined Ch'eng, 'and shouldn't cut so much wood as you do.'

Next day, after breakfast, Ch'eng slipped away to the hills and arrived at the place where Na was occupied with his usual task, to the great astonishment of the latter, who inquired what he was going to do. 'To help you cut wood,' replied Ch'eng. 'And who sent you?' asked his brother. 'No one,' said he. 'I came of my own accord.' 'Ah,' cried Na, 'you can't do this work; and even if you can you must not. Run along home again.'

Ch'eng, however, remained, aiding his brother with his hands and feet alone, but declaring that on the morrow he would bring an axe. Na tried to stop him, and found that he had already hurt his finger and worn his shoes into holes so he began to cry, and said, 'If you don't go home directly, I'll kill myself with my axe.'

Ch'eng then went away, his brother seeing him halfway home, and going back to finish his work by himself. He also called in the evening at Ch'eng's school and told the master his brother was a delicate boy, and should not be allowed to go on the hills, where, he said, there were fierce tigers and wolves. The master replied that he didn't know where Ch'eng had been all the morning, but that he had caned him for playing truant. Na further pointed out to Ch'eng that by not doing as he had told him, he had let himself in for a beating. Ch'eng laughed, and said he hadn't been beaten; and the very next day off he went again, and this time with a hatchet.

'I told you not to come,' cried Na, much alarmed, 'why have you done so?' Ch'eng made no reply but set to work chopping wood with such energy that the perspiration poured down his face. When he had cut about a bundle he went away without saying a word. The master caned him again, and then Ch'eng told him how the matter stood, at which the former became full of admiration for his pupil's kind behaviour and no longer prevented him from going.

His brother, however, frequently urged him not to come, though without the slightest success; and one day, when they went with a number of others to cut wood, a tiger rushed down from the hills upon them. The woodcutters hid themselves, in the greatest consternation; and the tiger, seizing Ch'eng, ran off with him in his mouth. Ch'eng's weight caused the tiger to move slowly, and Na, rushing after them, hacked away at the tiger's flanks with his axe. The pain only made the tiger hurry off and in a few minutes they were out of sight.

Overwhelmed with grief Na went back to his comrades, who tried to soothe him; but he said, 'my brother was no ordinary brother, and, besides, he died for me. Why, then, should I live?' Here, seizing his hatchet he made a great chop at his own neck, upon which his companions prevented him from doing himself any more mischief. The wound, however, was over an inch deep, and blood was flowing so copiously that Na became faint, and seemed at the point of death. They then tore up their clothes and, after having bandaged his neck, proceeded to carry him home.

His stepmother cried bitterly, and cursed him, saying, 'You have killed my son, and now you go and cut your neck in this make-believe kind of way.' 'Don't be angry, mother,' replied Na. 'I will not live now that my brother is dead.' He then threw himself on the bed, but the pain of his wound was so great he could not sleep, and day and night he sat leaning against the wall in tears. His father, fearing that he too would die, went every now and then and gave him a little nourishment; but his wife cursed him so for doing it, that at length Na refused all food, and in three days he died.

Now in the village where these events took place there was a magician who was employed in certain devil-work among mortals, and Na's ghost, happening to fall in with him, related the story of its previous sorrows, winding up by asking where his brother's ghost was. The magician said he didn't know, but turned round with Na and showed him the way to a city where they saw an official servant coming out of the city gates. The magician stopped him, and inquired if he could tell them anything about Ch'eng. The man drew out a list from a pouch at his side, and after carefully examining it, replied that among the male and female criminals within there was no one of the name of Ch'eng. The magician here suggested that the name might be on another list; but the man replied that he was in charge of that road and surely ought to know. Na, however, was not satisfied and persuaded the magician to enter the city where they met many new and old devils walking about, among whom were some Na had formerly known in life. So he asked them if they could direct him to his brother; but none of them knew where he was.

Suddenly there was a great commotion, the devils on all sides crying out, 'P'u-sa* has come!' Then, looking up, Na beheld a most beautiful man descending from above, encircled by rays of glory, which shot forth above and below, lighting up all around him.

'You are in luck's way, sir,' said the magician to Na. 'Only once in many thousand years does P'u-sa descend into hell and banish all

* A corrupted form of the Bodhisatva in China. Generally used to describe any deity of any kind.

suffering. He has come today.' He then made Na kneel, and all the devils began with clasped hands to sing songs of praise to P'u-sa for his compassion in releasing them from their misery, shaking the very earth with the sound. P'u-sa himself, seizing a willow-branch, sprinkled them all with holy water, and when this was done the clouds and glory melted away, and he vanished from their sight. Na, who had felt the holy water fall upon his neck, now became conscious that the axe-wound was no longer painful; and the magician then proceeded to lead him back, not quitting him until within sight of the village gate.

In fact, Na had been in a trance for two days and when he recovered he told them all that he had seen, asserting positively that Ch'eng was not dead. His mother, however, looked upon the story as a make-up and never ceased reviling him. As he had no means of proving his innocence, and his neck was now quite healed, he got up from the bed and said to his father, 'I am going away to seek for my brother throughout the universe; if I do not find him, never expect to see me again, but I pray you regard me as dead.' His father drew him aside and wept bitterly. However, he would not interfere with his son's design and Na accordingly set off.

Whenever he came to a large town or populous place he used to ask for news of Ch'eng; and by and by, when his money was all spent, he begged his way on foot. A year had passed away before he reached Nanking and his clothes were all in tatters – as ragged as a quail's tail, when suddenly he met some ten or a dozen horsemen, and drew away to the roadside.

Among them was a gentleman of about forty, who appeared to be a mandarin, with numerous lusty attendants and fiery steeds accompanying him before and behind. One young man on a small palfrey, whom Na took to be the mandarin's son, and at whom, of course, he did not venture to stare, eyed him closely for some time. At length he stopped his steed and jumping off, cried out, 'Are you not my brother?' Na then raised his head and found that Ch'eng stood before him. Grasping each other's hands, the brothers burst into tears, and at length Ch'eng said, 'My brother, how is it you have strayed so far as this?' Na told him the circumstances, at which he was much affected; and Ch'eng's companions, jumping off their horses to see what was the matter, went off and informed the mandarin. The latter ordered one of them to give up his horse to Na, and thus they rode together back to the mandarin's house.

Ch'eng then told his brother how the tiger had carried him away and how he had been thrown down in the road, where he had passed a whole night; also how the mandarin, Mr Chang, on his return from the capital had seen him there, and observing that he was no common-looking youth, had set to work and brought him round again. He had explained to Mr Chang that his home was a great way off and Mr Chang had taken him to his own home, and finally cured him of his wounds. Eventually, having no son of his own, he had adopted him. And now, happening to be out with his father, he had caught sight of his brother.

As he was speaking Mr Chang walked in and Na thanked him very heartily for all his kindness. Ch'eng, meanwhile, went into the inner apartments to get some clothes for his brother. Wine and food was placed on the table and while they were chatting together the mandarin asked Na about the number of their family in Honan.

'There is only my father,' replied Na, 'and he is a Shantung man who came to live in Honan.'

'Why, I am a Shantung man too,' rejoined Mr Chang. 'What is the name of your father's native place?'

'I have heard that it was in the Tung-ch'ang district,' replied Na.

'Then we are from the same place,' cried the mandarin. 'Why did your father go away to Honan?'

'His first wife,' said Na, 'was carried off by soldiers and my father lost everything he possessed. So, being in the habit of trading to Honan, he determined to settle down there for good.'

The mandarin then asked what his father's other name was. When he heard the name, he sat some time staring at Na, and at length hurried away within. In a few moments out came an old lady, and when they had all bowed to her, she asked Na if he was Chang Ping-chih's grandson. On his replying in the affirmative the old lady wept, and turning to Mr Chang, said, 'These two are your younger brothers.' Then she explained to Na and Ch'eng as follows: 'Three years after my marriage with your father, I was carried off to the north and made a slave * in a mandarin's family. Six months afterwards your elder brother here was born, and in another six months the mandarin died. Your elder brother being his heir he received this appointment, which he is now resigning. I have often thought of my native place and have not unfrequently sent people to inquire about my husband, giving them the full particulars as to name and clan; but I could never hear anything of him. How should I know that he had gone to Honan?' Then, addressing Mr Chang, she continued, 'That was rather a mistake of yours, adopting your own brother.'

'He never told me anything about Shantung,' replied Mr Chang. 'I suppose he was too young to remember the story; and I only looked at

---

* According to Giles, slavery existed in China up to the turn of the century. Giles reports having seen evidence of children selling themselves on public thoroughfares. Parents, having absolute power over their children, had complete liberty to sell them as slaves or bond servants to wealthier neighbours. The chief source of slaves, however, was through kidnapping.

the difference between our ages.' For he, the elder of the brothers, was forty-one; Ch'eng, the younger, being only sixteen; and Na, twenty years of age. Mr Chang was very glad to get two young brothers and when he had heard the tale of their separation, proposed that they should all go back to their father. Mrs Chang was afraid her husband would not care to receive her back again, but her eldest son said, 'We will cast our lot together – all or none. How can there be a country where fathers are not valued?'

They then sold their house, packed up, and were soon on the way to Honan. When they arrived Ch'eng went in first to tell his father, whose third wife had died since Na left, and who now was a desolate old widower, left alone with only his own shadow. He was overjoyed to see Ch'eng again, and looking fondly at his son, burst into a flood of tears. Ch'eng told him his mother and brothers were outside and the old man was then perfectly transfixed with astonishment, unable either to laugh or to cry. Mr Chang next appeared, followed by his mother; and the two old people wept in each other's arms, the late solitary widower hardly knowing what to make of the crowd of men and women servants that suddenly filled his house.

Here Ch'eng, not seeing his own mother, asked where she was. When he heard she was dead he fainted away and did not come round for a good half-hour. Mr Chang found the money for building a fine house and engaged a tutor for his two brothers. Horses pranced in the stables and servants chattered in the hall – it was quite a large establishment.

P'u Sung-ling (Ch'ing Dynasty)
From *Liao Chia Chih I*

The Poyang Murder Case

Yeh, a peasant in Poyang, married a widow and had by her a son, Fu-lai. Yeh died, leaving in addition a posthumous son, who was named Fu-teh. Mrs Yeh, unable to remain a second time a widow, took another husband by the name of Yen Mo-sheng, who, however, came to her home to live. After staying with her for five years, he returned to his own home with her and the two stepsons.

The farmland – one-third of an acre – left by Yeh was now cultivated by Yen Mo-sheng, who used the return to support the family of four. Owing to continual floods the income was insufficient for their maintenance; thereupon, Fu-lai, already nine years old, was apprenticed to a tailor and Fu-teh sent to a well-to-do farmer to tend buffaloes. The tailor and the farmer lived in the same village, some fifteen miles away from the stepfather's place.

On the twenty-fifth day of the twelfth moon in the third year of Kuang Hsu, Mo-sheng went to the village to bring the two boys home to pass the New Year. Next day the three started on their homeward tramp, Fu-lai shouldering a bag of blue cotton cloth containing a silver dollar and 1,000 copper cash, and Fu-teh a white bag with some rice. Meeting rain on the way, they sought shelter in a roadside arbour, where they had to take a rest anyway as the stepfather was suffering from an epileptic fit.

They met there a man by the name of Lei, a farmhand in the same house where the younger son worked, also on his way home which was in the vicinity of their own. Lei had two baskets with him, which he carried with a bamboo pole on his shoulder.

'As I am not feeling well,' said Mo-sheng to the farmhand, 'please look after the two boys as they go along with you. I'll resume my walk as soon as I get better.' He placed the money and the rice in Lei's baskets, and the three departed. When they arrived at the spot known as the Love Birds' Tomb, Lei said to the boys that their paths parted there and that they could await their father, while he would pursue his way. He returned both the money and the rice to them.

In the meantime Mo-sheng rested in the arbour until he was fully recovered and the rain had stopped. It was getting dark as he hastened home by a bypath and it was late in the night when he arrived there. On questioning his wife he learned that the two boys had not returned.

The next morning Mrs Yeh urged her husband to call at the farmhand Lei's home to make inquiries, and he was told that the man and the boys separated at the Love Birds' Tomb. He found no trace of the lads when he visited the mentioned spot.

A man by the name of Ouyang declared that on the twenty-seventh day he encountered two boys on the road who asked the way and he gave them some general directions, but he did not know where they went after that. Another man, a draper, who kept a stall by the roadside, admitted that on the same day two hungry boys came to him begging for something to eat, then left, but he also denied knowing what became of them.

He was asked if anyone else was present at the stall at the same time, and he mentioned a certain Fa-lieh, who took his departure as the boys did, and said that Fa-lieh probably saw them later.

On the following day the boys were found dead at Chenkung Slope, not far from their home. One had wounds on the cheeks, the ears and the neck, and the other was injured in the lower part of the body. Both the rice and the money were there, nor was anything else missing.

The murderer was unknown, but people suspected the draper and the man who was in his stall; so Mo-sheng accused both of them before the magistrate as the murderers of his stepsons. Meanwhile, the members of the Yeh clan, to which the boys' deceased father belonged, charged the stepfather with the crime, the motive, they asserted, being to succeed to the land, which it was the boys' legitimate right to inherit. The two cases dragged on for a long time in the court and no verdict could be reached.

The following year my relative by marriage, Mr Peng, Vice-Minister of State in Peking, arrived at Jaochou Prefecture whereof Poyang was a county, on a tour of inspection, and the two complaining parties petitioned at once to him to vindicate justice. As was the usage and in accordance with precedents, Vice-Minister Peng handed the petitions to the local prefect to deal with.

Two years later, Mr Peng visited the provincial capital, and all the high officials went to welcome him on the wharf. Mrs Yen, mother of the two boys, seized the opportunity to approach him with an appeal for justice but, rudely reprimanded and pushed aside by the mounted escort, she threw herself into the river. At the vice-minister's order she was rescued. After reading her petition, he mentioned the case to the provincial governor, the supreme local authority.

The crime had in fact become notorious, and most of the higher officials believed that it was Yen Mo-sheng the stepfather who committed the murder. Because the victims, being only young boys, could have no enemies and, if they had been killed with robbery as motive, why were the money and the rice left intact? There seemed little doubt from this reasoning that the stepfather was the criminal.

At any rate, the case having been tried for three years and being of so heinous a character, orders had been issued to have it transferred to the provincial capital – a move anticipating perhaps the arrival of the vice-minister.

Now the new magistrate of Poyang, Wang, was a very intelligent man. As soon as he assumed office, he deeply regretted that such a serious case should have been dragging on in his county for so many years with the culprit still at large, causing much distress to his superior, the prefect. He, therefore, adopted more energetic steps in the case, employing detectives to watch closely the parties involved, including the witnesses, then all detained in the county gaol, studying every move they made and recording every word they said.

By the fifth moon it was rumoured that the vice-minister would arrive at the county seat and personally preside at the trial. Fa-lieh, the man who left the roadside stall at the same time as the boys, seemed worried at hearing the news, and repeatedly asked the jailers for information. On the eighth day of the moon the vice-minister arrived.

Now just before this, a man had been caught with counterfeit seals, issuing false passports and pretending that he had been in the service of the vice-minister. After a prompt trial and found guilty, he was summarily executed. This news made Fah-lieh still more nervous.

'Things are looking bad,' he muttered again and again in his dreams.

When this was reported to the magistrate, he became convinced that Fah-lieh was the murderer of the two boys. In a private room he set up the tablet of the City God and prayed fervently for a revelation. That night he dreamed that he visited a spot where he smelt the odour of corpses but saw none. Then he noticed a man who seemed to be using his body to conceal them; on taking a closer look, he recognized the man as Fa-lieh.

The next day he had all the prisoners brought to the Temple of the City God. 'You are the murderer,' he said, pointing to the suspected man. 'The City God has already informed me.'

Although Fa-lieh did not confess at once, he changed colour visibly.

A second trial took place at the temple, when the prisoners weeping loudly called on the City God to execute vengeance on the guilty party. But Fa-lieh remained silent.

That night, however, he shouted loudly, 'I will confess: I dare not deceive the City God.'

It was then revealed that since the Love Birds' Tomb where the farmhand parted with the two boys was still ten miles from their home, the boys spent the night in a temple nearby. The following day they continued on their journey, meeting Ouyang and asking him the way, and then begging for a meal at the roadside stall, where they encountered Fa-lieh.

Attracted by the youthfulness and innocence of the two boys, Fa-lieh formed the wicked design of kidnapping and selling them. He, therefore, followed them from the stall, offering to be their guide and took them to his own place, hiding them in a dugout in his outside yard so that even his own people had no knowledge of the boys' presence.

At dawn of the twenty-eighth day he led them away from his place, but when they were passing over the top of a little hill, Fu-lai, the elder boy, suddenly saw their home village not far away, and refused to go with the self-appointed guide any further. The ruffian then tried to force them to do so, first with threats, followed by violence, and when resisted, choked Fu-lai to death. 'He's killed my brother,' shouted the younger, running for dear life. Presently the man caught him, kicked and mortally injured him.

Fa-lieh opened the two bags and saw the cash and rice, but he was too cunning to take them for fear of drawing suspicion on himself.

The magistrate, having thus solved the mystery of the murder, rushed a report to Vice-Minister Peng, who was visiting a temple on an isle in the Yangtze River. After reading it, Mr Peng gave a shout of satisfaction and, seizing a pen, indited the following comment in reply:

'My mystification and uneasiness due to the shocking murder which remained unsolved for many years is now removed. I salute you, wise magistrate, and on behalf of the departed souls of the two lads, I thank you very heartily for bringing the murderer to justice. I only wish that there were more conscientious magistrates like you to avenge the deaths of many other innocent people, as you have done in the present instance.'

That year His Excellency came to Soochow, and knowing that I was engaged in chronicling current and historical events, showed me the records of the Poyang Murder Case, from which I have abstracted the above account.

Yu Yueh (Ch'ing Dynasty)

A Chinese Solomon

CHAPTER I

HOW A MAGISTRATE LED DISPUTANTS TO MAKE PEACE

In the first year of the Emperor Yung Ch'ing of the Manchu (Ch'ing) Dynasty, a new official was appointed to be the District Magistrate of Po Yang in Chiu Chau (Swatow).

This man was very clear in his judgments.

Now in a village of the Po Yang District there was a man, Chan Jee, who had two sons named Ah Ming and Ah Ting. When they were young they went to school together, and when they grew up they worked together in the fields, ploughing and sowing. They were very affectionate to one another.

After they were married the family property was divided between them and they lived in separate houses.

Their father retained seven acres of fertile land which was for his own maintenance until his death, and after that they were to become the property of the elder son. But after his death, the brothers quarrelled about these seven acres, and neither their wives nor their relatives were able to settle their dispute.

They therefore brought the case before the District Magistrate for his decision.

The magistrate inquired from them the cause and origin of their dispute and Ah Ming said, 'When my father divided the property between us, he promised that at his death the seven acres of land in dispute should come to me and here is the entry in the book as proof,' and the book was handed to the magistrate. The record stated that the property should be given to the eldest son after the old man's death.

When the magistrate asked Ah Ting to state his case, he said, 'Although my brother has the deed of division, I also have a codicil or certificate on the subject. When my father was ill, and saw that I was very attentive to him and waited on him very well, he said that I was a filial son, and on his deathbed he wrote that the seven acres of fertile land were to be given to me to hold in perpetuity and to cultivate.' He also handed in the codicil.

'According to your evidence,' said the magistrate, 'you brothers are both right, and it was really your father who was wrong. You should therefore break open your father's coffin and ask him to explain why he had gone back on his word and so caused you two brothers to quarrel.'

When he spoke like this, Ah Ming and Ah Ting dared not speak a word.

The magistrate then said, 'Land is a small matter, but for brothers to quarrel is a heinous offence. I do not know what is the best way to decide this matter.'

After a moment's thought, the magistrate said, 'I suggest that each of you put out one leg, and let the two legs be tied together, and be squeezed between the pressing boards [used for torture]. Whichever can stand the pain longest and not mention it, the fields shall go to him.

'But as I do not know whether your left foot or your right foot feels pain most, you may each choose for yourselves which leg (left or right) you will submit to the test. Put out the leg that does not feel pain.'

They both said, 'Both of our legs feel pain.'

The magistrate said, 'It is really very strange that both of your legs feel pain. Your body is like your father; as you regard your left foot, so your father regards Ah Ming; and as your body regards your right leg so your father regards Ah Ting.

'As neither of you is willing to give up a leg, would your father, with two sons, be willing to give up one of them? I will adjudicate this matter on another day.'

He then ordered the lictors to bring an iron chain and lock together a foot of each of the brothers. He ordered that the locks must be sealed and must not be secretly unlocked.

So the two brothers must sit on the same seat, eat at the same table, sleep on the same bed, get up together, walk together, and perform all their natural functions together. They were thus very close together and could not be separated for a single moment.

He also sent officers to watch them, and note their movements and times of rest, their speech and their attitudes to one another, and to report to him each day.

At first the two brothers seemed to be very angry, and were much embarrassed. They did not speak to one another, but turned their backs on one another, one looking east and the other west.

On the second day they gradually began to face one another, and the third day they felt very much ashamed, and bent down their heads and did not dare to look up. The elder said, 'I am sorry that I did not listen to the advice of the elders of our clan.' His brother sighed and said, 'I am sorry that I did not listen to the members of my mother's family.'

On the fourth day they spoke to one another, and in the evening, when taking their meal, they invited one another to eat and drink.

The officers reported all this to the magistrate, and when he learned the state of affairs, he ordered the lictors to bring them before the court again.

He asked, 'Have you any sons?' and Ah Ming said, 'I have two sons, one about seventeen years of age and the other fourteen.' Ah Ting said, 'I also have two sons about the same ages as my brother's sons.'

The official ordered the police to bring the four sons to court. He then addressed Ah Ming and Ah Ting, saying, 'Your father ought not to have had two sons like you and so cause the unhappy state of affairs that we see today. If he had only had one son, all the fields and possessions would have gone to the one. What a happy state of affairs that would have been!

'Now it is your misfortune that you each have two sons, and in time to come they will grow up and quarrel and strive against one another, wishing to stab and kill one another. There will be no end to such strife. This will cause you deep sorrow and pain in your hearts. Now I have been thinking about your case and have prepared a plan for your benefit. You should each have only one son, that will be quite enough.

'Ah Ming is the elder and may keep the elder son, and part with the second son,' the magistrate ordered. 'Ah Ting, being the second in the family, may keep his second son and send away the elder one.'

Then he ordered the lictors to take Ah Ming's second son and Ah Ting's elder son and place them in the poor house, handing them over to the chief of the beggars so that they might become his sons, and a certificate must be issued to him so that the case may be on record.

'As beggars they will have no fields to work in and then what could they have to quarrel about!' the magistrate said. 'When there is only one person left in your family, trouble may be avoided in the future. Is this not a simple and inexpensive method of dealing with the case?'

When Ah Ming and Ah Ting heard this decision their hearts were filled with fear. They bowed to the ground, kowtowed and wept, saying, 'Your honour, we dare not dispute any longer.'

The magistrate asked, 'What do you mean by saying you dare not?'

Ah Ming said, 'I know that I have been in the wrong. I am willing to yield up the fields to my younger brother and never quarrel with him again till I die.'

Ah Ting said, 'I dare not accept the fields. I am willing to yield the fields to my elder brother and never regret it all my life.'

The magistrate said, 'I cannot really be certain that you are both telling the truth. I dare not trust you.'

The two men again kowtowed and said, 'It is true, it is true. If it is false may Heaven punish us and earth destroy us.'

The magistrate continued, 'Well, you two people perhaps may be telling the truth, but your wives may be unwilling to yield. Go home then and discuss the matter with your wives, and in three days time come and settle the matter about giving up the fields.'

CHAPTER 2

THE WIVES DISCUSS THE PROPOSAL

The two brothers were released so that they might go home, and that night Ah Ming told his wife all that the magistrate had said.

His wife said, 'My second son is the better one. He is clever and bright and good looking. I love him best. How is it that the magistrate is of such a new type, and that he wants to take my son and hand him over to the beggars? Is my son so despicable? How is it that he is so clever in his judgments? I must go to see him and ask him how he explains the fact that he is an official.'

Ah Ming said, 'He explained everything in detail to us. I have thought the matter over, and it really was I who was in the wrong. When you go with your sister-in-law in a few days time to see him, do not speak too loudly. If you trust to your ready tongue, and will not submit to him, he will take you two sisters-in-law, and chain one leg of each of you, so that you are bound together. Then you will both have to lie on one bed, and must sleep together and sit down together, and stand up together. That will be a terrible bondage and most inconvenient; you will soon know what it is to be afraid.'

His wife said, 'I will not let him lock me up.'

'If you do not allow him to do it,' Ah Ming said, 'he will call the lictors to beat you.'

His wife asked, 'Has he beating boards very handy?'

Ah Ming said, 'Do you think they are not convenient? Rattan canes are convenient, pressing boards are handy, cangues are provided, locks are at hand. You can choose which you like.'

His wife said, 'This year I am forty-one years of age, and have never seen an official. I need not be afraid of him.'

'It is said that there is no need to fear a governor, but there is fear of being governed [taken in hand and dealt with]. If you are not afraid, I am,' Ah Ming retorted. 'Your two sons are now detained in the police quarters. They are scared green or white, and their spirits are quite gone.'

His wife in great fear said, 'What can we do? We have struck our heads against a beam. My two boys will be frightened to death.' Then she wept and was very angry with her husband and said, 'Why did you not tell me all this before?'

Ah Ming said, 'Do you think the magistracy [Yamen] is like a flower boat, and that I could tell you all about it? It is not strange that the only thing you know about is being happy.'

His wife said, 'When you first went off to take the case to the official, I noticed that you spoke very bravely, saying that in this case you were sure to win, and that the seven acres of land were practically already in your grasp. You said that when you returned you would burn some paper money as a thanks-offering to the gods, and you would invite all our relations to a feast. That morning you drank two small pots of wine, and you were very sprightly, and very pronounced and definite in your ideas about it all. You took your bedding off to the boat, and I thought that when you arrived at the magistracy the police would respect you and wait on you and invite you to drink wine and to feast; that the official would sit down with you, because you said, you would explain the case to him. I thought it would be like children asking their parents for things, or nephews asking their uncles. There would be no stiffness, and no ceremony, you could stand or sit just as you pleased, and talk in a free and easy way.

'Besides,' she went on, 'you said you would go to court and literally beat the official, and I thought that if the magistrate did not do as you wished, you would seize him and beat him. You are very strong and the official would be afraid of you, and have to do as you told him. You would then put out your hand and seize the fertile fields, and so that day I was very happy. Who could have supposed that the official would beat you and not you him? Really you have yourself come to grief without any good result. If I had known before that we should experience this sorrow, why should we not have yielded to your brother a little?'

When Ah Ming heard this he felt inclined to be angry and also to laugh. Then he struck the pillow and said angrily, 'You foolish woman, you do not know the smallest thing that is before your eyes, what is the use of you?'

His wife replied, 'My eyes do not see a Yamen. For a woman not to understand these matters is excusable, but when brothers live together in a house and are constantly before one another's eyes, and though calling themselves men, do not understand what is right – that is really inexplicable.

'Now, because of a feud over a field you have caused my son to be taken away, what sort of fertile fields do you want to talk about? I only regard them as a sandbank out in the sea, or a cave away up in the high mountains. What is the use of them? Tomorrow you must go at once and bring my children back.'

Ah Ming said, 'I am discussing this with you for that very purpose.'

Again, in the case of Ah Ting, he also talked with his wife and informed her of the decision of the magistrate, and that their two sons were being detained in the police quarters at the magistracy, awaiting her decision and will in the matter.

His wife said, 'I advised you not to go to court; you would not be persuaded. It would have been very good if you had listened to your uncles, and you two brothers had each taken half of the fields. Would not that have saved all this trouble? But you two brothers, the elder would not yield, nor the younger obey, and now you have been before the official and been tried and disgraced before everyone.

'Why should you, being a man, have no sense of shame? I feel very much ashamed before people, and your only feelings are about the benefits you may get and your own desires, and you do not think of the family and your relations.

'You do not realize that when you pass by people point at you and say you are a pig elder brother and a dog younger brother. Really, you are not a man. Now you have gone into this lawsuit, and my elder son is to be given over to the beggars. I ask you, can you bear this?'

Ah Ting said, 'That is the decision of the magistrate; it was not my desire. I am now quite unwilling to have the fields, and I only wish to get my son back.

'The magistrate is afraid that you women will not agree in your hearts, and he requires you to go yourself with your sister-in-law, so that all may talk the case over clearly.'

His wife said, 'Do I prefer to have the fields and not have my son? My elder son is almost a man now, and can be of great service to us. Not to mention seven acres of fertile land, I should even regard a thousand ounces of yellow gold as old scrap iron in this case. Tomorrow morning we must go at once to the magistracy to see my son. If the others will not go I will go myself.'

Next morning the two sisters-in-law invited the two elders of the Clan, Messrs Chan Tak Tsun and Chan Tak Yee to go with them to the magistracy to ask for a settlement of the case.

The two ladies assisted one another on the way and together knelt before the bench and wept, agreeing that from that time forward, they would be for ever at peace with one another and they agreed that neither of them should have the fields.

Ah Ming and Ah Ting also wept and said, 'We brothers are foolish, and do not know right principles of life, and we have given your Honour great trouble in teaching us.

'We are now like men awaking from a dream; we are very much ashamed, and wish to die, and there is no place of repentance. Neither of us brothers now wishes to receive the fields.'

The official said, 'If you do not want the fields, what shall be done with them?'

They replied, 'We are willing to present the fields to a monastery to be used for incense and oil for the reverence of Buddha.'

The official struck the table and scolded them saying, 'Disgusting! Disgusting! This is most unfilial. When you talk of presenting the fields to a monastery, I ought to use the large bastinadoes and beat you to death.

'Your father worked hard all his life, he was industrious and very economical, enduring much hardship before he could purchase these fields for the sake of his children and grandchildren.

'Before you understood this, you strove together and quarrelled and accused one another; and now that you do understand you want to hand them over to priests, so that they may sit down and eat and be at rest. Will your father's spirit in the lower regions be able to close his eyes and be at rest?

'The elder brother should yield to the younger, and the younger to the elder. If neither of you will receive the land, then it should be returned to your father.

'Now these fields must be regarded as property for your father's ancestral fund. You brothers may receive the rents in turn for use year by year in the spring and autumn sacrifices. Thus your progeny for generations to come will not have any cause for disputes. Is not this the most excellent way?'

Then the elders, the brothers and their wives, all kowtowed and said it was very good.

They all returned home with joyful hearts, and that evening the brothers killed fowls and bought meat and worshipped the family gods and invited all the spirits of their paternal and maternal ancestors to partake. Afterwards the whole family gladly drank together, and they made a very happy party.

Little Chu

A man named Li Hua dwelt at Ch'ang-chou. He was very well off and about fifty years of age, but he had no sons, only one daughter named Hsiao-hui, a pretty child on whom her parents doted. When she was fourteen, she had a severe illness and died, leaving their home desolate and depriving them of their chief pleasure in life. Mr Li then bought a concubine and she, by and by, bore him a son who was perfectly idolized and called Chu, or the Pearl. This boy grew up to be a fine manly fellow, though so extremely stupid that when five or six years old he did not know rice from corn and could hardly talk plainly. His father, however, loved him dearly and did not observe his faults.

Now it chanced that a one-eyed priest came to collect alms in the town, and he seemed to know so much about everybody's private affairs that the people all looked upon him as superhuman. He himself declared he had control over life, death, happiness, and misfortune and consequently no one dared refuse him whatever sum he chose to ask of them. From Li, he demanded one hundred ounces of silver, but was offered only ten, which he refused to receive. This sum was increased to thirty ounces, whereupon the priest looked sternly at Li and said, 'I must have one hundred, not a fraction less.'

Li now got angry and went away without giving him anything. The priest rose up in a rage and shouted after him, 'I hope you won't repent.'

Shortly after these events, little Chu fell sick and crawled about the bed scratching the mat, his face being of an ashen paleness. This frightened his father who hurried off with eighty ounces of silver and begged the priest to accept them. 'A large sum like this is no trifling matter to earn,' said the priest smiling, 'but what can a poor recluse like myself do for you?'

So Li went home to find that little Chu was already dead and this worked him up into such a state that he immediately laid a complaint before the magistrate. The priest accordingly was summoned and interrogated and the magistrate would not accept his defence and ordered him to be bambooed. The blows sounded as if falling on leather. The magistrate then commanded his lictors to search him and from the priest's clothes they drew forth two small wooden men, a small coffin, and five small flags. The magistrate here flew into a passion and made certain mystic signs with his fingers. When the priest saw them he was frightened, and began to excuse himself, but the magistrate would not even listen to him and had him bambooed to death.

Li thanked him for his kindness and taking his leave proceeded home. In the evening after dusk he was sitting alone with his wife when suddenly in popped a little boy who said, 'Papa! Why did you hurry so fast? I couldn't catch up with you.' Looking at him more closely they saw that he was about seven or eight years old and Li, in some alarm, was on the point of questioning him when he disappeared, reappearing again like smoke and curling round and round and getting upon the bed. Li pushed him off, and he fell down without making any sound, crying out, 'Papa! Why do you do this?' and in a moment he was on the bed again.

Li was frightened and ran away with his wife, the boy calling after them, 'Papa, Mama, boo-oo-oo.' They went into the next room and bolted the door after them, but there was the little boy at their heels again. Li asked him what he wanted, to which he replied, 'I belong to

Suchou and my name is Chan. At six years of age I was left an orphan. My brother and his wife couldn't bear me, so they sent me to live at my maternal grandfather's. One day, when playing outside a wicked priest killed me by his black art underneath a mulberry tree. He made of me an evil spirit and doomed me to everlasting devildom without hope of transmigration. Happily, you exposed him and I want to remain with you now as your son.'

'The paths of men and devils,' replied Li, 'lie in different directions. How can we remain together?'

'Give me only a tiny room,' cried the boy, 'a bed, a mattress, and a cup of cold gruel every day. I ask for nothing more.'

So Li agreed to the great delight of the boy who slept by himself in another part of the house, coming in the morning and walking in and out like any ordinary person. Hearing Li's concubine crying bitterly, he asked how long little Chu had been dead, and she told him seven days. 'It's cold weather now,' he said, 'and the body can't have decomposed. Have the grave opened and let me see it. If it's not too far gone, I can bring him to life again.'

Li was only too pleased and went off with the boy and when they opened the grave they found the body in perfect preservation. But while Li was controlling his emotions, lo, the boy had vanished from sight. Wondering very much at this, he took little Chu's body home and hardly laid it on the bed when he noticed his eyes move. Little Chu then called for some broth which put him into a perspiration and then he got up. They were all overjoyed to see him come to life again, and what is more, he was much brighter and cleverer than before.

At night, however, he lay perfectly stiff and rigid without showing any signs of life, and as he did not move when they turned him over and over, they were much frightened and thought he had died again. But towards daybreak he awakened as if from a dream, and in reply to their questions said that when he was with the wicked priest there was another boy named Ko-tzu, and that the day before when he had been unable to catch up to his father, it was because he had stayed behind to bid adieu to Ko-tzu. He added that Ko-tzu was now the son of an official in Purgatory named Chiang, and very comfortably settled. He had invited Chan to go and play with him that evening and had sent him back on a white-nosed horse.

His mother then asked if he had seen little Chu in Purgatory to which he replied, 'Little Chu has been born again. He and our father here had not really the destiny of father and son. Little Chu was merely a man named Yen Tzu-fang from Chin-ling, who had come to reclaim an old debt.'

Now Mr Li had formerly traded with Chin-ling and actually owed money for goods to a Mr Yen, but he had died and no one else knew anything about it, so that he was now greatly alarmed when he heard this story. His mother next asked little Chu if he had seen his sister, Hsiao-hui. He said he had not and promised to go again and inquire about her.

A few days afterwards he told his mother that Hsiao-hui was very happy in Purgatory, being married to a son of one of the judges and that she had any quantity of jewels * and crowds of attendants when she went anywhere.

'Why doesn't she come home to see her parents?' asked his mother.

'Well,' replied the boy, 'dead people, you know, haven't any flesh or bones. However, if you can only remind them of something that happened in their past lives, their feelings are at once touched. Yesterday, I did manage to get an interview with Hsiao-hui and we sat together on a coral couch, and I spoke to her of her father and mother at home, all of which she listened to as if she was asleep. I then remarked, "Sister, when you were alive you were very fond of embroidering double-stemmed flowers, and once you cut your finger with the scissors and the blood ran over the silk, but you brought it into the picture as a crimson cloud. Your mother has that picture still hanging at the head of your bed, a perpetual souvenir of you. Sister, have you forgotten this?" Then she burst into tears and promised to ask her husband to let her come and visit you.'

His mother asked when she would arrive, but he said he could not tell. However, one day he ran in and cried out, 'Mother, Hsiao-hui has come with a splendid equipage and a train of servants. We had better get plenty of wine ready.' In a few moments he came in again saying, 'Here is my sister', and at the same time asked her to take a seat and rest. He then wept, although none of those present saw anything at all.

By and by, he went out and burnt a quantity of paper money † and made offerings of wine outside the door, returning shortly and saying he had sent away her attendants for a while. He also added that Hsiao-hui had asked if the green coverlet, a small portion of which had been burnt by a candle, was still in existence. 'It is,' replied her mother, and going to a box she at once produced the coverlet. 'Hsiao-hui would like a bed

* The ultimate success for many Chinese women.

† Chinese silver is called *sycee* from the Cantonese *sai-see*, 'fine silk', because of its use in casting 'shoes' weighing from one to one hundred ounces. If the silk is pure it is drawn into fine silk threads under heat and then cast. Paper imitations of these objects of high value were abundant and used as offerings to the spirits in the world below. The sharp edges of a 'shoe' of sycee were created by the mould containing the molten silver being gently shaken until the metal had set.

made up for her in her old room,' said her brother. 'She wants to rest awhile, and will talk with you again in the morning.'

Now their next-door neighbour, named Chao, had a daughter who was formerly a great friend of Hsiao-hui's, and that night she dreamt that Hsiao-hui appeared with a turban on her head and a red mantle over her shoulders and that they talked and laughed together precisely as in days gone by. 'I am now a spirit,' said Hsiao-hui, 'and my father and mother can no more see me than if I was far separated from them. Dear sister, I would borrow your body, from which to speak to them. You need fear nothing.'

On the morrow when Miss Chao met her mother, she fell on the ground before her and remained some time in a state of unconsciousness, at length saying, 'Madam, it is many years since we have met and your hair has become very white.'

'The girl's mad,' said her mother in alarm, and thinking something had gone wrong, proceeded to follow her out of the door. Miss Chao went straight to Li's house and there with tears embraced Mrs Li who knew not what to make of it.

'Yesterday,' said Miss Chao, 'when I came back I was unhappily unable to speak with you. Unfilial wretch that I was to die before you and leave you to mourn my loss. How can I redeem such behaviour?'

Her mother thereupon began to understand the scene and, weeping, said to her, 'I have heard that you hold an honourable position and this is a great comfort to me, but in living as you do in the palace of a judge, how is it that you are able to get away?' 'My husband,' replied she, 'is very kind and his parents treat me with all possible consideration. I experience no harsh treatment at their hands.' Here Miss Chao rested her cheek upon her hand exactly as Hsiao-hui had been wont to do when she was alive. At this time her brother came in to tell her that her attendants were ready to return. 'I must go,' said she, rising up and weeping bitterly all the while. And then she fell down and remained unconscious for some time as before.

Shortly after these events Mr Li became dangerously ill, but no medicines were of any avail, so that his son feared that they would be unable to save his life. Two devils sat at the head of his bed, one holding an iron staff and the other a nettlehemp rope four or five feet in length. Day and night his son implored them to go, but they would not move and Mrs Li in sorrow began to prepare the funeral clothes.*

Towards evening her son entered and cried out, 'Strangers and

* Death was regarded in ancient China as a summons from the authorities of Purgatory. Lictors are sent to arrest the doomed man, armed with a warrant similar to those on earth from a magistrate's yamen.

women leave the room! My sister's husband is coming to see his father-in-law.' He then clapped his hands and burst out laughing. 'What is the matter?' asked his mother. 'I am laughing,' answered he, 'because when the two devils heard my sister's husband was coming they both ran under the bed like terrapins drawing in their heads.'

By and by, looking at nothing, he began to talk about the weather and to ask his sister's husband how he had done it, and then he clapped his hands and said, 'I begged the two devils to go but they would not. It's all right now.'

After this he went out to the door and returned saying, 'My sister's husband has gone. He took away the two devils tied to his horse. My father ought to get better now. Besides, Hsiao-hui's husband said he would speak to the Judge and obtain a hundred years' lease of life for both you and father.'

The whole family rejoiced exceedingly at this, and when night came Mr Li was better and in a few days quite well again. A tutor was engaged for little Chu, who showed himself to be an apt pupil and at eighteen years of age took his bachelor's degree.

He could also see many things of the other world and when anyone in the village was ill, he pointed out where the devils were and burnt them out with fire, so that everybody got well. However, before long he himself became very ill and his flesh turned green and purple, whereupon he said, 'The devils afflict me thus because I let out their secrets. Henceforth I shall never divulge them again.' And then Chu died.

P'u Sung-ling (Ch'ing Dynasty)
From *Liao Chai Chih I*

4 Love and Marriage

The Painted Wall

While wandering about the capital one day, Chu and his friend, Meng Lung-t'an, came upon a monastery. But within they found no spacious halls or meditation chambers. It seemed deserted, when suddenly an odd-looking priest, bent with age, emerged and approached them. While the priest tried in vain to straighten out his dishevelled clothes, he courteously agreed to show them about the monastery. Chu and his friend were pleased with their luck.

They were led into the chapel where they saw an image of Chih Kung and beautifully painted walls on either side with representations of men and animals so real as to be out of life itself. On the east side were pictured a number of fairies, and among them, a young girl whose maiden tresses were not yet bound up into the matron's knot. The girl had a gentle smile on her cherry-red lips as she picked flowers, and the moisture of her eyes seemed about to overflow.

Chu gazed at her for a long time without taking his eyes away, until at last he became unaware of anything but his thoughts of this girl with the cherry-red lips. Suddenly, he felt himself floating in the air, as if riding on a cloud, and then found himself passing through the very wall. Halls and pavilions stretched out before him, one after another. This place was not like any mortal abode.

Chu went forward until he came to a crowd listening to an old priest preaching the law of Buddha. He joined them, but after a few moments received a gentle tug at his sleeve. He turned around to see the girl with the cherry-red lips walking away and laughing. At once, Chu followed her. After a time, he passed by a winding balustrade and arrived at a small apartment beyond which he dared not venture.

The young lady, however, looked back and beckoned him on with the flowers in her hand. He entered and found her alone. Then, as if it had always been meant to be, they both fell to their knees and worshipped heaven and earth and rose up as man and wife.* But to Chu's dismay, his bride soon departed, bidding him keep quiet until she returned.

The girl's visits back and forth to Chu during the next few days began to arouse her friends' suspicions. Following her back to Chu, they discovered him in his hiding place. They all laughed with great delight and turning to the girl urged her to change her coiffure. 'You are a married woman now,' they said, 'and you must act accordingly.'

So they produced the proper hair pins and head ornaments and bade her go bind her hair at once. She blushed greatly, but did as she was told. Then one of them said with a giggle, 'We must be off, my sisters. We are making a crowd here when there should only be two!' And away they went.

Chu found his wife much improved by the alteration of her hair style. The high top-knot and the coronet of pendants suited her. But his loving admiration was interrupted by the sound of clanking chains, the tramping of heavy-soled boots and angry voices. His bride jumped up in fright, and ran to him. Together, they peeped out the window in fright. They saw a man clad in golden armour, with a face as black as jet, carrying in his hands chains and whips, and surrounded by all the girls.

'Are you all here?' he demanded. 'All,' they replied. 'If you are concealing any mortal among you,' he said fiercely, 'denounce him at once, and lay not up more sorrow upon yourselves.'

But they all answered as before that there was no one. The gold-armoured man made a move as if he was about to search the place. Chu's bride became dreadfully alarmed and turned grey with fear. 'Hide yourself under the bed,' she said, and opening a small lattice in the wall, disappeared.

Under the bed, Chu hardly dared draw a breath; the boots tramped into the room and out again, and then everything sounded fainter and fainter in the distance. This reassured him, but the voices of people still travelled back and forth outside. Having been cramped so long, Chu's ears began to sing as if a locust were in them, and his eyes burned with fire. Still, he remained waiting the return of his bride.

Meanwhile, Meng Lung-t'an suddenly noticed the disappearance of Chu from the chapel. He asked the priest where his friend had gone. 'He has gone to hear the preaching of the Law,' replied the priest mysteriously. 'Where?' asked Meng. 'Oh, not very far,' smiled the priest.

* A marriage witnessed by heaven alone.

With his finger, the old man tapped the wall and called out, 'Friend Chu! Why are you staying so long?' At this, the likeness of Chu appeared figured upon the wall painting, his ear inclined in the attitude of listening. 'Your friend has been waiting for you for some time now,' added the priest. Whereupon Chu descended from the wall, standing transfixed like a block of wood, his eyes staring and limbs shaking.

His amazed friend asked him quietly what had happened. What had happened was that while hiding under the bed, Chu had heard a noise resembling thunder, had left his hiding place, and rushed out to see what was happening. Then suddenly he was back in the chapel – bewildered.

They all turned to the wall painting and noticed that the maiden's tresses had changed in style, and she now wore the coiffure of a married woman. Chu was astonished, and begged the old priest to explain.

The monk smiled and answered slowly. 'Visions have their origin in those who see them. What else can I tell you?' Chu found this answer very unsatisfactory, as did his friend, who by this time was thoroughly frightened. Together, they both ran down the steps of the temple and fled.

P'u Sung-ling (Ch'ing Dynasty)
From *Liao Chai Chih I*

Love and Loyalty of a Courtesan

Li Shih-shih was the daughter of a dyer by the name of Wang Ying, who lived in the eastern suburbs of Kai-feng, then the capital of the Sung Empire. Her mother died soon after giving birth to her, and it was her father who raised her on millet gruel for want of milk. She rarely cried as a baby.

According to the local custom, children deeply beloved by their parents must be nominally adopted by some Buddhist temple in order to be saved from dying early, and as Wang Ying was very fond of his baby girl, he had her adopted by the Temple of the Sacred Nimbus.

'Don't you know what sort of a place this is, and yet you dare to come here?' said the old monk, gazing at the infant.

At these words the child commenced to cry. Then the priest rubbed the crown of her head with the palm of his hand and she stopped crying. Her father was delighted, saying that she was certainly destined to be a Buddhist disciple. Now the disciples of Buddhism were familiarly called *shih* (teacher), so she was given the name Shih-shih.

When she was four years old, her father was sentenced for some criminal offence, and died in the prison. The child was left without a home, and Old Lady Li, a keeper of a house of pleasure, adopted her. As she grew in age, she excelled both in physical beauty and in her vocal art, and became the most famous of all the courtesans in the capital.

Now the Emperor Hui Tsung of the Sung dynasty, who had just assumed the imperial yellow, initiated a reign of luxury and extravagance. The Prime Minister Tsai Ching and his gang had succeeded, in the name of restoring some of the financial reforms of the preceding reigns, in introducing various onerous taxes to raise funds for court expenditures. The capital took on a false and superficial air of wealth and prosperity. The duty on spirits alone amounted daily to ten thousand strings of cash, and the imperial treasury overflowed with gold, silver, jade and silks. The courtiers and favourites pandered to the young sovereign with the pleasures of wine, women and song, of hunting dogs and racing ponies, and with the lavish construction of palaces and gardens. Exotic and rare plants, bizarre and costly rocks, were transported from all over the empire to beautify the imperial pleasure grounds. To the north of the city a luxurious mansion was built, where His Majesty and his boon companions spent days and nights in wild dissipation.

However, the emperor was soon surfeited with these orgies and diversions, and desired to visit incognito the houses of joy in the capital. A eunuch, Chang, an imperial favourite, used to be a gay young blade before he mutilated himself and entered the service of the palace. He knew Old Lady Li very well, as he had frequented many such houses in former days, hers among them, and he boasted to the emperor of the extraordinary beauty and talent of Li Shih-shih.

The emperor fell to the temptation, and the following day ordered Chang to convey to Old Lady Li valuable gifts of silks, velvet, pearls and silver shoes, all from the imperial treasury, and to inform her that a wealthy merchant by the name of Chao Yi would like to visit her house. Impressed with the presents, she gladly assented to the proposal. At night His Majesty changed his clothes and mingling among some two score of eunuchs who accompanied him, left the palace by the Tung Hua

Gate, arriving soon at Li's establishment. At the door he waved his hand at the others to return, while he and Chang boldly entered.

The house was a small and modest one, but the mistress was exceptionally warm in the reception of her guests. She set forth before them freshly cut pieces of lotus root, dates * as large as eggs, and many other kinds of fruit rarely seen even in the palace. The emperor helped himself to one of each kind, while the old lady continued to entertain him with gossip and small talk. But Shih-shih was nowhere to be seen though His Majesty patiently waited.

After a while the eunuch retired, and Li conducted her guest to a small kiosk, charmingly furnished and with windows elegantly curtained, through which he could see young bamboo plants in the moonlight gently wafted by the breeze and casting their shadows here and there. The emperor was much delighted with the cosy boudoir and waited contentedly, though Shih-shih still failed to show herself.

Then Old Lady Li took the distinguished visitor to a room in the rear, where were laid out on a dining table many dishes of venison, chicken, fish and lamb, all deliciously prepared, with rice of special fragrance, whereof he partook a bowl, she continuing to entertain him. Again, His Majesty was disappointed in that the famous beauty did not appear in his presence.

At this moment of bewilderment he was invited by the old lady to take a bath, which he refused.

'Don't be offended,' she whispered to him, 'but my dear daughter has a passion for cleanliness!'

His Majesty could not help but follow the old woman into a small bathroom, and after making his ablutions, was led back to the dining room where the table had been set anew with dainties and refreshments. He was urged to drink to his fill, but all by himself!

After another long wait, Old Lady Li, holding a lighted candle, introduced him to a bedchamber, where he saw a lonely lamp standing behind the door curtain. He was more than amazed, but concealed his annoyance by reposing himself now in a chair, now on the couch. After long last Li returned to the room, leading by the hand a young woman, who walked slowly and hesitatingly. She wore her natural complexion, using neither powder nor rouge, and seemed to have emerged fresh from a bath. She was as pretty as a lily on the surface of the water, but she manifested little interest in her visitor. In fact, she held herself in rather a cold and haughty posture and hardly acknowledged his presence.

* Chinese 'dates' are not palm dates but a fruit. In dried form they are like dates in colour, and delicious in flavour.

'Please don't take offence,' Li whispered in the guest's ear. 'My child is obstinate by nature.'

His Majesty stared at her intently in the lamplight, and was deeply impressed by her beautiful face and the brilliancy of her eyes, which shone with an air of surprise. He asked to know her age, but she made no reply, and when he insisted, she merely shifted to another seat. Li again told the visitor under her breath that the girl did not like to talk much, and that he should not mind her seeming rudeness. She then retired.

Shih-shih left her chair to remove her outer coat of yellow satin and, rolling up the sleeves of her soft clinging gown, reached for her lute hanging on the wall. Placing the instrument on a long table and sitting down by its side, she played the classical tune of the *Wild Geese's Descent on the Smooth Sands*, and the melody as well as the lightness of touch of her fingers fascinated the imperial ears, making him forget his drowsiness.

By the time she finished the third and last part of the piece, the cocks had begun to crow. The emperor hurriedly raised the door curtain to leave, and the old lady reappeared, bringing cakes and almond sauce. He took his departure shortly after, his escort waiting discreetly at the door, and returned to the palace. This happened on the seventeenth day of the eighth moon in the third year of the Ta Kuan period.

When alone by themselves Li complained cautiously to Shih-shih. 'That Mr Chao,' she said, 'treated you not badly; why were you so cool and indifferent?'

'Why,' she answered angrily, 'he is nothing but a contemptible shop-keeper. What did he expect of me?'

'You are stiff-necked enough to qualify you to be a censor,' retorted the old woman with a laugh.

Before long, gossip began to circulate in the capital about the imperial nocturnal visit to the house of joy, and when Li heard of it, she was terrified. She wept day and night, saying to Shih-shih that if the report was true, it meant the death of her entire family.

'Never fear,' said Shih-shih, 'if His Majesty deigned to call on me, he would surely not kill me. Moreover, he put no compulsion of any kind on me that night, proving that he had pity and love for me. What saddens me is that my fate in life is ill-starred – lowering me to such a social level as to bring infamy by association to the noble sovereign. For my being guilty of this, even death itself cannot atone. There is no need of fear of punishment for having offended His Majesty, because, the whole affair being one of gallantry, the emperor would surely try to keep it quiet.'

When the New Year came, His Majesty bestowed on Shih-shih the ancient and renowned instrument known as the Lute of the Snake's Skin (a treasure of the palace, so-called because the woodwork was varnished in the pattern and colour of a serpent's skin) and, in addition, fifty taels of pure silver.

In the third moon of the following year His Majesty paid his second incognito visit to Shih-shih. When the latter, still plainly dressed, met the imperial guest on her knees, he smilingly raised her to her feet. He noticed that the house had been entirely renovated and extended, and the rooms he previously visited had their furniture covered with satin embroidered with the imperial dragon. The quiet kiosk had been transformed into a big pavilion with vermilion columns and bright red railings, losing completely its former air of elegance.

Old Lady Li hid herself somewhere inside, and when summoned to the imperial presence, trembled all over, all her previous familiarity and loquacity having vanished. His Majesty, inwardly displeased, put on an appearance of amiability, addressing her as Old Mother, and informing her that all the three of them being now of one family, she should not feel constrained or nervous. She prostrated herself on the floor to express her gratefulness.

His Majesty was then conducted to a newly built hall and Shih-shih, falling on her knees, begged the emperor to dedicate it. His eyes were met by the apricot trees in full bloom in front of the building, so he wrote three big characters meaning 'The Hall of Intoxicating Apricot Blossoms'.

Soon the table was set; Shih-shih waited on His Majesty, while on bent knees Old Lady Li offered wine in honour of the emperor's longevity. Shih-shih was granted a seat on one side and commanded to play on the royal gift of the famous lute, the tune she chose being the classical *Playing Thrice for the Plum Blossoms*. Drinking and listening, His Majesty applauded heartily when the melody ended.

The emperor noted that the table-wares were painted with dragons and phoenixes, like those employed in the palace, and inquired where they originated. He was informed by Li that they were specially ordered at her own expense after the model provided by the cooks of the imperial household. Annoyed by the information, he warned her to continue in her former plain style of living and not indulge in ostentation. The dinner broke up somewhat abruptly on account of the incident.

His Majesty used to honour the Imperial Academy of Fine Arts with personal visits, when he would test the artists by commanding them to paint pictures with lines of poetry as themes. One or two pictures would be crowned each year with imperial awards. That year in the ninth moon a picture was painted having for its subject the following two lines:

Chewing bits of gold the ponies neigh softly on the grass-green sward,
While in the House of Jade, the Lady drinks to the apricot flowers.

This painting was bestowed on Shih-shih. In addition she was given highly precious and artistic lanterns, ten of each kind, having such fanciful names as Silken Fibres of the Lotus Root, Warming Up in the Snow, Fragrant Tulip, and the Fiery Phoenix Holding a Pearl in the Mouth; four sets of bejewelled wine-cups, ten in each set; a hundred pounds each of three kinds of exquisite tea; different makes of delicious cakes; and one thousand taels of gold and silver.

The affair soon became the topic of gossip in court circles. Her Majesty the Empress Cheng, getting knowledge of it, remonstrated with the Emperor, appealing to his good sense which, she pleaded, should not allow him to associate with a courtesan. Besides, she pointed out, going out of the palace incognito at night might lead to some untoward incident. His Majesty nodded in approval of her words. For almost two years he refrained from leaving clandestinely the palace precincts, but there continued a stream of messages and gifts for Shih-shih.

In the second year of the Hsuan Ho period His Majesty again honoured Shih-shih with a visit, and saw the painting which he had bestowed on her hung up in the Hall of Intoxicating Apricot Blossoms. Gazing at it for a long while, he suddenly turned and caught sight of Shih-shih. 'Hello,' he laughingly cried, 'the beauty in the picture responds to my call.'

He had brought from the palace wonderful hairpins of gold, strings of pearls, a handmirror ornamented with a dancing phoenix and an incense-burner encircled by a golden dragon. To these gifts were added the next day a stone inkslab carved with the phoenix, blocks of ink manufactured by the famous inkmaker Li Ting-kuei, writing brushes of fine hair and jade holders, and paper made of silk. Old Lady Li received as present a large sum of silver.

The eunuch Chang now slyly suggested to His Majesty that visiting surreptitiously at night the home of Shih-shih was after all inconvenient and could not be often repeated. Now, he said, the imperial château outside of the capital and her house were separated only by a piece of vacant public land, a few hundred yards in length. If a private enclosed passage were built between the two places, the problem would be solved. His Majesty commanded the eunuch to execute the scheme.

Using as pretext that the palace guards were obliged to live in the open, Chang and a few others in a formal petition recommended the building of barracks for the soldiers on the vacant public land, to be surrounded with a high wall. When the building was completed a safe and secret access was provided for His Majesty to Shih-shih's quarters, and on account of the presence of the guards the populace kept away from the neighbourhood.

In the third moon of the fourth year the emperor commenced his visits to Shih-shih by the newly provided route. He again showered presents on her, including dominoes and dice of ivory, a chessboard of jade and chess pieces of precious green and white stones, elegant fans painted by the artists of the Imperial Academy of Fine Arts, expensive mats and curtains of fine bamboo with hooks of jade. Losing good-humouredly to her in both games of dice and chess, he presented to her two thousand taels of pure silver. On her birthday she received two filigrees richly bedecked with pearls, and two gold bracelets, a box of precious stones, bolts of brocades, silks and another thousand taels of silver. On a subsequent occasion celebrating the military victory over the Northern barbarians, when honours and promotions were generally conferred on civil and army officials, Shih-shih received her bountiful share of gifts, including curtains of purple gauze with brightly coloured tassels, bed covers of brocade, a thousand taels of gold and jars of famous wines. In all she and Old Lady Li received gifts of objects and money amounting in value to one hundred thousand taels of silver.

Once His Majesty and the court ladies were assembled at a banquet. 'What is this Li woman who seems to have bewitched Your Majesty?' he was quietly asked by the imperial consort Wei.

'Oh, nothing,' he replied, 'but if the hundred of you ladies discarded your gorgeous costumes and replaced them with simple dresses, with Shih-shih standing in your midst, you will find her absolutely different. She has an air of quiet elegance and a carriage of sylphs and fairies, entirely aside from her wonderful complexion and features.'

Some years later His Majesty abdicated, adopting the title of Pope of the Taoist Church and residing in an independent palace. He lost interest in the vain and idle pleasures of the flesh.

'You and I,' observed Shih-shih one day to her mother, 'live so happily that we have no idea when a sudden disaster will bring us to ruin.'

Li asked her what they should do then.

'You had better live in a place which nobody would know, and let me do the rest according to my own judgement,' Shih-shih replied.

At the time the Chin nomadic tribes had already started hostilities against the empire, and north China appealed for military aid. Shih-shih gathered together all the gold and silver bestowed on her by the emperor and sent it, accompanied by a letter addressed to the Prefect of Kaifeng, as a contribution to the war-chest. At the same time, through bribing the eunuch Chang, she got word to His Majesty for permission to become a nun, and the latter bestowed on her the Temple of the Merciful Cloud outside the North Gate.

Before long the Chin invaders captured the capital. Their commanding general went in search of Shih-shih, for the King of the Chins had heard of her name and insisted on having her captured alive. For many days she could not be discovered, then the traitor officials Chang Pang-chang and others trailed her to the temple, and offered her to the Chin commander.

'I am but a humble woman of the house of joy,' Shih-shih railed at them bitterly. 'But since I have been honoured by the love of His Majesty, I have no ambition now other than to die. You people have occupied high official positions and received handsome emoluments; in what way has the throne treated you unkindly that you do your best to destroy the dynasty? You now serve as slaves to the wretched savages, hoping to find in me a suitable present with which to ingratiate yourselves with them. I will never let myself be the vicarious lamb or the sacrificial wild goose for you blackguards.'

She took her gold hairpin and pierced her throat with it, but failed to kill herself; then she bent and swallowed it, finding her death that way.

Later when the former emperor in exile heard of her tragic death, he wept inconsolably.

Anonymous (Sung Dynasty)

The Faithless Widow

Mr Niu was a Kiangsi man who traded in piece goods. He married a wife from the Cheng family, by whom he had two children, a boy and a girl. When thirty-three years of age he fell ill and died, his son Chung being then only twelve and his little girl eight or nine. His wife did not remain faithful to his memory,* but, selling off all the property, pocketed the proceeds and married another man, leaving her two children almost in a state of destitution with their aunt, Niu's sister-in-law, an old lady of sixty, who had lived with them previously, and had now nowhere to seek a shelter. A few years later this aunt died, and the family fortunes began to sink even lower than before.

Chung, however, was now grown up and determined to carry on his father's trade, only he had no capital to start with. His sister marrying a rich trader named Mao, she begged her husband to lend Chung ten ounces of silver, which he did, and Chung immediately started for Nanking. On the road he fell in with some bandits, who robbed him of all he had, and consequently he was unable to return. But one day when he was at a pawnshop he noticed that the master of the shop was wonderfully like his late father, and on going out and making inquiries he found that this pawnbroker bore precisely the same names. In great astonishment, he forthwith proceeded to frequent the place with no other object than to watch this man, who, on the other hand, took no notice of Chung; and by the end of three days, having satisfied himself that he really saw his own father, and yet not daring to disclose his own identity, he made application through one of the assistants, on the score of being himself a Kiangsi man, to be employed in the shop. Accordingly, an indenture was drawn up. But when the master noticed Chung's name and place of residence he started, and asked him whence he came. With tears in his eyes Chung addressed him by his father's name, and then the pawnbroker became lost in a deep reverie, by and by asking Chung how his mother was. Now Chung did not like to allude to his father's death and turned the question by saying, 'My father went away on business six years ago and never came back; my mother married again and left us. Had it not been for my aunt our corpses would long ago have been cast out in the kennel.'

The pawnbroker was much moved and cried out, 'I am your father!' seizing his son's hand and leading him within to see his step-mother.

This lady was about twenty-two, and having no children of her own she was delighted with Chung, and prepared a banquet for him in the inner apartments. Mr Niu himself was, however, somewhat melancholy and wished to return to his old home. But his wife, fearing that there would be no one to manage the business persuaded him to remain; so he taught his son the trade, and in three months was able to leave it all to him.

He then prepared for his journey, whereupon Chung informed his

* Only under exceptional circumstances is it considered permissible in China for widows to marry again. If they do remarry, it is considered a lapse in virtue.

step-mother that his father was really dead, to which she replied in great consternation that she knew him only as a trader to the place, and that six years previously he had married her, which proved conclusively that he couldn't be dead. Chung then recounted the whole story, which was a perfect mystery to both of them. Twenty-four hours afterwards in walked his father, leading a woman whose hair was all dishevelled. Chung looked at her and saw that she was his own mother, and Niu took her by the ear and began to revile her, saying, 'Why did you desert my children?' to which the wretched woman made no reply. He then bit her across the neck, at which she screamed to Chung for assistance, and he, not being able to bear the sight, stepped in between them. His father was more than ever enraged at this, when, lo! Chung's mother had disappeared. While they were still lost in astonishment at this strange scene, Mr Niu's colour changed. In another moment his empty clothes had dropped upon the ground and he himself became a black vapour and also vanished from their sight. The step-mother and son were much overcome. They took Niu's clothes and buried them.

After that Chung continued his father's business and soon amassed great wealth. On returning to his native place he found that his mother had actually died on the very day of the above occurrence and that his father had been seen by the whole family.

P'u Sung-ling (Ch'ing Dynasty)
From *Liao Chai Chih I*

The Heartless Lover

During that period of the Tang dynasty known as Ta Li there lived in Kansu a young scholar by the name of Li Yi. He had barely reached twenty years of age when he obtained the much coveted doctorate in the imperial examinations, and the following summer in the sixth moon he arrived at Changan, the capital of the empire, for the civil service examination, taking lodging in the Street of New Prosperity. Li Yi came from a renowned literary family. He was possessed of a brilliant intellect, and was particularly accomplished as a poet and essayist, unequalled in reputation by any other scholar of his time.

Highly pleased with himself and his literary attainments, he had only one regret, and that was his inability to find a congenial and accomplished girl after his own heart. He roved a great deal among the famous courtesans of the city, hoping to meet a sweetheart acceptable to his taste and worthy of his love, but a prolonged hunt resulted in nothing.

At this stage, there lived in Changan a well-known mistress of courtesans and matchmakers, Mrs Pao, a former bondmaid in the house of one of the emperor's sons-in-law, who had bought her freedom and had been married for a dozen years or so. She was a crafty woman, clever of speech and acquainted with all the distinguished families of the city – in fact, the queen of her profession. Entrusted by Mr Li with the task of finding for him a lady friend and loaded with valuable presents from him, she tried her best to fulfil his yearning.

One late afternoon as the young scholar was whiling away his time in an arbour of the garden of his house, someone knocked impatiently at the gate. The janitor opened it and reported to him that the caller was Mrs Pao. Li hurriedly went forward and received her.

'How is it, Madame, that you are here?' he asked.

'Your fondest dream has come true,' she said. 'A goddess has been banished to this sorry earth: she seeks no wealth but only love and romance. Such beauty and sentiment fulfil all your requirements.'

'I am willing to be her slave all my life,' cried the young scholar, dancing with delight and seizing Mrs Pao's hands to show his gratefulness. He asked for her name and address.

'She is Miss Jade, the youngest daughter of the late Prince Huo,' she explained. 'Her mother, by the name of Purity, was a favourite bondmaid and, later, concubine of His Highness and when he died his legitimate heirs considered the girl as born of a woman of humble status and refused to recognize her. The mother was given some money and sent away. She changed her name to Cheng, thus concealing her and the girl's antecedents. She is the most beautiful young woman I have ever laid my eyes on, noble in her sentiments and artistic in her temperament – in short, superior in every way. She possesses numerous accomplishments, being a poet as well as a musician, and is intellectually highly qualified. I have been commissioned by her mother yesterday to find a suitable mate for her, and I immediately mentioned your name. She had also heard of you as the famous romantic Master Li, the Tenth Favourite Son of the Li family, and was very much pleased with my suggestion. She lives in the house with wide portals to the south of the Old Temple in Sheng Yeh Street. I have arranged a meeting for tomorrow noon: you can easily find the house, because a servant-maid will watch for your arrival.'

After the departure of the caller, the young gallant made careful preparations for the coming interview. He sent his page to borrow from his cousin Shang, who was on the staff of the Metropolitan Garrison Headquarters, a coal-black pony equipped with a gold bit, and that night he bathed and completed his coiffure, being so exhilarated that he could not sleep a wink. As soon as it was dawn he tried on his most becoming hat and gown, looking repeatedly in the mirror to see if all was in order and he was appearing at his best. He walked nervously about in the courtyard, waiting for the arrival of the hour of departure. Then he mounted his steed and galloped rapidly to the appointed spot.

A girl in black stood at the gate. 'Are you Master Li the Tenth?' she queried, and led him inside the premises, locking the gate. Mrs Pao was the first to appear.

'How dare you, stranger, invade these sacred precincts?' she chided him smilingly.

He was conducted to the second gate, where he saw before him a courtyard with four cherry trees, in the north-west corner of which hung a cage with a parrot therein.

'Guest has come. Raise the curtain!' cackled the parrot.

By nature timid and retiring, and feeling somewhat nervous, Li was so taken by surprise when he heard the words of the parrot, that he dared not take a step further. The girl's mother now stepped down from the terrace to welcome him and invite him inside. She was just turned forty, still an attractive woman, and showed herself a charming talker.

'I have heard a great deal of your scholarly attainments and romantic personality,' she declared cordially, 'and now I perceive that you are also very handsome – indeed, you do not belie your reputation. My daughter, while not highly educated, is far from being a homely person, and would really make a suitable companion for you. Mrs Pao has transmitted to me your proposal for my daughter's hand, and I am quite ready to order her to wait on you as her lord and master.'

'I am an ignorant and mediocre person, unworthy of your kind notice,' politely responded the young man, 'and I feel highly honoured now and hereafter to receive such a kind welcome from you, Madame.'

Drink and food was then brought to celebrate the occasion, and Miss Jade was summoned to meet the visitor. She entered from an adjoining chamber on the east side of the reception room. Master Li bowed profoundly to her. The two of them made an exceedingly handsome pair, like two matching pieces of beautiful art, diffusing radiance at each other and at the others in the room. She took a seat by the side of her mother.

The mother turned to the daughter: 'You love to repeat the lines:

Pushing aside the curtain I note the bamboos waving in the breeze;
Methought it a harbinger of the arrival of a dear friend!

'These lines, my dear, were composed by our friend Master Li. Is not his actual presence here today more interesting to you than mere recitation of his poetry?'

'What I have heard of him is really enough to make me enchanted,' she lowered her head and replied in a soft voice. 'Seeing him or not does not make much difference, for how can a talented scholar lack good looks?'

'You love masculine talent and I adore female beauty,' declared gallantly the handsome suitor, rising from his seat and making a bow before the girl, 'we thus complement each other in our ideals.'

Mother and daughter smiled understandingly at each other at this gracious compliment. After several rounds of wine, Master Li arose and requested Miss Jade to favour him with a song. She modestly declined, but when her mother insisted, she complied. She possessed a rich and clear voice and the tune sounded unusually melodious.

The merry gathering lasted till evening, when Mrs Pao conducted the young scholar to his quarters in the west courtyard, where he found the rooms quiet but elegantly furnished. Two young maids waited on him, assisting him to disrobe and retire for the night. Miss Jade did not keep him long waiting. She showed herself to be gentle and affectionate and tried her best to please him. She became his mistress that night and they were very happy together.

But in the middle of the night she commenced to weep. 'I am,' she avowed to her lover, 'but a common girl and I realize that I am socially not your equal. You love me for my looks, but I fear that as my beauty fades, so, too, will your sentiments fade, so that I shall resemble a vine with nothing to cling to, or like a fan that is abandoned with the passage of summer. In my hour of supreme bliss, I am overwhelmed by dark foreboding.'

He was much agitated by her frank statement of her tragic presentiment.

'I have found my ideal love,' he said to comfort her, using his arm to serve as her pillow. 'I swear solemnly never to forsake you. If I do, may my bones be reduced to ashes and my body be broken into a thousand pieces. Why do you talk to me in the way you have done? Let me have a piece of white silk and I'll write down in ink what I have just sworn.'

Cherry, the maidservant, was summoned, and she brought a yard of white satin, together with a writing brush and a stone inkslab. The elegant implements for writing came originally from her father, the Prince. Jade was literarily inclined, always fond of books, and the collection she owned also came from her father.

In the bright candlelight the scholar-lover composed and penned an original statement, in which he called on the mountains and the rivers, and the sun and the moon to bear witness to his eternal fidelity to his lady love. Every word and every sentence bore the imprint of his profound affection for and attachment to Jade, and when she eagerly read it, she sighed with great contentment. The piece of precious silk was then carefully locked away in her jewel-box.

Like a couple of love-birds, they spent happily two years together, hardly ever separated from each other, be it day or night. In the spring of the third year Mr Li passed the civil service examination, and was appointed Clerk of the Cheng County, and in the fourth moon he prepared to proceed to his post. A dinner was held to celebrate the occasion, and many local friends and acquaintances made it a point to be present. It was near the end of spring and the beginning of summer, and Nature was at its best. When the wine was finished and the guests had said their adieus, the young couple were left to themselves.

'You are admired by the whole world,' said Jade sadly to her sweetheart, 'for your talent, your social position and your literary renown, and many a father would be proud to have you as son-in-law. Your beloved parents await keenly your return, and as there is no daughter-in-law to assist in the management of the household, you will surely get married when you are back at home. As to the troth exchanged between us and your solemn oaths, they are but vain and empty words. But I have just one tiny wish to make known to you, and in view of the deep and genuine affection I have for you, you will perhaps be willing to listen.'

'In what way have I shown myself remiss that you address yourself thus to me?' cried Master Li, much taken aback and honestly pained. 'I'll gladly listen to anything you desire to say to me.'

'I am eighteen years of age,' she began, 'and you are twenty-two: there remain still eight years to elapse before you reach the traditional age of marriage. Let us two enjoy to the full our blissful love in this period: it will not be too late then for you to contract your marriage with some lady of quality. As for me, I will shave off my hair and don the costume of a nun for the rest of my days, thus consummating happily my original vow.'

'The oath I swore to the celestial bodies,' he exclaimed, tears flowing down his cheeks, 'I will fulfil were it to cost my life. How can I possibly think of other loves, when the good fortune has been granted me to satisfy my longing for you and to grow old with you alone? Let not your heart doubt for an instant my eternal constancy. Stay here and wait patiently. By the eighth moon I shall surely arrive at Huachow, when I will send my people for you. It will not be long before we shall be again in each other's arms.'

In a few days he left eastward for his post, and after a fortnight there he asked for leave to visit his parents in Loyang, the ancient East Capital.

He had been home for little more than a week, when his mother informed him of a match which she had arranged between him and his cousin Miss Lu. As the old lady was very punctilious and conservative in such matters, he hesitated to express any objection, still less opposition, but was on the contrary constrained to thank her for the matrimonial arrangements she had completed for him. The wedding, she said, would take place at an early date.

Now the Lu family belonged to the aristocracy, and when marrying away one of its daughters demanded always an enormous sum as settlement from the groom or his family. If this sum was not forthcoming, the wedding would be indefinitely postponed. As the Li family was not wealthy, Li Yi was obliged to raise the wedding gift to the bride by loans from friends and relatives. Using this as a pretext, he travelled further eastward, then southward, from the autumn till the next summer.

Realizing now that he had violated his oath to Jade and broken his promise to meet her soon, Li decided not even to correspond with her, so as to put an end once and for all to her hopes, and, moreover, cowardly requested his friends and acquaintances to keep everything about his doings secret from her.

Poor Jade did her best to obtain news of her lover after he had failed to fulfil his promise. The little she succeeded in discovering would sometimes prove later to be false, or else the information would be contradictory. She consulted all kinds of oracles and fortune-tellers without success, and finally after a year of sorrow and disappointments she fell desperately ill, becoming a confirmed invalid confined to her bedroom. Though no letter ever arrived from her former lover, her hope of seeing him again never faded. She cajoled and bribed his friends to assist her in retracing him, so that she had to spend a large part of her resources. Repeatedly she sent her maids with jewellery and ornaments for sale to a second-hand shop kept by a man by the name of Hou. She was the lucky owner of a valuable hair ornament of purple jade, which on the way to the shop was seen by a court jeweller.

'Why,' he exclaimed with surprise, 'that piece of jade is of my handiwork: when the youngest daughter of Prince Huo was to put up her hair, His Highness ordered me to make the pin, and gave me ten thousand copper cash for it. I remember the incident distinctly. Who are you and where did you get it?'

'My mistress,' replied the maid with some hesitation, 'is that lady.'

She related the story of how the daughter of the Prince had been seduced and abandoned by her lover for nearly two years, and how she was trying to raise some money so as to get news of his whereabouts. The jeweller felt much saddened by the story and took the girl to the Palace of Princess Yen Hsien, who, sympathizing with the unhappy lot of Miss Jade, offered to buy the pin at ten times the original price.

At this time Miss Lu, the future bride of Li Yi, was also residing at Changan. Li, having succeeded in raising the fund for his wedding, returned to his post, and in the twelfth moon he asked for leave to get married. Proceeding secretly to Changan, he rented a house in a quiet neighbourhood, not letting anyone know of his presence.

However, he had in the city a cousin by the name of Tsui, a master of arts and a highly honourable man, who used to drink with him at Jade's home and have merry times with him. Whenever he received any letter from Li, he would honestly transmit the contents to Jade, who reciprocated by sending him gifts of fuel and clothes, for which Tsui was exceedingly grateful. When Li secretly came to Changan for his marriage, Tsui broke the news to her.

'Can such dishonourable conduct be possible?' she cried, her grief mixed with anger.

She earnestly requested his friends to persuade him to call at her house, but he, ashamed of having broken his promise and knowing that she was ill and almost on the verge of death, hardened his heart and refused to see his former sweetheart. He went everywhere, leaving the house early in the morning and returning late at night, but he refused to call on her, while she wept bitterly at home, refraining from food and sleep, but hoping against hope for at least an interview. Her illness became graver with each passing day.

The story of Li's scandalous treatment of his mistress became widely known among the literary and romantic circles of Changan. One and all sympathized with and lauded Miss Jade for her deep attachment to her lover and condemned Li for his heartlessness.

By then it was in the third moon, and people went out to enjoy the splendid spring weather. Li and half a dozen of his boon companions made a visit to the Chung Ching Temple to inspect the celebrated peonies, strolling in the gardens and composing poems to commemorate the occasion.

'In this beautiful weather and with Nature at her best,' observed his good friend Wei Hsia-ching, 'it is nothing less than tragic that Miss Jade should be confined alone to her room, bearing her heavy grief. You must have a heart of stone to abandon her without any feeling of regret, and it is hardly manly on your part to act like this. I urge you to reconsider your attitude.'

While the two friends were thus conversing, a stranger wearing a yellow robe and carrying a cross bow accosted them. He had striking features and was elegantly dressed, being accompanied by a Central Asian boy. He bowed to young Li, and inquired if he was the well-known Master Li the Tenth.

'I am from Shantung,' he explained, 'and I am related to the royal family. Although I myself am no scholar, I admire learning, and having heard so much of your brilliant attainments, I am proud to make your acquaintance. My humble house is not far from here, and I can provide music to entertain you. In the house you will also find some pretty girls and in the stables a dozen steeds. You may have any of these if you will honour me with your visit.'

Hearing the invitation, Li's friends were eager to visit the house, and mounting their ponies they galloped after their genial host. After several turnings, the party found itself in Sheng Yeh Street and Li, realizing that they were in the vicinity of Jade's home, raised objections to proceeding any further. The stranger, saying that his house was only a few yards away, seized the bridle of Li's mount and dragged the animal along. In a few minutes the party arrived at Jade's door. The heartless lover made another attempt to escape, but the gallant stranger summoned his servants who were at hand, and had him carried, willy-nilly, inside. As soon as the party had entered the door was locked.

'Master Li the Tenth has come,' shouted the cavalier, and the entire Cheng household appeared in great amazement and rapture.

Now during the preceding night Miss Jade dreamed that her lover, borne by a yellow-robed man, paid her a visit and on their entry the stranger asked her to remove Li's shoes. In the morning she related the dream to her mother and interpreted it to herself as follows: shoe stood for harmony * – which meant that Li was to come to her, but removal meant parting for ever after the meeting. So she requested her mother to help her coiffure, which the latter did, simply to humour her, believing that in her serious illness her mind was not working normally. Soon after, however, Li actually arrived together with the party.

Although much enfeebled, Miss Jade seemed suddenly to recover her strength, and as soon as the visitors were announced, she jumped up

* The character for 'shoe' and that for 'harmony' have the same sound.

from her bed, dressed properly and went out to meet her ex-sweetheart, as if in a trance. For a while she stared at him with anger in her eyes then raised an arm to hide her face as if unable to sustain the sight of him. After a while, however, she glanced at Li from behind her sleeves, her eyes now expressing infinite sorrow and reproach. In spite of her brave front, she could not conceal from those present the ravages of her very serious malady, which only intensified their sympathy for her.

To the surprise of all, soon a magnificent repast was laid out. Inquiries elicited the information that it was provided by the same chivalrous stranger. After all had sat down, Jade, sitting sideways and gazing at her lover for a few minutes, took up her cup and poured the wine on the floor.

'I am only a woman of unhappy fate,' she cried, 'but you are an utterly heartless man. About to die of a broken heart in my young womanhood, I will no longer be able to support my beloved mother. Goodbye to my books and to my musical instruments! I have also to thank you, my faithless lover, for my coming suffering in purgatory. So adieu, Master Li! After my death, however, I shall become an evil spirit and return to this world to torment you and your wife, so that you will never know a day of peace and happiness.'

Grasping Li's arm with her left hand, she flung her winecup on the floor, breaking it into a hundred pieces. She gave several wails and moans, then expired. Her mother, placing the body of her daughter in Li's lap, urged him to try to revive her, but his efforts were unavailing.

Master Li went into deep mourning and showed great sorrow at Jade's death. On the eve of the interment he saw her once more appear behind the curtains which concealed the coffin: she was as beautiful as when she was alive, wearing her old skirt of the colour of pomegranate seeds, her purple jacket, and the shawl of red and green, holding in her hand the ribbons attached to her dress. She intimated to him that she appreciated his feelings in seeing her off from the world, and though now only a spirit, she still retained sentiments of regret and pity for him. Then she vanished and never appeared to him again. The following day her remains were buried in a Changan cemetery, Li walking behind the coffin all the way to the grave.

A month later Li married his cousin, Miss Lu, but not being able entirely to forget his previous love, he was not happy. The new couple went soon after to Li's post in Cheng County.

One night while in bed, he was suddenly awakened by a sound outside the curtains, and on looking out saw a handsome young man, beckoning to his wife from behind the window shades. Jumping out of bed, he looked for the intruder, but the latter had vanished. From that time on he suspected his wife of unfaithfulness, and a coolness arose between them. On the intervention of friends, however, he was induced to forget the incident.

About ten days later, on returning home, he found his wife playing on the lute in her boudoir, when all of a sudden someone threw into the room a small, elegant inlaid jewel-box, tied with a ribbon in the shape of a lover's knot. It fell into his wife's lap. Snatching it, he opened it. Inside he found love philtres and aphrodisiacs. The discovery made him violently angry. He roared like a wild beast, seized the lute and struck his wife with it, demanding an explanation of the affair, of which she herself was honestly unaware. After that incident, he assaulted her frequently, ending in their going to court and getting divorced. The handmaids and concubines who shared his bed later on fared no better at his hands, and one of them was actually killed by him in a fit of insane jealousy.

Visiting Yangchow, he married a concubine by the name of Miss Ying the Eleventh, a great beauty, who became his favourite. To frighten her into good behaviour he used to relate to her the fate of some of her predecessors – where he came to know them and how he got rid of them for their misdeeds. When he was obliged to leave the house, he would cover her in bed with a bathtub, sealing the edges. When he returned he would examine minutely the seals before permitting her to leave the bed. He kept always on his person a short sharp sword, showing it often to the handmaids and boasting that it was made of the finest steel and could easily sever the head of any woman who was unfaithful to him.

During his entire life he was obsessed with jealousy and suspicions concerning the women of his household, and though he married three times, the marriages all ended in great unhappiness for him.

Chiang Fang (T'ang Dynasty)

Miss A-pao; or Perseverance Rewarded

In the province of Kuang-si there lived a scholar of some reputation, named Sun Tzu-ch'u. He was born with six fingers, and such a simple fellow was he that he readily believed any nonsense he was told. Very shy with the fair sex, the sight of a woman was enough to send him flying in the opposite direction, and once when he was inveigled into a room where there were some young ladies, he blushed down to his neck and the perspiration dripped off him like falling pearls. His companions laughed heartily at his discomfiture, and told fine stories of what a noodle he looked, so that he got the nickname of Silly Sun.

In the town where our hero resided, there was a rich trader whose wealth equalled that of any prince or nobleman, and whose connections were all highly aristocratic.* He had a daughter of great beauty, A-pao, for whom he was seeking a husband. The young men of position in the neighbourhood were vying with each other to obtain her hand, but none of them met with the father's approval.

Now Silly Sun had recently lost his wife, and in joke, someone persuaded him to try his luck and send in an application. Sun, who had no idea of his own shortcomings, proceeded at once to follow this advice.

The father, though he knew him to be an accomplished scholar, rejected his suit on the ground of poverty. As the go-between was leaving the house, she chanced to meet A-pao and related to her the object of her visit. 'Tell him,' cried A-pao, laughing, 'that if he'll cut off his extra finger, I'll marry him.'

The old woman reported this to Sun, who replied, 'That is not very difficult,' and seizing a chopper, cut the finger clean off. The wound was extremely painful and he lost so much blood that he nearly died, it being many days before he was about again. He then sought out the go-between, and bade her inform Miss A-pao, which she did. A-pao was taken rather aback, but she told the old woman to go once more and bid him cut off the 'silly' from his reputation.

Sun got much excited when he heard this and denied that he was silly. However, as he was unable to prove it to the young lady herself, he began to think that probably her beauty was overstated and that she was giving herself great airs. So he ceased to trouble himself about her until the following spring festival, when it was customary for both men and women to be seen abroad. The young rips of the place would stroll about in groups and pass their remarks on all and sundry.

Sun's friends urged him to join them in their expedition and one of them asked him with a smile if he did not wish to look out for a suitable mate. Sun knew they were chaffing him, but he thought he should like

* There was no aristocracy of birth in China, as in the West. A man was considered aristocratic if he rose to prominence and official rank by his talents and literary tastes. Wealth was important but, as Herbert Giles writes, had little to do with rank. Trade was looked upon as ignoble and debasing – so much so that Giles reports that social intercourse between merchants and officials or highly regarded scholars was 'so rare as to be almost unknown'.

to see the girl that had made such a fool of him and was only too pleased
to accompany them. They soon perceived a young lady resting herself
under a tree with a throng of young fellows crowding round her and they
immediately determined that she must be A-pao, as in fact they found
she was. Possessed of peerless beauty, the ring of her admirers gradually
increased till at last she rose up to go.

The excitement among the young men was intense after she had gone.
They criticized her face and discussed her feet, only Sun remaining
silent. When they had passed on to something else, there they saw Sun
rooted like an imbecile to the same spot. As he made no answer when
spoken to, they dragged him along with them, saying, 'Has your spirit
run away after A-pao?' He made no reply to this either, but they thought
nothing of that, knowing his usual strangeness of manner, so by dint of
pushing and pulling they managed to get him home.

There he threw himself on the bed and did not get up again for the
rest of the day, lying in a state of unconsciousness just as if he were
drunk. He did not wake when called, and his people, thinking that his
spirit had fled, went about in the fields calling out to it to return.* However, he showed no signs of improvement. When they shook him and
asked him what was the matter, he only answered in a sleepy kind of
voice, 'I am at A-pao's house.' But to further questions he would not
make any reply, and left his family in a state of keen suspense.

Now when Silly Sun had seen the young lady get up to go, he could
not bear to part with her, and found himself first following and then
walking along by her side without any one saying anything to him. Thus
he went back with her to her home, and there he remained for three
days, longing to run home and get something to eat, but unfortunately
not knowing the way. By that time Sun had hardly a breath left in him
and his friends, fearing that he was going to die, sent to beg of the rich
trader that he would allow a search to be made for Sun's spirit in his
house. The trader laughed and said, 'He wasn't in the habit of coming
here, so he could hardly have left his spirit behind him', but he yielded
to the entreaties of Sun's family and permitted the search to be made.
Thereupon a magician proceeded to the house, taking with him an old
suit of Sun's clothes and some grass matting.

When Miss A-pao heard the reason for which he had come, she sim-
plified matters very much by leading the magician straight to her own
room. The magician summoned the spirit in due form and went back

* This was a common custom. In the case of an ill child, its mother would go
outside, into a garden or a field, and call out the child's name several times. The
belief was that the departing spirit would cease its wandering and return to the
body.

towards Sun's house. By the time he had reached the door Sun groaned and recovered consciousness. He was then able to describe all the articles of toilette and furniture in A-pao's room without making a single mistake. A-pao was amazed when the story was repeated to her and could not help feeling kindly towards him on account of the depth of his passion. Sun himself, when he got well enough to leave his bed, would often sit in a state of abstraction as if he had lost his wits; and he was for ever scheming to try and have another glimpse at A-pao.

One day he heard that she intended to worship at the Shui-yueh temple on the eighth of the fourth moon, that day being the Wash-Buddha festival, and he set off early in the morning to wait for her at the roadside. He was nearly blind with straining his eyes and the sun was already past noontide before the young lady arrived. But when she saw from her carriage a gentleman standing there, she drew aside the screen and had a good stare at him. Sun followed her in a great state of excite-ment, upon which she bade one of her maids to go and ask his name. Sun told her who he was, his perturbation all the time increasing, and when the carriage drove on he returned home. Again he became very ill, and lay on his bed unconscious, without taking any food, occasionally calling on A-pao by name, at the same time abusing his spirit for not having been able to follow her as before.

Just at this juncture a parrot that had been long with the family died, and a child, playing with the body, laid it upon the bed. Sun then reflected that if he was only a parrot one flap of his wings would bring him into the presence of A-pao; and while occupied with these thoughts, lo! the dead body moved and the parrot flew away. It flew straight to A-pao's room, at which she was delighted; and catching it, tied a string to its leg, and fed it upon hemp seed. 'Dear sister,' cried the bird, 'do not tie me by the leg: I am Sun Tzu-ch'u.' In great alarm A-pao untied the string, but the parrot did not fly away. 'Alas!' said she, 'your love has engraved itself upon my heart; but now you are no longer a man, how shall we ever be united together?' 'To be near your dear self,' replied the parrot, 'is all I care about.' The parrot then refused to take food from any one else, and kept close to Miss A-pao wherever she went, day and night alike.

At the expiration of three days, A-pao, who had grown very fond of her parrot, secretly sent some one to ask how Mr Sun was; but he had already been dead three days, though the part over his heart had not grown cold.

'Oh! come to life again as a man,' cried the young lady, 'and I swear to be yours for ever.'

'You are surely not in earnest,' said the parrot, 'are you?'

Miss A-pao declared she was, and the parrot, cocking its head aside, remained some time as if absorbed in thought. By and by A-pao took off her shoes to bind her feet a little tighter* and the parrot, making a rapid grab at one, flew off with it in its beak.

She called loudly after it to come back, but in a moment it was out of sight. She next sent a servant to inquire if there was any news of Mr Sun and then learned that he had come round again, the parrot having flown in with an embroidered shoe and dropped down dead on the ground. Also, that directly he regained consciousness he asked for the shoe, of which his people knew nothing; at which moment her servant had arrived and demanded to know from him where it was. 'It was given to me by Miss A-pao as a pledge of faith,' replied Sun; 'I beg you will tell her I have not forgotten her promise.'

A-pao was greatly astonished at this and instructed her maid to divulge the whole affair to her mother, who, when she made some inquiries, observed that Sun was well known as a clever fellow but was desperately poor, 'and to get such a son-in-law after all our trouble would give our aristocratic friends a laugh against us.' However, A-pao pleaded that with the shoe there as a proof against her, she would not marry anybody else. Ultimately, her father and mother gave their consent. This was immediately announced to Mr Sun, whose illness rapidly disappeared in consequence.

A-pao's father would have had Sun come and live with them but the young lady objected on the score that a son-in-law should not remain long at a time with the family of his wife, and that as he was poor he would lower himself still more by doing so. 'I have accepted him,' added she, 'and I shall gladly reside in his humble cottage, and share his poor fare without complaint.'

The marriage was then celebrated and bride and bridegroom met as if for the first time in their lives.† The dowry A-pao brought with her somewhat raised their pecuniary position and gave them a certain amount of comfort, but Sun himself stuck only to his books and knew nothing about managing affairs in general. Luckily his wife was clever in that respect and did not bother him with such things; so much so that by the end of three years they were comparatively well off, when Sun suddenly fell ill and died. Mrs Sun was inconsolable and refused either

---

* The rewinding of bandages was necessary at numerous times during the day and night – otherwise, reports tell us, 'the gait of the walker became unsteady'.
† Herbert Giles advises us that couples were not supposed to see each other before the wedding (though in most cases the intended manage to purloin a peep). This was only true of the upper classes. Among the poor, both sexes mixed as freely as in the West.

to sleep or take nourishment, being deaf to all entreaties on the subject, and before long, taking advantage of the night, she hanged herself.* Her maid, hearing a noise, ran in and cut her down just in time: but she still steadily refused all food.

Three days passed away, and the friends and relatives of Sun came to attend his funeral when suddenly they heard a sigh proceeding forth from the coffin. The coffin was then opened and they found that Sun had come to life again. He told them that he had been before the Great Judge, who, as a reward for his upright and honourable life, had conferred upon him an official appointment. 'At this moment,' said Sun, 'it was reported that my wife was close at hand. But the Judge, referring to the register, observed that her time had not yet come. They told him she had taken no food for three days. Then the Judge, looking at me, said that as a recompense for her wifely virtues she should be permitted to return to life. Thereupon he gave orders to his attendants to put to the horses and see us safely back.'

From that hour Sun gradually improved and the next year went up for his master's degree. All his old companions chaffed him exceedingly before the examination and gave him seven themes on out-of-the-way subjects, telling him privately that they had been surreptitiously obtained from the examiners. Sun believed them as usual and worked at them day and night until he was perfect, his comrades all the time enjoying a good laugh against him. However, when the day came it was found that the examiners, fearing lest the themes they had chosen in an ordinary way should have been dishonestly made public, took a set of fresh ones quite out of the common run – in fact, on the very subjects Sun's companions had given to him. Consequently, he came out at the head of the list. And the next year, after taking his doctor's degree, he was entered among the Han-lin Academicians. The Emperor, too, happening to hear of his curious adventures, sent for him and made him repeat his story – subsequently summoning A-pao and making her some very costly presents.

P'u Sung-ling (Ch'ing Dynasty)

* At the turn of the century this was still considered a creditable act on the part of a Chinese widow.

The Marriage Lottery

A certain labourer, named Ma T'ien-jung, lost his wife when he was only about twenty years of age and was too poor to take another. One day when out hoeing in the fields, he beheld a nice-looking young lady leave the path and come tripping across the furrows towards him. Her face was well painted,* and she had altogether such a refined look that Ma concluded she must have lost her way, and he began to make some playful remarks in consequence.

'You go along home,' cried the young lady, 'and I'll be with you by and by.' Ma doubted this rather extraordinary promise, but she vowed and declared she would not break her word. Ma went off, telling her that his front door faced the north and giving her careful directions.

At midnight the young lady arrived and then Ma saw that her hands and face were covered with fine hair, which made him suspect at once she was a fox. She did not deny the accusation and accordingly Ma said to her, 'If you really are one of those wonderful creatures you will be able to get me anything I want. I should be much obliged if you would begin by giving me some money to relieve my poverty.' The young lady said she would and next evening, when she came again, Ma asked her where the money was. 'Dear me!' replied she, 'I quite forgot it.' When she was going away, Ma reminded her of what he wanted, but on the following evening she made precisely the same excuse, promising to bring it another day.

A few nights afterwards Ma asked her once more for the money, and then she drew from her sleeve two pieces of silver, each weighing about five or six ounces. They were both of fine quality, with turned-up edges, and Ma was very pleased and stored them away in a cupboard. Some months after this, he happened to require some money for use and took out these pieces, but the person to whom he showed them said they were

* Only slave girls, women of the poorer classes and old women did not paint their faces.

only pewter, and easily bit off a portion of one of them with his teeth. Ma was much alarmed, and put the pieces away directly, taking the opportunity when evening came of abusing the young lady roundly. 'It's all your bad luck,' retorted she, 'real gold would be too much for your inferior destiny.'* There was an end of that, but Ma went on to say, 'I always heard that fox-girls were of surpassing beauty; how is it you are not?'

'Oh,' replied the young lady, 'we always adapt ourselves to our company. Now you haven't the luck of an ounce of silver to call your own, and what would you do, for instance, with a beautiful princess? My beauty may not be good enough for the aristocracy, but among your big-footed, bent-backed rustics, why it may safely be called "surpassing".'

A few months passed away and then one day the young lady came and gave Ma three ounces of silver, saying, 'You have often asked me for money but in consequence of your weak luck I have always refrained from giving you any. Now, however, your marriage is at hand and I here give you the cost of a wife, which you may also regard as a parting gift from me.'

Ma replied that he wasn't engaged, to which the young lady answered that in a few days a go-between would visit him to arrange the affair. 'And what will she be like?' asked Ma.

'Why, as your aspirations are for "surpassing" beauty,' replied the young lady, 'of course she will be possessed of surpassing beauty.'

'I hardly expect that,' said Ma. 'At any rate, three ounces of silver will not be enough to get a wife.'

'Marriages,' explained the young lady, 'are made in the moon; mortals have nothing to do with them.'

'And why must you be going away like this?' inquired Ma.

'Because,' answered she, 'for us to meet only by night is not the proper thing. I had better get you another wife and have done with you.' Then when morning came, she departed, giving Ma a pinch of yellow powder, saying, 'In case you are ill after we are separated, this will cure you.'

Next day, sure enough, a go-between did come and Ma at once asked what the proposed bride was like, to which the former replied that she was very passable-looking. Four or five ounces of silver was fixed as the marriage present, Ma making no difficulty on that score, but declaring

* Giles describes this curious phase of Chinese superstition as 'each individual is so constituted by nature as to be able to absorb only a given quantity of good fortune and no more, any superfluity of luck doing actual harm to the person on whom it falls'.

he must have a peep at the young lady. The go-between said she was a respectable girl and would never allow herself to be seen. However, it was arranged that they should go to the house together and await a good opportunity. So off they went, Ma remaining outside while the go-between went in, returning in a little while to tell him it was all right. 'A relative of mine lives in the same court, and just now I saw the young lady sitting in the hall. We have only got to pretend we are going to see my relative and you will be able to get a glimpse of her.'

Ma consented and they accordingly passed through the hall, where he saw the young lady sitting down with her head bent forward while some one was scratching her back. She seemed to be all that the go-between had said. But when they came to discuss the money it appeared the young lady only wanted one or two ounces of silver, just to buy herself a few clothes, which Ma thought was a very small amount. He gave the go-between a present for her trouble, which just finished up the three ounces his fox-friend had provided.

An auspicious day was chosen and the young lady came over to his house. But, lo! she was humpbacked and pigeon-breasted, with a short neck like a tortoise, and regular beetle-crushers, full ten inches long. The meaning of his fox-friend's remarks about the yellow powder then flashed upon him.

P'u Sung-ling (Ch'ing Dynasty)
From *Liao Chai Chih I*

5 Taoist Tales and Other Realms

A Taoist Priest Gives a Feast

Once upon a time there was a Mr Han, who belonged to a wealthy family and was fond of entertaining people. A man named Hsu, of the same town, frequently joined him over the bottle. On one occasion when they were together, a Taoist priest came to the door with his alms-bowl in his hand. The servants threw him some money and food, but the priest would not accept them, neither would he go away. Annoyed, the servants went inside and would take no more notice of him. Mr Han heard the noise of the priest knocking his bowl* going on for a long time and asked his servants what was the matter. They had hardly told him when the priest himself walked in.

Mr Han begged him to be seated, whereupon the priest bowed to both gentlemen and took his seat. On making the usual inquiries they found that he lived at an old tumble-down temple to the east of the town. Mr Han expressed regret at not having heard sooner of his arrival so that he might have shown him the proper hospitality of a resident. The priest said that he had only recently arrived and had no friends in the place, but hearing that Mr Han was a jovial fellow, he had been very anxious to take a glass with him.

Mr Han immediately ordered wine and the priest soon distinguished himself as a hard drinker. Hsu treated him all the time with a certain

---

* Beggars in China called attention to themselves by beating gongs or performing some other annoyance until they received something that satisfied them. Giles reports that some priests varied their performance and would swing dead cats (or any other animal) on the end of a string around and around over their heads until the 'miser' gave in. Beggars were so well organized that they had a guild to which a shopkeeper could pay a fee that would exempt him from visits by beggars in that district.

amount of disrespect in consequence of his shabby appearance while Han made allowances for him as being a traveller. When the priest had drunk over twenty large cups of wine he took his leave, returning subsequently whenever any jollification was going on, no matter whether it was eating or drinking.

Even Han began now to tire a little of him and on one occasion Hsu said to him sardonically, 'Good priest, you seem to like being a guest, why don't you play the host sometimes for a change?'

'Ah,' replied the priest, 'I am much the same as yourself – a mouth carried between a couple of shoulders.' This put Hsu to shame and he had no answer to make, so the priest continued: 'But although that is so, I have been revolving the question with myself for some time, and when we do meet I shall do my best to repay your kindness with a cup of my own poor wine.' When they had finished drinking the priest said he hoped he should have the pleasure of their company the following day at noon.

At the appointed time the two friends went together, not expecting, however, to find anything ready for them. But the priest was waiting for them in the street, and passing through a handsome courtyard, they beheld long suites of elegant apartments stretching away before them. In great astonishment, they remarked to the priest that they had not visited this temple for some time and asked when it had been thus repaired, to which he replied that the work had been only lately completed. They went inside and there was a magnificently decorated apartment, such as would not be found even in the houses of the wealthy. This made them begin to feel more respect for their host. No sooner had they sat down than wine and food were served by a number of boys, all about sixteen years of age, dressed in embroidered coats, with red shoes. The wine and the eatables were delicious and very nicely served. When the dinner was taken away, a course of rare fruits was put on the table, the names of which it would be impossible to mention. They were arranged in dishes of crystal and jade, the brilliancy of which lighted up the surrounding furniture. The goblets in which the wine was poured were of glass,* and more than a foot in circumference.

The priest suddenly cried out, 'Call the Shih sisters.' One of the boys went out and in a few moments two elegant young ladies walked in. The first was tall and slim like a willow wand, the other was short and very young, both being exceedingly pretty girls. Being told to sing while the company were drinking, the younger beat time and sang a song, while the elder accompanied her on the flageolet. They played beautifully, and when the song was over the priest, holding his goblet bottom upwards

* Glass was first manufactured in China in AD 424.

in the air, challenged his guests to follow his example, bidding his servants pour out more wine all round. He then turned to the girls and remarked that they had not danced for a long time, asking if they were still able to do so. A carpet was spread by one of the boys and the two young ladies proceeded to dance, their long robes waving about and perfuming the air around. The dance concluded, they leaned against a painted screen, while the two guests gradually became more and more confused and were at last irrevocably drunk.

The priest took no notice of them, but when he had finished drinking he got up and said, 'Pray, go on with your wine. I am going to rest awhile and will return by and by.'

He moved away and lay down on a splendid couch at the other end of the room. Seeing this, Hsu became very angry and shouted out: 'Priest, you are a rude fellow,' at the same time making towards him with a view of rousing him up.

The priest then ran out and Han and Hsu lay down to sleep, one at each end of the room, on elaborately carved couches covered with beautiful mattresses.

At daybreak when they woke up they found themselves lying in the road. Hsu had his head in a dirty privy, and Han was embracing a stone. Terrified, they looked around. Close by were a couple of rush huts, but everything else was gone.

P'u Sung-ling (Ch'ing Dynasty)
From *Liao Chai Chih I*

A Dream and Its Lesson

In the nineteenth year of the reign of Kai Yuan in the T'ang dynasty, an old Taoist, on his journey to Hantan, arrived at a small inn. Spreading a mat on the *kang*, he unburdened himself of the bag from his shoulder and sat down. A young man by the name of Lu, wearing a short fur jacket and riding a pony, being on his way to tend his farm, also stopped at the inn for a brief rest. He made the acquaintance of the old Taoist and the two chatted pleasantly for some time.

Looking at his own shabby attire, the young man sighed in the middle of the conversation.

'It is a shame,' he complained, 'that a man like me should have no luck in life and be indigent like this.'

'Your face has a good colour, you seem to be well nourished and in excellent health, and you converse pleasantly, why should you sigh and complain of your hard luck?' rejoined the old man.

'I am barely hanging on to life,' was the moody reply, 'and there is practically no happiness to speak of.'

'If such as you are discontented with life,' observed the Taoist, 'with what should one then be satisfied?'

'A man should have the opportunity to render distinguished service to his country and acquire wide renown, either as a general or as a minister of state,' claimed the young man. 'He would then be wined and dined and entertained with music of his choice, his family and relations would become prosperous and influential, and he would be able to spend money freely in his household expenditures. Then and then only may one admit that he is contented. In my case I have devoted my time and energy to learning and I am also proficient in many arts. I believed at one time that I could pass with ease the imperial examinations and receive deservedly high official appointments. Today I am no longer young, and yet I have to toil in the fields from morning to night. If this is not misfortune, then I do not know what is.'

When he had finished his discourse, he was becoming somewhat drowsy and felt like taking a nap. As the innkeeper was then engaged in cooking some millet for his meal, the old Taoist reached for his bag and took from it a pillow which he handed to the young man.

'Put this pillow under your head,' he said, 'it will bring you all that you yearn for – honours, fame, wealth and what not.'

The pillow made of porcelain was hollow and the two ends were open. Lu placed his head on it and soon fell sound asleep.

In his dream he saw that the apertures of the pillow were enlarging to a size that would admit his body, and it was bright inside. Boldly he entered and soon found himself back at home. Before long a marriage was arranged between him and a Miss Tsui of Chingho, a wealthy and beautiful heiress, and from that time on he lived luxuriously, wearing rich and soft furs and going about in handsome equipages.

The following year he obtained the doctorate at the metropolitan examination and was appointed Imperial Compiler. Passing with flying colours the civil service test, he was nominated Magistrate of the Weinan

County, and breveted soon after as Censor, stepping into that post within three years. Rapid promotions followed, for he became Prefect of Tungchou, and was subsequently transferred to Shenchou.

Now Lu was keen on engineering projects and during his stay at Shenchou constructed a canal eighty *li* long, thus facilitating irrigation and transportation in that region. To commemorate this valuable service to the locality, the people erected honorific stone tablets. After occupying the higher post of Intendant of Pienchou, he was further honoured with the appointment of Governor of the Metropolitan District.

At the time the emperor was engaged in conflicts with the nomadic tribes in the north-west. The Khan of the Turfans had attacked and captured two important Chinese cities, killing the Chinese Commanding General Wang. The vast north-western territory being threatened with invasion, His Majesty sought for a capable military leader. The choice fell on Governor Lu, who smashed the barbarian onslaught, killed some seven thousand enemy troops, brought a territory of several thousand square *li* under imperial rule and constructed three big fortified cities as key points in this important strategical area. Thus the empire's frontiers on the north were made invulnerable, and Lu's exploits were engraved on stone to immortalize his name.

On his triumphant return to the capital he was showered with honours and received the appointment of Censor and Vice-Minister of Civil Service. Enjoying now high prestige and becoming an idol of the people, he incurred the jealousy of the Prime Minister, who tried his best by spreading malicious rumours to destroy the national hero. Lu was, as a consequence, demoted to Prefect of Tuanchow, and returned to the capital only after serving in the province for three years.

However, this time he was promoted to be Minister of Finance, later became Imperial Secretary, and, together with two others, was in control of state affairs for a period of ten years. He was consulted as often as three times a day by His Majesty on imperial problems, and his ripe experience and profound grasp of statecraft earned for him the reputation of being a very wise premier.

Once more his colleagues intrigued and plotted against him, accusing him of maintaining secret and improper relations with frontier military officers with a view to high treason. He was condemned to imprisonment. The police came to his house to arrest him. He was so frightened at the thought of the death penalty that he confessed his innermost thoughts to his wife.

'My family came originally from Shantung,' he said, 'we owned several hundred *mou* of fertile land, which was sufficient to feed and clothe us comfortably. Why did I then foolishly seek for official honours, only to arrive at such a pass? At this moment, it is not even possible for me to wear my short fur jacket and, mounting my pony, gallop gaily on the road to Hantan.'

He took a knife to commit suicide by cutting his throat but was prevented from killing himself by his wife. In the end, while all his fellow accused were beheaded, he was spared his life through friendly intervention, and later appointed Magistrate of Huan.

A few years afterwards His Majesty, realizing that Lu had been a victim of injustice, recalled him to the capital and restored him to the post of Imperial Secretary, besides ennobling him as the Duke of Chao. Once more he basked in imperial favour and was the envy of all official-dom. All his five sons held fat posts under the government, while his relatives by marriage belonged all to illustrious families of the empire. He was, moreover, the proud grandfather of more than a dozen boys.

Twice during his career he was banished to the provinces and twice he returned to power. He was a prominent figure in and out of the capital and he played a preponderating role around the throne. For thirty years he enjoyed to the full both renown and authority, and no other minister of state could boast of such a brilliant career.

In his later years he indulged freely in luxury and extravagance, and spent much time in his harem. The emperor bestowed on him huge estates and mansions, as well as beautiful women and noble horses. As he aged, he prayed to the emperor to be relieved of his important posts, but met only with refusals. Finally, he fell desperately ill. Medicines came to him from the imperial pharmacy. Noted physicians ministered to him. Visitors to his palace to inquire after his health arrived in a veritable procession. On his deathbed he prepared his last memorial to the throne.

'Your liege servant,' he modestly stated, 'started out in life as a humble scholar of Shantung, who occupied himself with farming and gardening, but through imperial patronage was enabled to enter the government service. He was promoted beyond his deserts and has received many honours and awards from the throne. Proceeding to the frontiers on a military mission, he was escorted by a forest of banners, and serving in the capital he was permitted to stand close to the Imperial Presence, thus basking in the imperial sunshine without making appreciable contribution to the Sacred Rule. Nevertheless, your servant battled on horseback not unsuccessfully against the barbarian invader, proceeding in his strategy with a prudence as if he were walking on thin ice over deep waters.

'One day thus followed another without your liege's noticing the rapid approach of old age: today he is over eighty, having attained one of the three highest posts in the government. The sands of his life are fast running out, and his old bones and shrivelled muscles can no longer stand the strain of work. He is confined to his bed breathing his last, feeling that he has reached the end of his efforts. Unable to repay any further his indebtedness to His Gracious Majesty, he craves on his knees to bid eternal and loving farewell to his Imperial Master and Sovereign.'

His Majesty the Emperor deigned to grant a gracious rescript:

'You have with your eminent talent and virtues nobly supported us in the government of the empire. Out on the distant frontiers you played the part of an impregnable rampart, while in the capital you contributed your invaluable counsel for promoting the peace and prosperity of the land. The well-being and security of the empire during a period of more than a score of years have been due to your wise statesmanship. When we heard of your illness, we had hoped that you would soon recover, but now we learn to our profound sorrow of its gravity. We are sending Field Marshal Kao to pay you a visit and inquire after your condition. We trust that for our sake you will continue to take good care of yourself, follow faithfully the advice of the physicians, and while placing no reliance on false hopes, await patiently a happy issue to the present struggle.'

That night the illustrious statesman died.

Now our young man Lu gave a yawn and awoke, finding himself lying in the inn. The old Taoist was sitting by his side, the millet which the innkeeper was cooking over the fire was not quite ready, and everything else in the room remained the same as before. He jumped up with a start.

'Was all this merely a dream?' he asked.

'All human affairs are like this,' replied the old man with a laugh.

For a long while the young man cogitated. Finally he spoke to the old Taoist.

'I thank you, sir, for the wonderful experience,' he said slowly. 'I fully grasp the meaning now of the cycle of honour and disgrace, of the principle of seeming loss and gain, and of life and death. You have taught me an invaluable lesson as regards personal ambitions, and I remain always your grateful and obedient pupil.'

He bowed profoundly and went to tend his farm.

Li Mi (T'ang Dynasty)

The Taoist Priest of Lao-shan

There lived in our village a Mr Wang, the seventh son in an old family. This gentleman had a *penchant* for the Taoist religion, and hearing that at Lao-Shan there were plenty of Immortals,* shouldered his knapsack and went off for a tour thither. Ascending a peak of the mountain, he reached a secluded monastery, where he found a priest sitting on a rush mat, with long hair flowing over his neck and a pleasant expression on his face. Making a low bow, Wang addressed him thus: 'Mysterious indeed is the doctrine: I pray you, sir, instruct me therein.'

'Delicately nurtured and wanting in energy as you are,' replied the priest, 'I fear you could not support the fatigue.'

'Try me,' said Wang.

So when the disciples, who were very many in number, collected together at dusk, Wang joined them in making obeisance to the priest and remained with them in the monastery.

Very early next morning, the priest summoned Wang, and giving him a hatchet, sent him out with the others to cut firewood. Wang respectfully obeyed, continuing to work for over a month until his hands and feet were so swollen and blistered that he secretly meditated returning home. One evening when he came back he found two strangers sitting drinking with his master. It being already dark and no lamp or candles having been brought in, the bold priest took some scissors and cut out a circular piece of paper like a mirror, which he proceeded to stick against the wall. Immediately it became a dazzling moon, by the light of which you could have seen a hair or a beard of corn.

The disciples all came crowding around to wait upon them, but one of the strangers said, 'On a festive occasion like this we ought all to enjoy ourselves together.' Accordingly he took a kettle of wine from the

* Taoist priests were believed to possess the elixir of immortality. Immortality in a happy land was held out as the highest, priestly example. This could be achieved by strict adherence to the doctrines of the Tao.

table and presented it to the disciples, bidding them drink each his fill. Our friend Wang began to wonder how seven or eight of them could all be served out of a single kettle. The disciples, too, rushed about in search of cups, each struggling to get the first drink for fear the wine should be exhausted. Nevertheless, all the candidates failed to empty the kettle, at which they were very much astonished.

Suddenly one of the strangers said, 'You have given us a fine bright moon but it's dull work drinking by ourselves. Why not call Ch'ang-ngo* to join us?' He then seized a chopstick and threw it into the moon, whereupon a lovely girl stepped forth from its beams. At first she was only a foot high but on reaching the ground lengthened to the ordinary size of woman. She had a slender waist and a beautiful neck, and went most gracefully through the Red Garment figure.† When this was finished she sang the following words:

Ye fairies; ye fairies! I'm coming back soon,
Too lonely and cold is my home in the moon.

Her voice was clear and well sustained, ringing like the notes of a flageolet, and when she had concluded her song she pirouetted round and jumped up on the table, where, with every eye fixed in astonishment upon her, she once more became a chopstick.

The three friends laughed loudly, and one of them said, 'We are very jolly tonight, but I have hardly room for any more wine. Will you drink a parting glass with me in the palace of the moon?' They then took up the table and walked into the moon, where they could be seen drinking so plainly that their eyebrows and beards appeared like reflections in a looking-glass. By and by, the moon became obscured, and when the disciples brought a lighted candle they found the priest sitting in the dark alone. The viands, however, were still upon the table and the mirrorlike piece of paper on the wall.

'Have you all had enough to drink?' asked the priest. They answered that they had. 'In that case,' said he, 'you had better get to bed, so as not to be behind-hand with your wood-cutting in the morning.' So they all went off, and among them Wang, who was delighted at what he had seen, and thought no more of returning home.

But after a time he could not stand it any longer, and as the priest taught him no magical arts he determined not to wait, but went to him and said: 'Sir, I travelled many long miles for the benefit of your instruction. If you will not teach me the secret of Immortality, let me at

* The beautiful wife of a legendary chieftain who flourished about 2500 BC.
† A famous dance of antiquity.

any rate learn some trifling trick and thus soothe my cravings for a knowledge of your art. I have now been here two or three months, doing nothing but chop firewood, out in the morning and back at night, work to which I was never accustomed in my own home.'

'Did I not tell you,' replied the priest, 'that you would never support the fatigue? Tomorrow I will start you on your way home.'

'Sir,' said Wang, 'I have worked for you a long time. Teach me some small art, that my coming here may not have been wholly in vain.'

'What art?' asked the priest.

'Well,' answered Wang, 'I have noticed that whenever you walk about anywhere, walls and so on are no obstacle to you. Teach me this, and I'll be satisfied.'

The priest laughingly assented and taught Wang a formula which he bade him recite. When he had done so he told him to walk through the wall. But Wang, seeing the wall in front of him, didn't like to walk at it. As, however, the priest bade him try, he walked quietly up to it and was there stopped. The priest here called out, 'Don't go so slowly. Put your head down and rush at it.' So Wang stepped back a few paces and went at it full speed, the wall yielding to him as he passed. In a moment he found himself outside. Delighted at this, he went in to thank the priest, who told him to be careful in the use of his power or otherwise there would be no response, handing him at the same time some money for his expenses on the way.

When Wang got home he went about bragging of his Taoist friends and his contempt for walls in general. But as his wife disbelieved his story, he set about going through the performance as before. Stepping back from the wall, he rushed at it full speed with his head down, but coming in contact with the hard bricks, he finished up in a heap on the floor. His wife picked him up and found he had a bump on his forehead as big as a large egg, at which she roared with laughter. Wang was over-whelmed with rage and shame and cursed the old priest for his base ingratitude.

P'u Sung-ling (Ch'ing Dynasty)

The Gambler's Talisman

A Taoist priest called Han lived at the T'en-ch'i temple, in our district city. His knowledge of the black art was very extensive and the neighbours all regarded him as an Immortal. My late father was on intimate terms with him, and whenever he went into the city invariably paid the priest a visit.

One day, on such an occasion, he was proceeding thither in company with my late uncle when suddenly they met Han on the road. Handing them the key of the door, he begged them to go on and wait awhile for him, promising to be there shortly himself. Following these instructions they repaired to the temple, but on unlocking the door there was Han sitting inside – a feat which he subsequently performed several times.

Now a relative of mine, who was terribly given to gambling, also knew this priest, having been introduced to him by my father. And once this relative, meeting with a Buddhist priest from the T'ien-fo temple, addicted like himself to the vice of gambling, played with him until he had lost everything, even going so far as to pledge the whole of his property, which he lost in a single night. Happening to call in upon Han as he was going back, the latter noticed his exceedingly dejected appearance, the rambling answers he gave and asked him what was the matter. On hearing the story of his losses, Han only laughed and said, 'That's what always overtakes the gambler, sooner or later. If, however, you will break yourself of the habit, I will get your money back for you.'

'Ah,' cried the other, 'if I can only win back my money, you may break the dice with an iron pestle when you catch me gambling again.' So Han gave him a talismanic formula, written out on a piece of paper, to put in his girdle, bidding him only win back what he had lost, and not attempt to get a fraction more. He also handed him 1000 *cash* on condition that this sum should be repaid from his winnings, and off went my relative, delighted.

The Buddhist, however, turned up his nose at the smallness of his means and said it wasn't worth his while to stake so little – but at last he was persuaded into having one throw for the whole lot. They then began, the priest leading off with a fair throw, to which his opponent replied by a better. The priest doubled his stake, and my relative won again, going on and on until the latter's good luck had brought him back all that he had previously lost. He thought, however, that he couldn't do better than just win a few more strings of cash, and accordingly went on.

But gradually his luck turned, and on looking into his girdle he found that the talisman was gone. In a great fright he jumped up and went off with his winnings to the temple. He reckoned up that after deducting Han's loan and adding what he had lost towards the end, he had exactly the amount originally his. With shame in his face he turned to thank Han, mentioning at the same time the loss of the talisman. Han only laughed and said, 'That has got back before you. I told you not to be over-greedy, and as you didn't heed me, I took the talisman away.' *

P'u Sung-ling (Ch'ing Dynasty)

Planting a Pear Tree

A countryman was one day selling his pears in the market. They were unusually sweet and fine flavoured, and the price he asked was high. A Taoist priest in rags and tatters stopped at the barrow and begged one of them. The countryman told him to go away, but as he did not do so he began to curse and swear at him. The priest said, 'You have several hundred pears on your barrow; I ask for a single one, the loss of which, sir, you would not feel. Why then get angry?'

The lookers-on told the countryman to give him an inferior one and let him go, but this he obstinately refused to do. Thereupon the beadle of the place, finding the commotion too great, purchased a pear and handed it to the priest. The latter received it with a bow and turning to

* Giles believes that gambling is the 'great Chinese vice, far exceeding in its ill effects all that opium has ever done to demoralize the country'.

the crowd said, 'We who have left our homes and given up all that is dear to us are at a loss to understand selfish niggardly conduct in others. Now I have some exquisite pears which I shall do myself the honour to put before you.'

Here somebody asked: 'Since you have pears yourself, why don't you eat those?'

'Because,' replied the priest, 'I wanted one of these pips to grow them from.' So saying, he munched up the pear. When he had finished, he took a pip in his hand, unstrapped a pick from his back, and proceeded to make a hole in the ground, several inches deep, wherein he deposited the pip, filling in the earth as before. He then asked the bystanders for a little hot water to water it with, and one among them who loved a joke fetched him some boiling water from a neighbouring shop. The priest poured this over the place where he had made the hole, and every eye was fixed upon him when sprouts were seen shooting up and gradually growing larger and larger. By and by, there was a tree with branches sparsely covered with leaves, then flowers, and last of all fine, large, sweet-smelling pears hanging in great profusion. These the priest picked and handed round to the assembled crowd until all were gone, when he took his pick and hacked away for a long time at the tree, finally cutting it down. This he shouldered, leaves and all, and sauntered quietly away.

Now, from the very beginning, our friend the countryman had been amongst the crowd, straining his neck to see what was going on, and forgetting all about his business. At the departure of the priest he turned round and discovered that every one of his pears was gone. He then knew that those the old fellow had been giving away so freely were really his own pears. Looking more closely at the barrow, he also found that one of the handles was missing, evidently having been newly cut off. Boiling with rage, he set out in pursuit of the priest, and just as he turned the corner he saw the lost barrow-handle lying under the wall, being in fact the very pear tree that the priest had cut down. But there were no traces of the priest, much to the amusement of the crowd in the market-place.

P'u Sung-ling (Ch'ing Dynasty)
From *Liao Chai Chih I*

The Painted Skin

At T'ai-yuan there lived a man named Wang. One morning he was out walking when he met a young lady carrying a bundle and hurrying along by herself. As she moved along with some difficulty,* Wang quickened his pace and caught her up, and found she was a pretty girl of about sixteen. Much smitten, he inquired whither she was going so early, and no one with her.

'A traveller like you,' replied the girl, 'cannot alleviate my distress. Why trouble yourself to ask?'

'What distress is it?' said Wang. 'I'm sure I'll do anything I can for you.'

'My parents,' answered she, 'loved money and they sold me as concubine into a rich family. The wife was very jealous, and beat and abused me morning and night. It was more than I could stand, so I have run away.'

Wang asked her where she was going, to which she replied that a runaway had no fixed place of abode. 'My house,' said Wang, 'is at no great distance. What do you say to coming there?' She joyfully acquiesced and Wang, taking up her bundle, led the way to his house.

Finding no one there, she asked Wang where his family were, to which he replied that that was only the library. 'And a very nice place, too,' said she, 'but if you are kind enough to wish to save my life, you mustn't let it be known that I am here.' Wang promised he would not divulge her secret, and so she remained there for some days without any one knowing anything about it. He then told his wife and she, fearing the girl might belong to some influential family, advised him to send her away. This, however, he would not consent to do.

Going into the town one day he met a Taoist priest, who looked at him in astonishment and asked him what he had met. 'I have met nothing,' replied Wang.

* This was, of course, because of the pain and difficulty involved in walking any distance with bound feet.

'Why,' said the priest, 'you are bewitched. What do you mean you have met nothing?' But Wang insisted that it was so, and the priest walked away, saying: 'The fool! Some people don't seem to know when death is at hand.'

This startled Wang, who at first thought of the girl. But then he reflected that a pretty young thing as she was couldn't well be a witch, and he began to suspect that the priest merely wanted to do a stroke of business.

When he returned the library door was shut and he couldn't get in, which made him suspect that something was wrong. He then climbed over the wall, where he found the door of the inner room shut too. Softly creeping up, he looked through the window and saw a hideous devil, with a green face and jagged teeth like a saw, spreading a human skin upon the bed and painting it with a paint-brush. The devil then threw aside the brush and giving the skin a shake out, just as you would a coat, threw it over its shoulders, when lo! it was the girl. Terrified at this, Wang hurried away with his head down in search of the priest, who had gone he knew not whither. Subsequently finding him in the fields, he threw himself on his knees and begged the priest to save him.

'As to driving her away,' said the priest, 'the creature must be in great distress to be seeking a substitute for herself;* besides, I could hardly endure to injure a living thing.' However, he gave Wang a fly-brush and bade him hang it at the door of the bedroom, agreeing to meet again at the Ch'ing-ti temple.

Wang went home, but did not dare enter the library, so he hung up the brush at the bedroom door, and before long heard a sound of footsteps outside. Not daring to move, he made his wife peep out. She saw the girl standing looking at the brush, afraid to pass it. She then ground her teeth and went away; but in a little while came back and began cursing, saying: 'You priest, you won't frighten me. Do you think I am going to give up what is already in my grasp?' Thereupon she tore the brush to pieces and bursting open the door, walked straight up to the bed, where she ripped open Wang and tore out his heart, with which she went away.

---

* A curious Chinese belief is that disembodied spirits from the underworld are permitted, under certain conditions of good conduct and proper time, to absorb the vitality of mortals. The mortal, thus destroyed in his human shell, exchanges places with the 'devil'. The devil does not, however, reappear on this plane of existence, as in cases of possession in the West, but is merely allowed rebirth by the virtue of his new-found vitality. This comes about because of the Chinese belief that there is only so much life energy available. It is a constant quality and cannot be diminished or enhanced – the devil, therefore, has to make do with the particular level of vitality he has come upon.

Wang's wife screamed out and the servants came in with a light – but Wang was already dead and presented a most miserable spectacle. His wife, who was in an agony of fright, hardly dared cry for fear of making a noise. The next day she sent Wang's brother to see the priest. The latter got into a great rage and cried out, 'Was it for this that I had compassion on you, devil that you are?', proceeding at once with Wang's brother to the house, from which the girl had disappeared without any one knowing whither she had gone. But the priest, raising his head, looked all round, and said, 'Luckily she's not far off.'

He then asked who lived in the apartments on the south side, to which Wang's brother replied that he did, whereupon the priest declared that there she would be found. Wang's brother was horribly frightened and said he did not think so. Then the priest asked him if any stranger had been to the house. To this he answered that he had been out to the Ch'ing-ti temple and couldn't possibly say: but he went off to inquire, and in a little while came back and reported that an old woman had sought service with them as a maid-of-all-work and had been engaged by his wife.

'That is she,' said the priest, as Wang's brother added she was still there, and they all set out to go to the house together. Then the priest took his wooden sword, and standing in the middle of the courtyard, shouted out, 'Base-born fiend, give me back my fly-brush!'

Meanwhile the new maid-of-all-work was in a great state of alarm and tried to get away by the door. But the priest struck her and down she fell flat, the human skin dropped off, and she became a hideous devil. There she lay grunting like a pig until the priest grasped his wooden sword and struck off her head. She then became a dense column of smoke curling up from the ground, when the priest took an uncorked gourd and threw it right into the midst of the smoke. A sucking noise was heard and the whole column was drawn into the gourd; after which the priest corked it up closely and put it in his pouch. The skin, too, which was complete even to the eyebrows, eyes, hands, and feet, he also rolled up as if it had been a scroll and was on the point of leaving with it when Wang's wife stopped him, and with tears entreated him to bring her husband to life. The priest said he was unable to do that. But Wang's wife flung herself at his feet and with loud lamentations implored his assistance. For some time he remained immersed in thought and then replied, 'My power is not equal to what you ask. I myself cannot raise the dead; but I will direct you to someone who can, and if you apply to him properly you will succeed.' Wang's wife asked the priest who it was, to which he replied, 'There is a maniac in the town who passes his time grovelling in the dirt. Go, prostrate yourself before him, and beg him to help you. If he insults you, show no sign of anger.' Wang's brother knew the man to whom he alluded, and accordingly bade the priest adieu, then proceeded thither with his sister-in-law.

They found the destitute creature raving away by the roadside, so filthy that it was all they could do to go near him. Wang's wife approached him on her knees. The maniac leered at her and cried out, 'Do you love me, my beauty?'

Wang's wife told him what she had come for, but he only laughed and said, 'You can get plenty of other husbands. Why raise the dead one to life?' But Wang's wife entreated him to help her, whereupon he observed. 'It's very strange: people apply to me to raise their dead as if I was king of the infernal regions.' He then gave Wang's wife a thrashing with his staff, which she bore without a murmur before a gradually increasing crowd of spectators. After this he produced a loathsome pill which he told her she must swallow, but here she broke down and was quite unable to do so. However, she did manage it at last, and then the maniac crying out, 'How you do love me!' got up and went away without taking any more notice of her. They followed him into a temple with loud supplications but he had disappeared, and every effort to find him was unsuccessful. Overcome with rage and shame, Wang's wife went home where she mourned bitterly over her dead husband, grievously repenting the steps she had taken and wishing only to die. She then bethought herself of preparing the corpse, near which none of the servants would venture, and set to work to close up the frightful wound of which he died.

While thus employed, interrupted from time to time by her sobs, she felt a rising lump in her throat, which by and by came out with a pop and fell straight into the dead man's wound. Looking closely at it, she saw it was a human heart. It then began to throb, emitting a warm, vapour-like smoke. Much excited, she at once closed the flesh over it and held the sides of the wound together with all her might. Very soon, however, she got tired, and finding the vapour escaping from the crevices, she tore up a piece of silk and bound it round, at the same time bringing back circulation by rubbing the body and covering it with clothes. In the night she removed the coverings and found that breath was coming from the nose. By next morning her husband was alive again, though disturbed in mind as if awaking from a dream and feeling a pain in his heart. Where he had been wounded, there was a cicatrix about as big as a cash, which soon after disappeared.

P'u Sung-ling (Ch'ing Dynasty)

A Visit to Inferno

CHAPTER 1

THE HOLIDAY

There was a scholar living in Cheung Chau in the Fukien Province who had gained the degree of Doctor of Literature. His name was Ting Laan Kat, and he also had the name Mung Ling, or the 'dream spirit'.

When he was still a young student, twenty-four years of age, it happened that on the ninth day of the ninth Moon (a day much observed among the Chinese as a great festival), he took the opportunity to ascend a mountain, according to custom. He took with him a bottle of wine for refreshment, and wandered over the hills admiring the scenery.

He was by himself and heard nothing but the movements of the leaves on the pine trees and the other trees of the wood, and the whispering sound of the falling leaves.

He sat down on the top of the hill and poured himself out a few cups of wine which he drank. Suddenly a great gust of wind rushed by, blowing the leaves about on the ground until they whirled about as if boiling, and almost as if they had their own ideas and sense.

Laan Kat said, 'This wind is very delightful and yet it is strange. Surely it cannot be a spirit or demon passing by?' But in case there might be such a thing he at once poured out three cups of wine as a libation. When the wine reached the ground, the wind and the leaves turned about and passed on.

CHAPTER 2

THE JOURNEY TO HADES

In a moment Laan Kat became as if he were drunk, and he slept, and then he appeared to observe a man dressed in a uniform of a bluish-grey colour who came before him and bowed, saying, 'Mr Ting, you really are a good man. Thank you very much for your gift of wine.'

Laan Kat replied, 'Honoured sir, who are you? Why do you speak thus?'

'I am not a man,' Bluecoat said, 'I am a messenger, a sort of police officer or runner from the nether world. I was on my way to a certain city with a dispatch to the God of the City Moat, and I was just passing this place.

'When I was in the world of men I had a great craving for wine, and today, when I suddenly smelt the fragrance of wine, I could not control my feelings, so I stayed near here and, thanks to your great generosity, my vinous throat has been irrigated and moistened. How can I repay such an expression of good will?'

Laan Kat raised his hands to salute the man, and said, 'Honoured sir, you are a responsible officer of the other world, and know all about the conditions of that world. I have heard that there are eighteen grades or stages in Hades or Hell: but I do not know the truth about these stages. I have always wanted to go and examine the place for myself, but there is no road by which one may go, and everything about that world is so mysterious. Could you possibly take me to walk about there and see the conditions?'

'That is as easy as picking up beans, in fact easier,' said Bluecoat, 'because in picking up beans one has to stoop down to pick them up.'

'If you take me there you must bring me back again,' said Laan Kat.

'That is a matter of course. Is it likely that I would take you away to death?' replied Bluecoat.

The Greatest Good and Evil

So they went along together, and after a time they reached a place where it grew darker, and they saw a great many people coming and going, and soon they came to a large palace, and stopped in front of the door.

Bluecoat said, 'You wait here while I go and give my report to the officials. After I have done that, I will take you for a walk to investigate the conditions. But when I go in, if it should happen that there is much business to be attended to, and I cannot come out soon, you need not worry. I shall certainly be able to manage it.'

He then went inside the palace, and Laan Kat waited outside. He saw a pair of scrolls on a large iron plate on which there were ten large characters in words in two antithetical sentences of five words each. One side read, 'Of all evils fornication or adultery is the chief', and on the other, 'Of all good deeds the principal one is filial piety'.

He also saw a great many people passing along. Some were sitting in sedan-chairs, some rode on horseback, some were in carriages, some were in cangues and some free, others were in chains. Some came sauntering along swaying their arms and limbs in an easy style, others again came with heads downcast as if in the depths of despondency.

He observed that some who came out of the palace seemed to be very pleased, as pleased as heaven and earth. Some howled and wept bitterly, some went by wearing long official robes, some had ragged coats and trousers.

Some were clad in cow's hide or skins of horses, and some in skins of dogs or sheep. Everything that was to be seen in the world was also to be seen in appearance in the nether world. One crowd was going, and another multitude was coming.

The mountain of knives, the tree of swords, the sea of bitterness and the lake of blood could be seen in the distance, yet they appeared to be close to the eye.

CHAPTER 3

THE ENTRANCE

After about half an hour, Bluecoat came out and said, 'I know that you have been kept waiting for me a long time. I have been delayed on account of various matters of business.'

Ting Laan Kat said, 'Well, well, there really is a nether world related to the world of men. I have read about this in books for a very long time, but I have been very sceptical about it. This was very wrong of me.'

To this Bluecoat replied, 'Well, people are in the world for less than a hundred years. Those who do good are rewarded by blessing, but the amount of their happiness and peace is limited. Those who do evil meet with calamity, but their bitterness and sorrow is also limited. Therefore, the Creator has ordained that those who are really good should be rewarded with great blessings and dwell in Heaven for thousands of years, and even for ever and ever.'

'As I listen to your conversation,' said Laan Kat, 'it is as if all the channels of my being are opened up. Will you please now take me to see those eighteen grades of Hades?'

Bluecoat led him to a place where the air was so terrible that it made people's hair stand on end. There was a man guarding the gateway, and this man called to Laan Kat and said, 'What have you come here for?'

Bluecoat answered the guard and said, 'He is my friend. I have brought him here to walk about and see the conditions in this place.'

The gatekeeper said, 'Is he a friend of yours? If so, he may go in.' And so they went on into the first stage.

CHAPTER 4

THE FIRST STAGE

As they entered they saw people, with heads of cows and faces of horses, who were as cruel as wolves and were beating the sinful spirits, the ghosts of men.

The sinners here were tied up with hempen cords and the demons who punished them had iron rods like pipe bamboos, about four feet long, with which they beat the sinners from head to foot, and after beating them let them down, and hung up other sinners whom they beat in the same way.

The spirits (ghosts) wept without ceasing, and cried out: 'We dare not offend any more!' 'Do not beat us so much!' 'Please hit with lighter blows!' 'We have had enough!' and such expressions, like children being beaten on the earth.

The cattle-headed Hell police said, 'You have beaten people a great deal, and it is now our turn to beat you. If you were not beaten, you would not know how painful and grievous it is to others to be beaten.'

Some of these sinful spirits were women, most of whom had been cruel to slave girls and concubines.

Many others were police and cruel people who had extorted money from others. Some, too, were masters who had ill-treated their apprentices, and others teachers who had been cruel to their pupils and, not having a heart of love, they had followed their own evil bent and unjustly punished those under them.

'YOUR HONOUR'

The offenders of different types came in turns. Suddenly a culprit was brought in who was wearing an official hat and official boots, and a long robe, and having a string of beads round his neck. He came stepping forward without any sense of fear.

The lictors took off his clothes and removed his hat and boots, but he kept trying to kick the lictors with his big feet. The lictors were afraid and said, 'What is the matter with you? Are you pretending to be mad?'

The prisoner said, 'You are mad; you do not know how to distinguish one person from another. You bold villains – taking off my clothes. Do you want to rob me?'

All the lictors put their hands to their mouths and laughed at him.

'Who do you think I am?' said he. 'I have been a magistrate and have governed the people, and been called a great man (or "Your Honour"). Do you think there is any comparison between you and me, you robbers?'

The lictors said, 'You were an official, but now you are an offender and a criminal.'

'What offence have I committed?' said the official, and the lictors replied, 'A short time ago your case was tried before the King of Hades, and it was said that you oppressed and robbed the people much worse than robbers do. Yet you come here and pretend that you know nothing about it, and that you are silly.'

Eight Hundred Strokes

One of them said, 'Why do you talk to him so much? It is simply a waste of breath, and absolutely useless. The King of Hades has ordered that he be beaten eight hundred strokes, so you must just beat him the full number. Why should there be all this talk about it? If an official has been a bad man, he should be beaten with greater severity. Hang him up.'

Now this official was fat, and his skin was white. He was fleshy but his bones were small. After he had been beaten a few strokes he cried aloud to heaven, and said in a loud voice, 'I will not claim to have been an official. I prefer to confess to being a robber.'

All the lictors broke out into loud laughter, and even women who were hung up near at hand undergoing torture could not refrain from laughing, though it was unintentional.

In this place there was also a very large and spacious shed in which people were hung up here and there. They were not more than five feet apart. One person would be hung up in a part of the shed and as the lictors beat him wildly with the rods, another near at hand would laugh at him.

Some were beaten three hundred strokes, some five hundred, some eight hundred or a thousand, the smallest number was two hundred. Some were men and some women, some old and some young, and as one lot went away another lot came in.

There was an official present marking off their names and punishments in a book, and when they had been beaten he sent them away to report themselves and afterwards they were led to the ruler of Hades, and according to his orders they were released, or changed into animals, or became men again, or they might be detained for further punishment.

CHAPTER 5

THE SECOND STAGE

He was then taken on to see the second stage or grade of Hell, and there he saw hundreds of beds laid crosswise.

Some had thorns laid all over the beds and those who were lying on the beds on their backs had large stones pressing on their chests. The hands and feet of those lying on the beds were also bound, so that they could not get up nor free themselves at all. They were in great pain and groaned day and night without ceasing. Some of them were on separate beds; in some cases two were in one bed, in some cases there were men only, and in other cases women only.

Sometimes there would be one man and one woman, sometimes one man and several women, and occasionally one woman and several men, sometimes there were seven or eight people, and sometimes more than ten or even many tens of people in one bed. The beds were of different sizes and the people of different ages.

Their faces were dry like charcoal and their bones were thin like wooden boards.

Ting Laan Kat asked for an explanation of all these things.

Bluecoat said, 'There are many kinds of sin. It is almost impossible to treat them as of one type. The evil of men proceeds from their evil hearts. It is by the mind that one may increase or reduce his wickedness.

'It may be that in going about during the day when one is busy, one cannot think over these matters very clearly; but at night when lying in bed, when the mind is settled, and the eyes are closed, and one contemplates things that cannot be fully realized, and the feelings that one cannot anticipate, many things strange and wonderful come into the mind, and all kinds of wickedness and villainy also come forth; in fact, most of the evil schemes originate in bed. Then they can be clearly planned, and one may begin cheating in secret, and as they develop the plans they may sleep in peace.

'Yet even in sleep one may think of acts of fornication, and enticing others by one's beauty, and enjoy the pleasure of lust in sleep.

'Joys are found in bed, and grief also comes to one in bed.

'It sometimes happens that a husband and wife, pillow-mates in bed, set one another on to do evil, and unfilial conduct often starts in this way, and dissensions among brethren also commence at such times. As for the others, they each have their own unclean minds and evil plans, so in their case each is on a separate bed. But in cases that are alike and where sins are similar, whether they be many or few, they are all placed together in one bed.'

CHAPTER 6

THE THIRD STAGE

When he had finished speaking, Bluecoat led Laan Kat away to the third stage, and the latter asked him why so many people were hooked at the roots of their tongues, or had their lips cut.

'These are the people who used to take pleasure in talking scandal, or those who cursed people with malicious words,' replied Bluecoat.

Laan Kat asked why some had their eyes gouged out, and the eyes of others were bleeding. To which Bluecoat replied, 'These people were such as had no proper method of distinguishing between honourable and mean conduct, and did not keep good men before their eyes as their examples.'

When asked why some had their arms and legs cut off, and others had fingers chopped off, he replied, 'This class of person used to steal things in secret, or brought false accusations against others; and as to those whose feet were cut off or others whose feet were cut away at the heels, they had practised kidnapping, or had offended by leading others into evil ways.'

Some too who had their breasts cut off or their chests cut open were people who had been braggarts, and compelled others to do wrong.

Others again had their hearts cut out, and their viscera drawn, these had been cheats and deceivers, whose fault had been playing false tricks on others.

There were some who were hooked in the back by weighing hooks, and some of whom the faces had been cut off with knives. These were people who had no backbone, or will to do good, and did not persevere in their work, and who had no sense of shame, that is, did not think about their faces.

Some had their lips moistened with molten brass, and others had filth thrown over their bodies, these were people who had coveted unjust gains, not considering their bad name.

Ting Laan Kat exclaimed, 'Seeing people in this condition arouses one's sense of pity.'

'You think of them with pity,' replied Bluecoat, 'but Im Wong, the king of Hades, thinks that their actions have been hateful, because they had no pity for others.'

CHAPTER 7

THE FOURTH STAGE

Then they went on to see the fourth grade of Hell, and here they saw people being put into a mill, and ground, so that blood and water flowed out of the mortar.

Other people were put into a pit or mortar and pounded, as rice is hulled in such pits, and as they were struck by the great pestle splinters of their flesh flew up.

Laan Kat inquired what sins these people had committed that they should receive such dreadful punishment.

Bluecoat replied, that these were people who had no proper feelings and did not consider their fathers and mothers, and disobedient sons who angered their parents. When Laan Kat asked why those who were unfilial should receive such terrible retribution, Bluecoat replied, 'Filiality is the chief virtue amongst men, and therefore it is clear that unfiliality must be the worst type of bad conduct.'

CHAPTER 8

THE FIFTH STAGE

They passed on further and entered into the next grade. On turning round a corner they saw a number of women naked and exposed, except that they each had a short loin cloth to cover them; all their other articles of clothing and their ornaments and shoes were thrown together in a heap.

Cow-headed lictors caught the women by their hair and pulled them into the middle of a great grindstone.

The mouth of this stone was about eighteen inches wide, large enough for one person to go in.

The women wept and wailed piteously and called out loudly, 'Save life', 'Help'. One of them gripped the base of the grindstone and refused to move, resisting the lictors who were pulling her up to the mouth of the mill. The lictors gave a great pull and placed her head in the mouth of the mill; her feet were pointing to the heavens, and the lictors turned her and pushed her in. Most of the women were treated in this summary manner.

This spectacle was so terrible that the eye could not bear to look on it.

Some of the lictors were forcing the women into the pit of the mortar, the mouth of which was about four feet wide. The women wept bitterly and would not go down, and lay on the ground and howled and kicked. In such cases, one lictor would seize the head and another the feet of the woman, and they carried them down into the pit of the mortar. Their bodies and legs were exposed, and they had only about five inches of cloth about their waists to cover their nakedness.

The great pestle came down on them, and the sound of their groans of pain was lengthened out until it seemed almost continuous; their arms and legs waved about and their flesh and blood were splattered all round the pit.

Laan Kat could not bear the sight; he turned away his face, and left the place asking why the women were treated so cruelly. He said, 'Speaking generally, women are of a meek and gentle disposition, they are not evil nor cruel, and never commit great offences such as murdering people in great ferocity. Why then do they receive such terrible punishment? Truly this is difficult to understand.'

Bluecoat replied saying, 'Well, as to women in the world, every one knows their good points, but people generally do not observe their evil deeds.

'For instance, some women hate their husbands when they take concubines, and they become very jealous. Such women would be willing to make the line of descent cease, and so cut off the sacrifices at the family altar, because there would be no son to carry on the succession unless the man took the concubine; they are angry too when their husbands spend money to support their parents, and purposely browbeat the parents, and give them insufficient food and clothing.

'Besides this, they do not treat the uncles of the family (including the husband's brothers) with proper respect, and are unkindly disposed to them. In this way the near relatives become as if they were distant relatives, and they repay kindness with enmity. In all these ways they help to increase the errors and sins of their husbands, and bring trouble on later generations, finally bringing the family to extinction.

'Women of this kind are not punished by the laws of the land, and it is difficult to control them by the ordinary law of the family or clan. There is only one way of dealing with such women, and bringing them to account, and that is by the pains and penalties of Hades.

'Besides these, there are some women who combine together to lead people on to fornication, and give themselves up to the evil practices of kidnapping and deceit. In what grade or depth of sin should they be classed?'

Bluecoat then led him on to a part of the fifth grade where he saw large numbers of great furnaces, from which fierce flames were belching forth, and there were large boilers over the fires in which there was a quantity of oily soup boiling up, the heat was intense, and yet constantly increased.

They went near to the boiler to see what was going on, and saw numbers of people rising and falling with the bubbling soup. Some were groaning, some weeping, some were sinking, and some rising, their very bones were being rotted away.

Laan Kat asked what class of sinners were subjected to this punishment, and what crimes they had committed to merit such treatment.

'Most of these people were local braves and bullies and villains,' replied Bluecoat; and in reply to the question as to how it was they made such fearful noises, as if they felt the pain and bitterness very intensely, he said, 'When people are in the world they regard the body as the nearest thing and therefore the most real, so they give all their attention to building up physical energy and the repair of blood vessels, and of skin and flesh, and omit entirely the building up of the clear and pure fabric of the spiritual part of their nature.

'Really,' said he, 'it is the spirit that makes men able to eat and drink, and to walk about and run. It is the spirit that makes men able to ascend into the heaven, and to go down into the earth, and to realize sorrow and joy. If their spirit should be lost, then they could not eat nor drink, nor could they go about, and whether the bones change or the whole frame disintegrate, in the end they are quite useless. Even if the whole body should remain they have a mouth but cannot speak; and ears but cannot hear; hands which cannot move; and feet which cannot walk. If you ask them anything they cannot reply, if you strike them they have no feeling and it does not hurt them.'

Ting Laan Kat jumped up and clapped his hands, saying, 'This is a most excellent discourse, and the doctrine is very sound. It is not surprising that you, sir, were a scholar in your former existence. You have exalted my mind, and illuminated my heart. It is like the saying, "To talk with you for half a day is better than studying in a school for ten years getting an ordinary education." I will go home now.'

CHAPTER 9

THE SIXTH GRADE

Bluecoat said, 'But you have not yet seen half of the eighteen grades. Why should you go home so soon? I will take you to see the sixth grade.'

Laan Kat did not wish to go, but Bluecoat seized him firmly by the hand, and went on, and they soon reached the sixth stage.

There they saw a great number of men and women, some of whom were standing on the ground, some sitting on stools, and some lying on beds.

All of them had nails driven into them, some in their heads, some in the feet or hands and some in their bodies, and the conditions and circumstances were quite different from any they had seen before.

As they suddenly turned a corner, Laan Kat saw his sister-in-law; she was sitting on a flat stone and was chained by an iron chain which was fastened to her feet, and a long iron nail was driven into her left breast.

When he saw this he was horrified, and perspiration broke out all over his head. He said, 'Ha! Ha! This is very strange! It is most wonderful! I remember that this very morning when I came out of the door my sister-in-law was still lying in bed, and crying about her pain and suffering. Can it be that she had died suddenly?' and the tears flowed freely down his face.

'Is that your sister-in-law?' said Bluecoat, and Laan Kat replied, 'Yes.'

The keeper of the prison in Hades said, 'Your sister-in-law is not yet dead, this is her living soul.'

Laan Kat asked when she was arrested and her soul dragged here.

The keeper said, 'About three years ago.'

Laan Kat said, 'It is not strange then that my sister-in-law has an abscess on her breast which has not healed for three years. We have used every possible means known to the medical profession, but without any effect. We have worshipped devils and spirits, and the whole house has been upset on her account. How could we tell that the keeper of the nether world had driven this nail into her? It will be very difficult for her to escape this retribution, but really what offence did my sister-in-law commit that she should receive such dreadful punishment?'

'The offence of your sister-in-law,' said the keeper, 'was a cruel deed done in secret. Your elder brother had no son, and so he took a concubine by whom he had a son, and your sister-in-law was afraid that the concubine, being honoured because of this son, might become proud and indolent and overbearing, and that her husband would love her very much, so she went into the concubine's room after the third morning, and finding that there was no one there with the baby, she took an embroidery needle, and stuck it into his navel. The child burst out crying, and the concubine, when she came into him, thought that the trouble must have been caused by injury to the cord when it was cut, and that this injury had caused wind in that region, and so irritation had set in and the child would not eat, but kept on crying continuously, and after a day and a night he died. The concubine only bemoaned her sad fate, and bethought herself that even after a son has been born it is difficult to bring him up. How could she know that there was another cause for the misfortune?

'The Kitchen God reported this affair to the Pearly Emperor, the King of Heaven, who passed it on to the nether regions for attention, and as she had used an embroidery needle to prick the child's navel, the King of Hades used a large nail to prick her breast. Do you not see that there is such a thing as a law of rewards and punishments?'

'Well, well,' said Laan Kat, 'how could one have suspected that she was so cunning and wicked? It is right that she should receive this punishment and tribulation. It is true that heaven has eyes.

'But the dead cannot come to life again. As my sister-in-law has now suffered for three years, is it not possible that her sin might now be remitted? Will you not please let me know by what method the nail may be removed from her breast?'

The keeper said, 'Absolutely not. We must submit to the will of the King.'

Laan Kat said, 'Is there no other plan?'

The keeper replied, 'The only possible way is to exhort her to do good deeds, then her sin may be expiated.'

'That is absolutely in accordance with all right principles,' said Laan Kat.

He then turned to Bluecoat and said, 'It is nearly night, I will not see any more but will hasten home.'

'Very well,' said Bluecoat, 'I will accompany you, and we can talk as we go along.'

CHAPTER 10

THE RETURN

Before long they had returned to the top of the hill, and Bluecoat said, 'Farewell, we shall meet again.'

'Elder brother,' said Ting Laan Kat, 'I thank you very much for your kindness and your company.'

Just then a bird was singing on the mountain, and this roused him. He looked about and saw his flask on the ground, but it was now empty. The sun was sinking in the West, so he quickly started for home, and was not long in reaching the house.

As he entered he heard his sister-in-law scolding the concubine, and saying, 'You are a useless person and not even worth your salt; you have no right to eat rice; you do not know how to infuse or decoct medicine, you use too little water and boil it dry. Do you want to poison me so that you may become the principal wife? Do you think I do not know the sort of secret malice you have in your heart?'

Laan Kat said, 'Sister-in-law, do not be so angry, just nourish yourself and take care of yourself.'

Yiu Shi, the sister-in-law, said, 'I am in great pain, and yet she comes and disturbs me, and makes me angry. How can I stand it?'

Laan Kat said, 'Ah so' (which is the right form of address for a young man when speaking to his sister-in-law), 'formerly you did not have this kind of pain, but really you were out to look for trouble.'

She replied, 'Where did I go to look for it? You, my brother-in-law, do not regard me as human. The concubine has no idea of using any method to help me; even you, my brother-in-law, do not treat me with the respect you should show to a sister-in-law. I know what is in your minds; you all think I ought to die.'

'Sister-in-law,' said Laan Kat, 'although you are not dead, you may be regarded as if you were dead.'

'Why should you regard me as already dead?' she replied.

'Your soul has been taken down to Hades, and you have had the pains of Hell for three years,' said Laan Kat.

'Have you seen my soul?' she asked in a loud voice.

He replied, 'Yes, I have, there is no mistake about it.'

'How did you see it?' she asked, and he replied, 'Well, I was out for a walk on the hill and owing to certain events that happened, I was taken to Hades and saw that you had an iron nail driven into you.'

She asked, 'What offence have I committed that they should treat me so? What secret villainy had I practised? Did I eat you or bite you?'

'You did not eat me, nor bite me,' he replied, 'but you caused the death of my nephew. Heaven cannot endure you, there is no place for you in Heaven.'

She was very angry and struck the bed, and called out in a loud voice, 'This is a most gross injustice. How dare you say that? Everyone knows that your nephew died on the third day of his life; there is nothing extraordinary in that. Many children die in that way. Now you have become mad and say that I caused his death. Am I that kind of person? Have I such an evil mind?

'Because of the death of that baby, I have shed many tears in secret; in fact, I may say that my eyes are never dry. When anyone just mentions a son, my heart is sore stricken, and yet you come here and say that I am such an unkind person. What proof have you for such a statement?

'If you tell stories like that, I shall be severely punished. If you are unjust to me, I can guarantee that you shall die first.'

Laan Kat laughed aloud and said, 'You, my sister-in-law, truly have a good heart! Formerly my younger sister-in-law (the concubine) had a good and healthy son; you were envious and jealous, and on the third day of his life, you took him up and said to him, "Baby, baby, you are a good boy." Then you took an embroidery needle and thrust it into his navel and he cried without ceasing until he died. Do you call that secret cruelty or not?'

When she heard these words, she was greatly afraid, her face turned very pale and she called out, 'You shall not be so unjust to me. I will call on the God of Thunder to strike you.'

'The Thunder God will not strike me, but the King of Hades will nail you. You know yourself whether you did it or not. I never knew it until today. If my brother had known sooner that you had such a wicked heart, I am sure that he would have punished you. I am afraid that even if you had died of your pain, he would not have had you treated for it.'

When she heard these words, she knew that the truth was out, and her mouth weakened, and she spoke in a low voice, and asked him quietly, 'Younger brother-in-law, are you telling the truth?'

'What I have said, I have said,' replied Laan Kat. 'Do you think I am making up a story to frighten you?'

CHAPTER 11

CONCLUSION

She bent down her head and spoke very quietly, and with bated breath said, 'Are you just trying to frighten me? Hearing you say all this makes me feel very much afraid. Perhaps my trouble and sickness may be the punishment for my sins. If one does not believe this, how can it be that though we have had so many doctors to see me, there has been no result, and I am just as ill as at first?

'Besides having doctors, we have tried many other methods. We have employed exorcists, blind people, and devil women; and still there has been no result. My brother-in-law, why was it that when you saw the nail driven into me, you did not pull it out for me?'

Laan Kat said, 'I wanted to pull it out, but the officer in charge would not allow me to do so.'

'Can it be that I am to continue in this pain until I die?' she said. 'I have been ill for three years. My pain is so great that it makes me feel very faint, in fact, it almost kills me. Is there not any other method to get cured?'

Laan Kat replied, 'The only possible way is that you should repent, and change your heart and put away all evil for the future. Perhaps if you did this you might get well, but I cannot say.'

When he had said this, he shook out his long sleeves in the usual Chinese way and went out.

His sister-in-law was in bed and thought the matter over and over, and came to the conclusion that her illness really was a punishment for her sins.

She thought to herself that when one comes to think about the world and the people in it, one feels that women are most kind-hearted, for whenever they hear that their relations have a son they are extremely glad and go and buy some pork or fowls for them, and when the completion of the first full month of the boy's life is celebrated, they send the meat and the fowls for the feast; and when the occasion for the ceremony of the lighting of the lamp arrives they send presents and congratulations. How then when one's own concubine gives birth to a son could one regard him as an enemy; besides when he should grow up, he might become wealthy, and serve and nourish one in one's old age; also I might in the future have had a daughter-in-law to wait on me.

Again, if he became an official, he would give presents to me before he assumed office, and at the end of my life when I become a hundred years old, he would worship me on the unlucky day of my funeral.

Many people adopt children and regard them as their own, and are good to them and love them. How much more should I have loved the child of my concubine, who would wear mourning for me for three years!

If I had not killed him when he was a baby, he would now be three or four years old, and would have been able to stand up and hold the side of my bed, and come to me and ask after my health; and if I died, I should have had a son to worship at my soul-tablet, and carry a branch of bamboo or some green tree which would have been blown about by the wind. He would also wear mourning and bow himself down and weep for me, calling me his mother.

Having thought matters over to this point, she could not refrain from weeping. She covered her mouth with her hand and in a low voice in her throat said, 'Ah! little one, I know you died in pain, I know I was cruel to your mother; now I repent, you are in the other world below the nine streams. Do not be angry with me.'

Having said this, she wept in secret for a long time. Afterward, she wiped her eyes and called the slave girl, and sent her to buy paper money, and candles and bring them out to be burnt in the open court of the house. Then she ordered the servant to take some of them out to the front of the house under the eaves, and she herself knelt down and prayed in secret there. No one knew what she was saying or what she was praying for. She struck her head wildly on the ground until her forehead was covered with sand and clay, and was greatly swollen.

After the worship was ended, she was assisted back to her bed, where she groaned terribly, and a cold sweat broke out all over her body.

From this time forward she treated the concubine like a sister, and they became as close to one another as bones and flesh. If there was anything on which they did not agree, she carefully explained matters to the concubine, never speaking to her roughly or in a loud voice as she did before; and the concubine was very glad to wait upon her continually.

Yiu Shi (the wife) knew that she had sinned and that her disease was caused by her sin, so she would not have a doctor to treat her, but used the powder from the incense bowl to poultice herself, and strangely enough in about ten days the abscess on her breast healed up; and it seemed as if she had received divine help.

After this, her whole nature was changed; she decided to do good deeds constantly, and whenever she heard of any philanthropic object, or anything for the benefit of others that it was possible for her to assist in, she would do what she could in the matter.

Three years later, she and the concubine each had a son, and the boys grew up and went to school and both became successful students and obtained degrees.

The *Shui-mang* Plant[*]

A young man named Chu was on his way to visit a same-year[†] friend of his when he was overtaken by a violent thirst. Suddenly, he came upon an old woman sitting by the roadside under a shed and distributing tea

[*] The *shui-mang* is a poisonous herb that grows in China. It is a creeper like the bean and has a similar red flower. Those who eat it die and are believed to become *shui-mang* devils, tradition asserting that they are unable to be born again unless they can find someone else who has also eaten of this poison to take their place.

[†] The common application of the term 'same-year man' is to persons who have graduated at the same time.

gratis.* He immediately walked up to her to get a drink. She invited him into the shed and presented him with a bowl of tea in a very cordial spirit. As the smell of the tea was not like ordinary tea, the young man became suspicious, refused to drink it and rose to leave.

The old woman stopped him and called out, 'San-niang! Bring some good tea.' Immediately a young girl came from behind the shed carrying in her hands a pot of tea. She was about fourteen or fifteen years old, with glittering rings and bracelets on her fingers and arms, and of very fascinating appearance. As Chu received the cup from her, his reason fled and drinking down the tea she gave him, the flavour of which was unlike any other kind, he proceeded to ask for more. Then, watching for a moment when the old woman's back was turned, he seized her wrist and drew a ring from her finger. The girl blushed and smiled. Chu, more and more inflamed, asked her where she lived. 'Come again this evening,' she answered, 'and you'll find me here.' Chu begged for a handful of her tea, which he stowed away with the ring and took his leave.

Arriving at his destination he felt a pain in his heart, which he at once attributed to the tea, and told his friend what had occurred. 'Alas! You are undone,' cried his friend, 'they were *shui-mang* devils. My father died in the same way and we were unable to save him. There is no help for you.'

Chu was terribly frightened and produced the handful of tea, which his friend at once pronounced to be the leaves of the *shui-mang* plant. He then showed him the ring and told him what the girl had said, whereupon his friend after some reflection said, 'She must be San-niang, of the K'ou family.' 'How could you know her name?' asked Chu, hearing his friend use the same words as the old woman. 'Oh,' replied he, 'there was a nice-looking girl of that name who died some years ago from eating of the same herb. She is doubtless the girl you saw.'

Here someone observed that if the person so entrapped by a devil only knew its name, and could procure an old pair of shoes, he might save himself by boiling them in water and drinking the liquor as medicine. Chu's friend thereupon rushed off at once to the K'ou family, and implored them to give him an old pair of their daughter's shoes, but they, not wishing to prevent their daughter from finding a substitute in Chu,

---

* This is by no means an uncommon form of charity. During the Canton up-heavals of 1877, Giles reports, large tubs of gruel were placed at convenient points throughout the city, ready for any poor person who wished to stop and eat. It is, thus Giles, tells us, and by similar acts of benevolence such as bridge building, repairing roads, and so forth, that the wealthy Chinese strives to maintain an advantageous balance in his record of good and evil.

flatly refused his request. So he went back in anger and told Chu, who ground his teeth with rage saying, 'If I die, she shall not obtain her transmigration thereby.'

His friend then sent him home. Just as he reached the door he fell down dead. Chu's mother wept bitterly over his corpse, which in due course was interred. Chu had also left behind a little boy barely a year old. His wife did not remain a widow long, for in six months she married again and went away, leaving Chu's son under the care of his grandmother who was quite unequal to any toil, and did nothing but weep morning and night.

One day she was carrying her grandson about in her arms, crying bitterly all the time when suddenly in walked Chu. His mother, much alarmed, brushed away her tears and asked him what it meant. 'Mother,' he replied, 'down in the realms below I heard you weeping. I have therefore come to tend you. Although a departed spirit, I have a wife who has likewise come to share your toil. Therefore do not grieve.'

His mother inquired who his wife was to which he replied, 'When the K'ou family sat still and left me to my fate, I was greatly incensed against them. So after death, I sought for San-niang not knowing where she was. I have recently seen my old same-year friend and he told me where she was. She had come to life again in the person of the baby daughter of a high official named Jen. But I went there and dragged her spirit back. She is now my wife and we get on extremely well together.'

A very pretty and well-dressed young lady here entered and made obeisance to Chu's mother, Chu saying, 'This is San-niang of the K'ou family.' Although San-niang was not a living being, Mrs Chu at once took a great fancy to her. Chu at once sent her off to help in the work of the house and, in spite of not being accustomed to this sort of thing, she was so obedient to her mother-in-law as to excite the compassion of all. The two then took up their quarters in Chu's old apartments and there they continued to remain.

Meanwhile, San-niang asked Chu's mother to let the K'ou family know of her return and this she did, notwithstanding some objections raised by her son. Mr and Mrs K'ou were much astonished at the news and, ordering their carriage, proceeded at once to Chu's house. There they found their daughter, and parents and child fell into each other's arms. San-niang entreated them to dry their tears, but her mother, noticing the poverty of Chu's household, could not restrain her feelings.

'We are already spirits,' cried San-niang, 'what matters poverty to us? Besides I am very well treated here, and am altogether as happy as I can be.' Then, looking at her husband, she added, 'Come, since you are the son-in-law, pay the proper respect to my father and mother, or what shall I think of you?' Chu made his obeisance and San-niang went into the kitchen to get food ready for them, at which her mother became very melancholy and went home, whence she sent a couple of maidservants, a hundred ounces of silver, and rolls of cloth and silk, besides making occasional presents of food and wine, so that Chu's mother lived in comparative comfort. San-niang also went from time to time to see her parents, but would never stay very long, pleading that she was wanted at home and such excuses. If the old people attempted to keep her, she simply went off by herself. Her father built a nice house for Chu with all kinds of luxuries in it, but Chu never once entered his father-in-law's door.

Subsequently a man of the village who had eaten *shui-mang*, and had died in consequence, came back to life to the great astonishment of everybody. However, Chu explained it saying, 'I brought him back to life. He was the victim of a man named Li Chiu, but I drove off Li's spirit when it came to make the other take his place.' Chu's mother then asked her son why he did not get a substitute for himself. He replied, 'I do not like to do this. I am anxious to put an end to this system rather than taking advantage of it. Besides, I am very happy waiting on you and have no wish to be born again.'

From that time on, all persons who had poisoned themselves with *shui-mang* were in the habit of feasting Chu and obtaining his assistance in their trouble. But in ten years' time, his mother died and he and his wife gave themselves up to sorrow and would see no one, bidding their little boy to put on mourning, beat his breast and perform the proper ceremonies.

Two years after Chu had buried his mother, his son married the granddaughter of a high official named Jen. This gentleman had had a daughter by a concubine, who had died when only a few months old, and now hearing the strange story of Chu's wife, came to call on her and arrange the marriage. He then gave his granddaughter to Chu's son, and a free intercourse was maintained between the two families.

However, one day Chu said to his son, 'Because I have been of service to my generation, God has appointed me Keeper of the Dragons, and I am now about to proceed to my post.' Thereupon four horses appeared in the courtyard, drawing a carriage with yellow hangings, the flanks of the horses being covered with scale-like trappings.

Husband and wife came forth in full dress and took their seats. While the son and daughter-in-law were weeping their adieus they disappeared from view.

That very day the K'ou family had seen their daughter who, bidding them farewell, had told them the same story. The old people wanted to keep her, but she said, 'My husband is already on his way,' and leaving the house parted from them forever.

Chu's son was named Ngo and his literary name was Li-chên. He begged San-niang's bones from the K'ou family and buried them by the side of his father's.

P'u Sung-ling (Ch'ing Dynasty)
From *Liao Chai Chih I*

Selected Bibliography

1. CLASSICAL LITERATURE

The Chinese Classics, 5 vols, translated by J. Legge. Hongkong, 1861–72.

The Texts of Confucianism, Sacred Books of the East, vols 3, 16, 27, 28, translated by J. Legge. Oxford, Clarendon Press, 1879–85. Also New York, Oxford University Press, 1961.

The Analects of Confucius, translated by A. Waley. London, George Allen & Unwin, 1937.

The Book of Songs (Shih-ching), translated by A. Waley. London, George Allen & Unwin, 1937.

The I Ching or *Book of Changes*, translated by R. Wilhelm; rendered into English by C. F. Baynes, 2 vols. London, Routledge & Kegan Paul, 1951. *I Ching*, translated by James Legge; newly arranged and edited with Introduction by Raymond Van Over. New York, New American Library, 1970.

The Sacred Books of Confucius and Other Confucian Classics, edited and translated by Ch'u Chai and Winberg Chai. New York, University Press, 1965.

2. GENERAL LITERATURE

An Introduction to Chinese Literature, Liu Wu-Chi. Bloomington, Indiana University Press, 1966.

Gems of Chinese Literature, translated by Herbert Giles. Shanghai, Kelly and Walsh, 1923. Paragon Books, 1964 (reprint).

Early Chinese Literature, Burton Watson. New York, Columbia University Press, 1962.

A History of Chinese Literature, Herbert Giles. London, Heinemann, 1901. Also New York, Grove Press, 1958.

A Treasury of Chinese Literature, Winberg and Ch'u Chai. New York, Appleton-Century, 1965.

Anthology of Chinese Literature, edited by Cyril Birch. New York, Grove Press, 1965. Also London, Penguin, 1967.

3. Prose Fiction in Translation

Traditional Chinese Tales, Wang Chi-chen. New York, Columbia University Press, 1944.

Stories from a Ming Collection, Cyril Birch. London, John Lane, 1958.

Strange Stories from a Chinese Studio (*Liao Chai Chih I*), P'u Sung-ling, translated by H. Giles, 2 vols. London, Thomas de la Rue, 1880. (Other editions: 1908, 1910, 1925.)

Contemporary Chinese Short Stories, Yuan Chai-hua and Robert Payne. London, Transatlantic Arts Co, 1946.

The Wisdom of China and India, Lin Yutang, 2 vols. London, Michael Joseph, 1944.

The Golden Casket, Wolfgang Bauer and Herbert Franke, eds. London, George Allen & Unwin, 1964.

Chinese Nights Entertainments, Brian Brown, ed. New York, Brentano's, 1922.

Modern Chinese Stories, W. J. F. Jenner, ed. London, New York, Oxford University Press, 1970.

Literature of the East, Eric B. Ceadel, ed. New York, Grove Press, 1959.

Translations from the Chinese, Arthur Waley. New York, Alfred A. Knopf, 1941.

PICADOR

Outstanding international fiction

THE NAKED i   60p
edited by Frederick R. Karl and Leo Hamalian

Fictions for the seventies. By twenty-five authors, including Leonard Cohen,
LeRoi Jones, Robert Coover, Carlos Fuentes, James Leo Herlihy, Sylvia Plath
and Ken Kesey.

THE EXISTENTIAL IMAGINATION   60p
edited by Frederick R. Karl and Leo Hamalian

An anthology of fiction, from de Sade to Sartre, which expresses existentialism.
The authors include Kafka, Proust, Beckett, Brecht, Malraux, Dostoyevsky and
Pavese.

A CHINESE ANTHOLOGY   50p
edited by Raymond Van Over

A collection of Chinese folktales, fables and parables which, by any standard,
can be termed definitive. It captures the elements which comprise the spirit of
Chinese culture – intensity of imagination, wit and humour, human concern.

CANNON SHOT AND GLASS BEADS   60p

Modern Black Writing *edited by* George Lamming

An anthology of the finest Black writing of our time, from Africa, Afro-America
and the Caribbean.

A PERSONAL ANTHOLOGY   45p
by Jorge Luis Borges

South America's major prose-writer makes his own selection of the pieces on
which he would like his reputation to rest.

THE ALEPH AND OTHER STORIES   50p
by Jorge Luis Borges

The most comprehensive collection of his work available in English. It contains
a long, specially written autobiographical essay as well as a brilliant selection of
fiction.

GENTLEMEN PREFER BLONDES 40p
by Anita Loos

The sparkling modern classic about a not-so-dumb gold-digging blonde. 'I reclined on a sofa reading *Gentlemen Prefer Blondes* for three days. I am putting the piece in place of honour. – JAMES JOYCE

THE THIRD POLICEMAN 50p
by Flann O'Brien

Wildly funny and chillingly macabre; the most extraordinary murder thriller ever written. 'Even with *Ulysses* and *Finnegans Wake* behind him, James Joyce might have been envious' – *Observer*

MURPHY 50p
by Samuel Beckett

Brilliant tragi-comic novel by the Nobel Prizewinner, of an Irishman's adventures in London.

MORE PRICKS THAN KICKS 50p
by Samuel Beckett

His first and most light-hearted novel. The adventures of a student in Dublin are explored by 'one of the greatest prose writers of the century'
–Times Literary Supplement

THE EXPLOITS OF THE INCOMPARABLE MULLA NASRUDIN 40p
by Idries Shah, *with drawings by* Richard Williams

A collection of stories about Nasrudin (an international folk hero of medieval origin but timeless appeal) which illustrate the philosophical teachings of the Sufis.

If you have any difficulty in obtaining Picador books please send purchase price plus 7p postage to PO Box 11, Falmouth, Cornwall.
While every effort is made to keep prices low, it is sometimes necessary to increase them at short notice. The publishers reserve the right to show new retail prices on covers, which may differ from those previously advertised in the text or elsewhere.